THE KINDERGARTEN OF THE MOVIES:

A History of the Fine Arts Company

by
Anthony Slide

The Scarecrow Press, Inc.
Metuchen, N.J., & London
1980

Also by Anthony Slide:

Early American Cinema (1970)
The Griffith Actresses (1973)
The Idols of Silence (1976)
The Big V: A History of the Vitagraph Company (1976)
Early Women Directors (1977)
Aspects of American Film History Prior to 1920 (1978)
Films on Film History (1979)

With Edward Wagenknecht:

The Films of D. W. Griffith (1975)
Fifty Great American Silent Films, 1912-1920 (1980)

Library of Congress Cataloging in Publication Data

Slide, Anthony.
   The kindergarten of the movies.

   Bibliography: p.
   Includes index.
   1. Fine Arts Film Company. 2. Griffith, David
Wark, 1875-1948. I. Title.
PN1999.F5S58   384'.8'065 79494   80-20391
ISBN 0-8108-1358-0

"Hail and farewell, Fine Arts! If Biograph was
the cradle, you have been the kindergarten of
the movies. Nor is this said in disrespect to
the discerning directors and the excellent actors
and the brilliant stories which have been beyond
your walls. You have held quality, and have
been exceptional in quantity. You have poured
forth simple, throbbing tales of human life.
You have taken boys and girls and made them
world-renowned. You have conquered the su-
premely necessary art of the subtitle as no one
else has conquered it. You have held to sincerity, naturalness, fidelity, always. You have
made fewer melodramas than most, but you
have thrust deeper at our hearts and intellects.
You will always be a chief foundation stone in
the great temple of sun-limned art just rising.
We do not mourn your end, for your renown
is durable as a diamond, and your splendid
people, your inspirations, your beliefs, have
gone into every corner of the reflection world. "

--Photoplay (July 1917)

CONTENTS

Introduction   vii

1.   Fine Arts and Triangle   1

2.   Supervised by D. W. Griffith   8

3.   The Films of 1915   20

4.   DeWolf Hopper   32

5.   Douglas Fairbanks: The Evolution of a Screen Legend   44

6.   The Films of 1916   69

7.   Enter Sir Herbert   95

8.   Fine Arts' Final Months, 1917   112

Appendixes   125

    A.   A Fine Arts Who's Who   127
    B.   Complete List of Fine Arts Productions during the Griffith Regime   165
    C.   Macbeth Credits   179
    D.   Intolerance: A Selected Commentary   180

Bibliography   220

Index   227

INTRODUCTION

The Fine Arts Film Company holds an important place in the story of film production in the Teens. It was not a long-lived company. It remained in existence for less than two years, and yet its productions were held on a par with those of such major competitors as Famous Players, Lasky, Metro, Vitagraph, World, and Fox, whose corporate activities spanned decades. It produced no broad comedies to be remembered in future eras, as were the Keystone comedies of Mack Sennett. It boasted no stars of the magnitude of Mary Pickford, Charles Chaplin, or Marguerite Clark. One would look in vain among the ranks of its contract directors for an established figure of the period, such as Sidney Olcott, Cecil B. DeMille, J. Searle Dawley, or Larry Trimble.

The importance of the Fine Arts Film Company can be linked, primarily, to its production head, D. W. Griffith. The director, at this time, was probably at the most important period of his career: The Birth of a Nation was completed and creating controversy and excitement wherever it was screened, and Griffith was at work on the planning and production of what was to be his finest achievement, Intolerance. Whether or not he took an active part in the direction of any of the Fine Arts productions, there can be no question that he played an important role in the overall supervision of the films, and his "touch" is forever apparent. It was the Griffith influence that established Fine Arts productions as quality productions. They might have their faults, but it is doubtful that the cinema, before or since, has produced five-reel program pictures in such quantity, boasting the production values or the dramatic content of the Fine Arts productions. From a purely quality point of view, there is not a fault to be found in a Fine Arts film, from the historical sweep of Martyrs of the Alamo through the comedy-drama of Let Katy Do It or Hoodoo Ann. The storylines might be slight at times and the direction may occasionally lack luster, but one is ever aware that here are quality motion pictures,

quite definitely aimed at raising the standards of film production from a nickelodeon amusement to a theatrical event.

Assisting D. W. Griffith in the quest for quality was
a group of directors of varying talents, whom Griffith tried
to mold in his image. Some, such as Lloyd Ingraham, Paul
Powell and Chester Withey, had their moments of glory at
Fine Arts and then fell by the wayside; others, particularly
Jack Conway and Sidney Franklin, continued as quality film
producers in the years ahead. It should also be noted that
it was at Fine Arts that Erich von Stroheim, acting and generally assisting in the productions, probably learned the craft
of film making.

Finally, the Fine Arts Film Company stands preemi-
nent in the creation of stars--not the beautiful, dumb creatures who drifted across the cinema screen so much during
the silent era, but intelligent actors and actresses whose
talent, brought to the fore by Griffith and Fine Arts, made
of them stars. The stock company of Fine Arts boasted
Lillian and Dorothy Gish, Robert Harron, Norma and Constance Talmadge, Gladys Brockwell, Jewel Carmen, Fay
Tincher, George Walsh, Seena Owen, Bessie Love, Mae
Marsh, and Alma Rubens. From the stage came DeWolf
Hopper, Marie Doro (about to embark on a major screen
career), and Sir Herbert Beerbohm Tree. Also from the
stage came Douglas Fairbanks, who became a major motion
picture star with his first Fine Arts production, The Lamb,
and who was to strengthen his film career with the other
Fine Arts productions which followed.

The Kindergarten of the Movies--an apt description of
Fine Arts coined presumably by Photoplay's Julian Johnson--
chronicles the activities of the Fine Arts Film Company, concentrating on its productions, its directors and its stars.
The life of the company is, of necessity, closely allied to
that of the Triangle Film Corporation, its releasing arm and
its financial provider. The Triangle Film Corporation does
figure in this volume, but The Kindergarten of the Movies is
not a history of Triangle, whose rise and fall (along with
that of its chief mentor, Harry Aitken) has been chronicled
by Kalton C. Lahue in Dreams for Sale (A. S. Barnes, 1971).
Although overly romantic, with each chapter deliberately
reading like the title of a Mack Sennett comedy, Lahue's book
does provide a good, general overview of Triangle and the
career of Harry Aitken, a quite extraordinary entrepreneur
in an age of extraordinary entrepreneurs. The chief fault of

<u>Dreams for Sale</u> is that Lahue does not separate the three
production arms of Triangle: Griffith's Fine Arts Company,
Thomas H. Ince's Kay Bee Productions and Mack Sennett's
Keystone Comedies.   In Lahue's book, players are always
Triangle stars first and foremost, regardless of their studio
affiliations, thus Seena Owen and Pauline Starke have the
dubious distinction of rubbing shoulders--or to be more pre-
cise, pages--with Louise Fazenda, Charlie Murray and Ben
Turpin. <u>The Kindergarten of the Movies</u> goes to the opposite
extreme by placing the Fine Arts Film Company and its productions where they belong, above and separate from Triangle,
Harry Aitken, Thomas H. Ince, and Mack Sennett.

In the preparation of this book, I have made extensive
use of the two major trade papers of the period: <u>The Moving
Picture World</u> and <u>Motion Picture News</u>.   J. C. Jessen's
column, "In and Out of West Coast Studios, " in the latter
periodical was of value.   I have also relied heavily on <u>Vari-
ety</u>, <u>Photoplay</u>, <u>Picture-Play</u> Magazine, <u>Motion Picture Maga-
zine</u>, <u>Motion Picture Classic</u>, and, of course, <u>The Triangle</u>.
For contemporaneous critical opinion, Julian Johnson's literate comments in <u>Photoplay</u> have proved trustworthy and reliable, and I have quoted at length throughout the book from
the man who was the cinema's first serious critic.   Special
mention should also be made of the "California's City of the
Fine Arts" section in <u>The New York Dramatic Mirror</u>, Vol.
75, No. 1948 (April 22, 1916), pages 26-31.

The following institutions provided the research tools
--films and photo stills, trade periodicals, and personal
papers--that I used: the Margaret Herrick Library of the
Academy of Motion Picture Arts and Sciences, the Library of
Congress (Barbara Humphrys and Emily Sieger), the Museum
of Modern Art (Eileen Bowser, Mary Corliss and Charles
Silver), and the Wisconsin Center for Film and Theatre Research (Susan Dalton and Maxine Fleckner).   I must also
thank George Pratt of George Eastman House for carefully
checking my filmography, and Bill Doyle, who constantly
proves to be an invaluable source for biographical data.

Personal reminiscences came from Karl Brown, Bessie Love, Carmel Myers, Colleen Moore, and Margery Wilson.   As always, Robert Gitt and Herb Sterne offered their
encouragement.   To all my thanks!

Anthony Slide
Studio City, California
November 1979

Chapter 1

FINE ARTS AND TRIANGLE

The Triangle Film Corporation was the brainchild of
Harry E. Aitken, a film entrepreneur who could only have
existed in the era of the silent screen when artistic integrity
and business acumen could somehow survive side by side,
and when it seemed as if anyone with the desire, if not the
intelligence, to succeed in the film industry could and did.
In these days of conglomerates and multi-billion dollar cor-
porations controlling the motion picture industry, it is hard
to comprehend how one man could enter the film industry in
1905 by the simple expedient of opening four nickelodeons in
downtown Chicago, and within ten years have "produced" the
most famous film of all time, The Birth of a Nation. But
this Harry E. Aitken did--and a lot more beside.

Harry E. Aitken died in Chicago, where his career
had begun, on August 1, 1956, at the age of seventy-nine.
He had first come to national prominence in the film industry
in 1911, when his recently-formed Majestic Company was able
to lure Mary Pickford away from Carl Laemmle's IMP Company, presumably by offering the star more money and,
equally if not more importantly, promising the actress's ego-
tistical husband, Owen Moore, the chance to direct his wife.
(In fact, Miss Pickford made only five films for Majestic,
released between November 1911 and February 1912, before
returning to her alma mater, the American Biograph Company, and to her mentor, D. W. Griffith.)

In 1912 Aitken created the Mutual Film Corporation,
with its famous slogan of "Mutual Movies Make Time Fly"
and its trademark of a winged clock dial, as a distribution
arm chiefly for his own production companies of Majestic and
Reliance. When D. W. Griffith tired of his affiliation with
American Biograph (because of that company's failure to

1

realize that the future of the film industry lay in multi-reel
productions), Aitken was able to persuade the director to sign
with him, and in December of 1913 Griffith began production
of his first Reliance-Majestic feature, The Escape, in a tiny
loft converted into a studio at 29 Union Square in New York
City.   Because of the illness of The Escape's leading lady,
Blanche Sweet, production was temporarily suspended, and
the director turned to another project, The Battle of the
Sexes, which was completed and released some two months
prior to The Escape.

After two further Reliance-Majestic six-reel features,
Home, Sweet Home and The Avenging Conscience, Griffith
began production of his first masterwork, The Birth of a Nation.   Although the producer must have had certain misgiv-
ings as to its cost, Harry Aitken had obviously approved of
the project, and eventually created a separate company, the
Epoch Producing Corporation--incorporated on February 8,
1915, with Aitken as President and D. W. Griffith as Vice-
President--to finance and distribute the feature.

In the meantime, Aitken had become involved with two
other legendary entrepreneurs of the early silent screen,
Adam Kessel, Jr. and Charles O. Baumann.   Creators of
the New York Motion Picture Corporation, these two men
had Thomas Ince, for whose early financial success they
were largely responsible, and Mack Sennett under contract.
They had at one time been a part of Carl Laemmle's Universal Film Manufacturing Company, but in June 1912 with-
drew from Universal and released their films through Aitken's
Mutual Film Corporation.   The New York Motion Picture
Corporation was reorganized in the spring of 1913 with Kessel as President, Baumann as Vice-President, Charles Kessel as Secretary, C. J. Hite (of the Thanhouser Company)
as Treasurer, and Harry E. Aitken as Assistant Treasurer.
It was their proud boast that in 1913, the New York Motion
Picture Corporation turned out twenty-one million feet of
film.   In his 1914 volume The Theatre of Science (Broadway
Publishing Company), Robert Grau wrote that "The Mutual
Film Corporation has impressed itself upon the minds of all
as one of the most alert and progressive as well as the fast-
est growing and most stable among motion picture concerns."

It was due to Aitken's progressiveness that the Triangle Film Corporation came about.   On July 3, 1915, The
Moving Picture World announced that, "Having withdrawn
from the presidency of the Mutual Corporation, H. E. Aitken

will figure in a new alliance for the production of feature pictures in which Adam Kessell [sic] and C. O. Baumann, with
D. W. Griffith, Thomas H. Ince and Mack Sennett as the
chief directors will be the most important factors.   The new
$4,000,000 company is being organized at the present time
and probably the first program will be ready for release
early in September, on the expiration of the New York Motion Picture Company's contract with Mutual." It was further
announced that the new organization would be called The Sig
Motion Picture Company, taking its name from the initials of
its three creative heads: Sennett, Ince and Griffith.

      Griffith and Ince were each to supervise the production
of one five-reel feature a week, while one two-reel comedy
a week would be produced under Mack Sennett's supervision.
Motion Picture News (July 17, 1915) reported:

> These pictures will be distributed to motion picture
> theatres under what is known as the "lock reel"
> system.   That is to say, one five-reel feature and
> one two-reel comedy will constitute an evening's
> program for a theatre and the same feature will
> play with the same comedy wherever shown.   Thus
> the exhibitor is furnished with a complete show.
> By producing two big features and two big comedies
> a week (an incorrect statement), two complete shows
> will be furnished a week.   Contracts will be signed
> with motion picture theatres all over the country
> for the service.   These contracts will be based
> upon the size of the theatre and the size of the city
> or town.   In cities with two theatres capable of
> playing the same show for a week's run, two the-
> atres can be signed up, because each can be given
> a show without conflict.   In cities where public de-
> mands still dictate a change of program twice
> weekly only one theatre can be served.   The ser-
> vice will be exclusive.   The exhibitor can advertise
> his attractions in advance without fear of any other
> theatre duplicating his show or playing it first. 55*

Admission prices were set at a minimum of 25 cents and a
maximum of two dollars.   Some theatres were encouraged to
screen both the Griffith and the Ince features on the same
program, while those with a policy of running the same

---

*Superior numbers in the text refer to the bibliography.

ninety-minute program for an entire week were allowed to
select either the Griffith or the Ince feature.

The Triangle program was, of course, a form of
block booking, allowing theatres to screen only the distribu-
tor's product, and meaning that a theatre might have the box
office advantage of a William S. Hart feature one week but
would have to offset that the following week with, say, a
feature starring J. Barney Sherry. Block booking was to
plague the film industry in the Teens--and later--but Triangle's contribution to that evil was nothing compared with
Paramount activities in the field, which, under Adolph Zukor's
guidance, made almost an art of block booking.

On July 20, 1915, an auspicious meeting took place
in the small town of La Junta, Colorado, between Aitken
and Griffith, Ince and Sennett. The Sig Motion Picture Company became the Triangle Film Corporation, which was now
a five million dollar company. Its trademark was a triangle,
with the words "Triangle Plays" at its center; the origin of the
name is, of course, obvious and presumably did away with the
problem of deciding whose name or initial should come first.

On September 4, 1915, Harry E. Aitken, president
of the newly-formed corporation, announced that the initial
screening of Triangle releases would take place at the Knickerbocker Theatre on New York's 42nd Street on September 18,
1915. The Knickerbocker was intended to be the first of a group
of "model" theatres that would demonstrate "the Triangle idea
of adequate motion picture presentation,"[66] one aspect of which
was the use of specially arranged or composed musical ac-
companiment. (Other model theatres were to be the Stu-
debaker in Chicago, the Chestnut Street Opera House in Philadelphia and the Olympic in St. Louis.) That same day it
was also announced that the subjects to be produced by D.
W. Griffith would be known as Fine Arts Films. The Lily
and the Rose and The Sable Lorcha were beginning production, while Martrys of the Alamo and Old Heidelberg were
being completed. Mack Sennett productions were dubbed
Keystone comedies, but no special name was given the Ince
productions.

The Triangle for November 13, 1915, published the
following list of Triangle-Fine Arts stars: Mary Alden,
Frank Campeau, Elliott Dexter, Marie Doro, John Emerson,
Douglas Fairbanks, Dorothy Gish, Lillian Gish, Jane Grey,
Robert Harron, DeWolf Hopper, Thomas Jefferson, Orrin

Johnson, Mae Marsh, Tully Marshall, Norma Talmadge, Sir
Herbert Beerbohm Tree, Sarah Truax, and Helen Ware. A-
mong Ince's stars were noted William S. Hart, Dustin Farnum, Henry B. Warner, Julia Dean, Louise Dresser, Mary
Boland, and George Beban. At Ince's Culver City studios
work was in progress on The Coward, "a civil war story
with a punch," which was intended to be the first Ince release on the Triangle program. At the time it was hailed
because of the fame of its star, Frank Keenan, but today
his performance appears stilted and overly melodramatic, and
the film is best known as the feature which brought Charles
Ray to prominence.

Mack Sennett's Keystone Company boasted Raymond
Hitchcock, Eddie Foy, Weber and Fields, Fred Mace, and
Mabel Normand among its contract stars. "With this list
of artists," commented The Moving Picture World, "it has
been found advisable to discard much of the old Rabellaisian
tricks upon which so-called 'comedy' pictures have mainly
depended and everyone is delighted with the new order of
things."66

The following were the executive staff for the Triangle
Corporation: J. N. Naulty, General Manager; George W.
Sammis, Business Manager; William Furst, Musical Direc-
tor; Henry MacMahon, General Press Representative; W. M.
Powers, Assistant Press Representative; and Florence Mac-
Cormack, Librarian. Griffith, Ince and Sennett, together
with Charles O. Baumann, were Vice-Presidents of the or-
ganization, and Adam Kessel was Secretary.

With the creation of Triangle, Harry E. Aitken had
become one of the top--if not the top--producer-businessmen
in the film industry. He may probably be judged as holding
more power than the heads of Vitagraph, Universal and Fox.
He certainly towered over the companies that formed the
General Film Company. Only one man was his superior in
the film industry and that was Adolph Zukor, the head of
Paramount Pictures. In fact, it is interesting to note, as
has Seymour Stern before me, that with the demise of Triangle it was Zukor who bought up its biggest assets, Griffith, Ince, Fairbanks, William S. Hart, and Mack Sennett.

Thursday, September 23, 1915, marked the first Triangle presentation at the Knickerbocker Theatre. It drew a
star-studded audience, which included Otto Kahn, Ignace Paderewski, William Randolph Hearst, Howard Chandler Christy,

James Montgomery Flagg, Irvin S. Cobb, Rupert Hughes, and
the production heads of various rival companies, including
Universal and Fox.   The program began with Thomas Ince's
production of The Iron Strain, featuring Dustin Farnum and
Enid Markey, which was substituted for The Coward because,
according to Ince in Motion Picture News (September 11,
1915), "The Iron Strain is a bigger and more forceful production ... the whole action is swifter and more compelling
than The Coward."   Mack Sennett's production of My Valet,
starring Raymond Hitchcock, supported by Mabel Normand,
Fred Mace and Sennett himself, provided the middle portion
of the program, and to close came the Griffith-supervised
production of The Lamb, directed by W. Christy Cabanne,
and featuring Douglas Fairbanks and Seena Owen.

       The trade papers were unanimously enthusiastic, with
most agreeing that The Lamb was the highspot of the evening's entertainment, which surprised Aitken and Griffith, the
former because he had thought the Dustin Farnum vehicle
far superior and the latter because he had been disappointed
in Fairbanks' antics.   Variety's Jolo (October 1, 1915) found
The Iron Strain "a very good feature," and The Lamb, "the
classiest kind of melodramatic comedy, wonderfully staged,
brilliantly acted and humorously captioned."   Of My Valet,
Jolo wrote, "The audience screamed with laughter at the innumerable sure-fire situations, which owe their origin to
the old-time 'nigger' acts."   "All in all," commented The
Moving Picture World (October 9, 1915), "it was a successful opening."   Harvey F. Thew in Motion Picture News (October 9, 1915), raised an interesting point when he wrote,
"Good as the pictures were, they were glorified by the advertising; by virtue of it, they had been before the New York
public for a couple of weeks, and when the spectators as-
sembled for the first view, a species of entente between picture and spectator had already been established.   It is possible that they were actually better pictures because of this
advertising."

       Outside of the trade press, reviewers were less favor-
ably impressed.   The critic for The New York Times (September 24, 1915) wrote, "Each [film] is an example of nicely
accomplished motion picture photography, no one of them
reveals anything amazing or unprecedented in this now hugely
popular form of entertainment.   Anyone who went to the
Knickerbocker last evening looking for that must have come
away disappointed."   The Times went on to single out Fairbanks for praise, describing him as "a new movie actor who

is certain to build an enormous following in that considerable
multitude which is possessed of a passion for the cinema."
Julian Johnson, writing in Photoplay (December, 1915), had
very mixed feelings concerning Triangle's initial offerings.
"Are these pictures, as so far shown, 'two dollar pictures?' "
he asked--and answered, "No." Johnson thought the second
bill of Triangle releases, consisting of The Coward, Old
Heidelberg and a Mabel Normand comedy, Stolen Magic, far
superior, "and should have been an opener to strike the
triple keynote of splendor, fun and power."

The first Triangle program received its Los Angeles
premiere at Clune's Auditorium--the home of The Birth of
a Nation for many weeks--on November 8, 1915. A few
days later, it was screened at the Triangle Theatre, located
at Fulton Street and Flatbush Avenue in Brooklyn.

Minor negative comments notwithstanding, Harry Aitken
must have been pleased with the beginnings of his organization.
and doubtless saw little reason why it should not succeed
and prosper. The entrepreneur had created an organization
to distribute quality motion pictures produced almost on a
conveyor belt system. Aitken had the three leading producers
of the film industry under contract, and yet, within two years
these men would be out of Triangle, within five years Triangle would cease to exist, and within seven years Harry Aitken would be back in his home town of Waukesha, Wisconsin,
with his sole assets limited almost entirely to certain rights
in The Birth of a Nation and the Mabel Normand vehicle,
Mickey. Harry Aitken had not taken into account his own
need to interfere in the creative happenings of his colleagues
and the ambitious plans of one colleague in particular, D.
W. Griffith.

Chapter 2

SUPERVISED BY D. W. GRIFFITH

"As far as the general public is concerned," wrote
Julian Johnson in Photoplay (December, 1915), "Mr. Griffith is head and front of Triangle, and the reason-in-chief
for a $2 entrance fee. Mr. Sennett and Mr. Ince, probably
very busy men, have time to direct their own pictures.
Why cannot Mr. Griffith do the same? We understand that
he is working on a vast feature to be called The Mother and
the Law--still, why call a thing a triangle when for all prac-
tical purposes it has only two sides?"

Johnson's comment sums up a major problem facing
any film historian investigating the history of the Fine Arts
Company. To what extent was Griffith involved in the production of its features, and did he in any way participate in
their direction? It is a question to which there is no easy
answer, and certainly no concrete answer. There can be
little doubt that many, if not all, of the extant Fine Arts
features bear definite signs of Griffith's influence in their
direction and even in their sub-titling. Several Fine Arts
films were in fact written by, or at least based on original
stories by, D. W. Griffith working under the pen name of
Granville Warwick. The Griffith influence was most certainly there, but was the man himself also present in the
production of Fine Arts' features?

One contemporary account of the making of a Fine
Arts production comes from Bessie Love, who recalls that
on the films in which she appeared Griffith never appeared
on the set, but would always take the last rehearsal in company with the film's director. She also comments that "Griffith had a great deal to do with the cutting," and that she is
sure he screened and OK'd each production prior to its release. As confirmation of Griffith's overseeing of the cut-

ting and presumed viewing of the rushes, Bessie Love remembers that scenes would often be retaken and, if necessary, sets would be rebuilt if a scene did not meet with the
producer's approval and a retake was imperative. Miss
Love also asserts that the directors had nothing to do with
the running of the studio, and that Griffith handled casting
of the leading roles. "D. W. Griffith ran that studio, and
if anything was changed, he changed it," she maintains.

One of the Fine Arts directors, Allan Dwan, recalled
that Griffith's supervision only manifested itself

> in a pleasant way. When we were going to make
> a picture, we'd all go into a room with two or
> three of the actors assigned and the script we
> were going to do--or a synopsis of it--and we'd
> go over it. Sometimes we'd play a scene, discuss
> this and that. And he was just seeing that I wasn't
> going to do the same thing one of the other fellows
> was doing. Or seeing if maybe I should use Lil-
> lian Gish instead of Mae Marsh, or someone out
> of the stock company. After that we got whatever
> we wanted and were completely independent. 8

Another version of how Fine Arts films were conceived
comes from Carmel Myers:

> Griffith had a very unusual way of preparing his
> pictures. He would take stock girls and stock men
> to play the leads and the director who was going
> to direct the picture would direct them for five
> weeks almost, block out all the studio sets, this
> is the living room, this is the bedroom, this is
> the door, etc. Anyway, Winifred Westover came
> to me one day and said, "Carmel, they want me
> to do this thing, to stand in for Lillian Gish in a
> picture called The House Built upon Sand, and I
> want to go shopping. If you'll do this for me, I'll
> give you $5.00." Well, I had just got to Griffith's
> and I was delighted! I said, "You'll give me $5.00!
> I'll give you $5.00 if you will let me do it." So
> I had five weeks of the most exciting.... Here
> I'm playing a star part, which I wasn't going to
> play, as a stand-in, and the man who was playing
> Bobby Harron's part was one from stock. And
> I remember one scene in it, where he was supposed
> to be having tea with me, this gentleman, and to

denote the passing of time, he piled up five cups
one on top of the other--kind of a silly thing. Then
at the end of five weeks, Mr. Griffith, Miss Gish
and Bobby Harron came in to watch us go through
this, and it was really a thrilling time for me,
to play a starring role. I'd just come to the studio
one month before. Mr. Griffith sat there with his
hat pulled down over his eyes in his usual way--
you wondered how he could see anything, but he
could see alright--and at the finish he thanked us,
and I guess I was alright because the next day I
got a lead in a picture.

Colleen Moore, whose second film was Fine Arts'
An Old Fashioned Young Man, tells me, "I never worked for
Mr. Griffith and met him only years later after I had became a star. I bumped into him in the lobby of a theatre
in New York and he said something to the effect that he was
certainly a great picker of stars as I had fulfilled his predictions. We both laughed as we both knew that I received
a Griffith contract only as payment to my uncle Walter Howey,
editor of the Hearst paper in Chicago. I was a payoff for
the favors my uncle did for Mr. Griffith in getting The Birth
of a Nation and Intolerance past the censors in Chicago."

Writing in his autobiography, DeWolf Hopper commented, "Perhaps if Don Quixote had fallen under the direction of D. W. Griffith it might have been a mark to date
from in pictures, but Griffith's heart and most of his time,
as far as I could observe, were going into his spectacle Intolerance. In her autobiography, Lillian Gish goes into more
detail,

During this period, a typical day might start with
a story conference with "Daddy" Woods, head of
the scenario department. Then, between work on
Intolerance, Mr. Griffith would supervise in detail
the rehearsals, shooting, and editing of films made
by his assistants. Late into the night he would
watch the daily rushes and lay out the next day's
schedule. 22

Certainly there were periods when Griffith spent little
time on the Fine Arts productions. From the formation of
the company through the completion of Intolerance in the summer of 1916, the director was obviously primarily concerned
with his second masterwork. In late November and early

D. W. Griffith during his Fine Arts period.

December of 1915, Griffith was coping with his mother's
death and funeral. Late in 1916 and early in 1917, he was
busy promoting Intolerance. Consider his schedule: In New
York at the Liberty Theatre opening of Intolerance, September 5, 1916; in San Francisco at the Columbia Theatre opening of Intolerance, October 9, 1916; in Chicago at Colonial
Theatre opening of Intolerance, November 28, 1916; in Chicago, January 22, 1917; in Washington, D.C., January 25,
1917.

   Yet, even with Intolerance being the number one production on his mind, Griffith was still finding time for Fine
Arts. On April 1, 1916, Motion Picture News quoted Harry Aitken, "The activity of Mr. Griffith in supervising the
product of this studio is unquestionable. I found his energy
manifest everywhere in speeding up production." However,
Aitken then went on to describe Griffith's work in directing
battle scenes with 2,500 extras, scenes which could only be
for Intolerance.

   The Triangle published a lengthy description of Griffith's supervision of The Flying Torpedo:

     Griffith, Emerson and O'Brien are seated together
     at one side of the room and the players are grouped
     around the table in the center. Presently W. E.
     Lawrence appears at a far corner ducking behind
     an imaginary hedge, and Viola Barry goes through
     the pantomime of trying to find him.
       "Let's get away from the 5 and 10 cent stuff!"
     shouts Griffith at this point. "That peek-a-boo
     stuff is as old as the hills." He thinks rapidly
     for a moment.
       Then Mr. Lawrence and Miss Barry are re-
     hearsed in an entirely new scene in which Lawrence
     appears at the gate with a bunch of books and blue-
     prints under his arm. He sits down to study a problem
     in aerial mechanism, the girl trips quietly up be-
     side him and joins his studies and then, when the
     problem is solved, there is a love-making scene
     between them.
       Mr. Griffith certainly wrought marvels with the
     character that was next taken up. In the scenario
     as staged by O'Brien, Bessie Love, "Our Mary,"
     as Griffith called her, was just an ordinary ser-
     vant of the conventional society-play type. In fact,
     it was thought she would not do for the part and
     there was talk of dismissing her.

That afternoon Mr. Griffith took "Our Mary" in hand. There was no private rehearsal of the novice. The supervisor simply said: "You are a terrible Swede. Your eyes are popping, your mouth is agape, and your mind is filled with raw interest in the detective story you are reading." As the visitor enters and the maid raises her eyes from the book, she recognizes John Emerson as its author. "Look at him like this!" Mr. Griffith made a ridiculous mouth. "My hero! That is what your expression should say more plainly than words. Now Mr. Emerson, the story writer, gives you another book, another of his precious crime romances. You are his slave. You would jump through the window for him if he asked you to."

Next came the death of the old inventor of the flying torpedo, who is killed by the explosion of a formulating cap attached by one of the outlaws to the telephone instrument. "Our Mary" is the first to discover the casualty. She is supposed to rush outside, run to Emerson's house and inform him of it. The point was how to get the crude frenzy of the Swedish servant girl expressed by her gestures, liniaments and action.

"By yiminy, he yumped to hell!"

"You want me to say that?" "Our Mary" looked in real wonder at the boss.

"Yes," consoled Griffith, "some of them cuss like troopers, especially on occasions of strong excitement. Use those funny words with all the force you have in you. They will give your face and mouth the expression."

"By yiminy, he yumped to hell."

Bessie Love had worked herself up into a frenzy of excitement to which the words furnished a most amusing anti-climax. All the members of the company laughed convulsively. A gale of mirth swept over the room.

"Mary, that's fine," said the supervisor. "Now go ahead and try it under Mr. O'Brien. Remember you are always a Swede, you have just landed in the city from the wilds of Minnesota or North Dakota, that you think John Emerson the greatest ever, and with your native shrewdness you are up to all sorts of tricks at conning the old druggist and the other people whom he is trying to run down."

Then came a red hot discussion over how The
Flying Torpedo should wind up. O'Brien presented
one plan of campaign, Emerson another, Griffith
a third.   There were to be attacks on the American positions in Southern California, victories for
the Yellow Men, launching of hundreds of Flying
Torpedoes, and finally destruction of the enemy
armies and ships through this awful instrument of
death.   The differences were as to technical detail, order of events and so forth.   Nothing was
settled that day.
As a result of the supervisor's efforts, The Flying Torpedo somehow seemed to get away from the
melo-dramatic conventionality and assumed art
proportions. [34]

In The New York Dramatic Mirror (April 22, 1916),
Frank Woods gave his explanation of Griffith's contribution
to Fine Arts:

There are three distinct departments which go to
produce the output from this studio.   These three
departments comprise that of David W. Griffith,
that of the Fine Arts, and that of the Reliance.
The plant is rightly called that of Mr. Griffith, for
it is here that he creates the distinctive pictures
that bear his trademark.   The Birth of a Nation
does that--but you have seen it on no other picture
since the making of that one.   The Mother and the
Law will bear the Griffith trademark; it will have
taken a year in the making.   So you see the Griffith output is but an average of one picture a year,
and Mr. Griffith himself shapes the play and personally directs the actors in the rehearsing and
filming of every scene.
Of the Fine Arts Corporation, Mr. Griffith is
vice-president and director general.   This corporation releases one five-reel photoplay each week
for the Triangle service.   For the making of these
features, there is a staff of directors which ranks
at the very top of the profession--William Christy
Cabanne, Allan Dwan, John Emerson, Lloyd Ingraham, Edward Dillon, Paul Powell, and C. M.
and S. A. Franklin.   Several of these men have
had their training under Mr. Griffith and are im-
bued with his spirit and are grounded in his technique.

To each of the Fine Arts five-reel pictures, Mr. Griffith gives a measure of supervision both before and after they are filmed. But it is the policy of the organization to give to the individual directors the fullest possible freedom to work out their own artistic salvation. It is "up to them" individually, and when one of these features is called a "Griffith picture," it is a misnomer. The Fine Arts directors are selected on merit and because they are deemed qualified to maintain the highest existing standards of the photo-drama. As opportunity is given them to express themselves freely in their work, a production made by one could not be mistaken for that of any other of the Fine Arts directors.

Thus the term, "a Griffith director" is quite as significant as the often misunderstood "supervised by David W. Griffith." For, while this supervision is actual, both before and after the filming of a picture, it is the director whose production it really is.

The third division of this studio is that of the Reliance Company. It is an individual producing corporation of which the Sir Herbert Beerbohm Tree production of <u>Macbeth</u> is the most recent output. The Reliance is the oldest of the three companies which go to make up the Fine Arts Studio, and shares with the Fine Arts Company a general supervision by Mr. Griffith.

It should be obvious, I think, that no one individual can watch every detail of so large a volume of production, and that intricate administrative machinery is required to keep such a triple organization as this spinning along at high speed without interference or a lowering of standards.

Many departments naturally dove-tail or overlap. There is no duplication of mechanical divisions; such things as costumes are all under one roof, and the various stages are common possessions. Properties, for the most part, come from a common store and the players are largely interchangeable, though under centralized control.

Efficiency and economy of administration has thus been carried to a high degree in studios like this. Such large consolidations of production make this possible despite the great sums of money required to make a modern feature picture of the

first class. These lavish expenditures have given
rise to a great cry of wastefulness in film production, but elaborate and costly photoplay is made
possible and profitable by the centralizing of large
production in bulk in just such institutions as ours.

Interestingly, The Triangle--the official Triangle publicity journal--lists the following films, and the following
films only, as being "supervised by D. W. Griffith": Let
Katy Do It, The Missing Links, The Wood Nymph, Susan
Rocks the Boat, and Mr. Goode, the Samaritan. No other
films publicized in The Triangle, not even the aforementioned
The Flying Torpedo, contain references to Griffith in their
credits. One film with which Griffith was particularly concerned was apparently Hoodoo Ann, with a screenplay by Griffith as Granville Warwick--and many of the sub-titles have
a distinctly Griffith ring to them. According to The Moving
Picture World (March 25, 1916), "Active as he is in the
supervision of Fine Arts pictures for the Triangle program,
David W. Griffith has surprised his associates on the Coast
by the active direction he has given to the forthcoming Mae
Marsh release, Hoodoo Ann. Miss Marsh has been in great
favor with the director since The Birth of a Nation days, and
her long siege of ill health has prevented the fruition of many
ambitious plans which he had for 'the little sister of the
films.' But now, apparently, Miss Marsh is again able to
resume her work, and Griffith is determined that her first
appearance as a Triangle star shall be a success." The
direction of the film is actually credited to Lloyd Ingraham,
a nondescript director of dubious talents.

Griffith's public disavowal of Fine Arts productions
and his general disinterest in the company began with the
completion and initial screenings of Intolerance. It is almost
as if, buoyed by the critical success of his masterpiece, he
had decided that he did not need Fine Arts and, more importantly, he did not need his one-time financial savior, Harry Aitken. Certainly this is the most likely reason for the
number of statements from this point onwards, statements
which do not ring true and do a disservice to both Griffith's
name and the Fine Arts Films.

The comments started mildly enough with an interview
in Chicago on August 30, 1916--reported in Variety--in which
the director stated that he was considering the suggestion
that in the future he devote himself entirely to the directing
of three or four big features a year, leaving the regular

Triangle releases to the work of Thomas H. Ince and Mack
Sennett. Arriving back in Los Angeles on October 4, he
told The Moving Picture World that "I am going to some
lonely spot where I can be all by myself and rest. I am
going to do a lot of thinking and I must have a rest. But
right now I am without a plan for the future."

On October 1, he had been interviewed in Chicago
(the stopover in Chicago for transfer to and from the Twentieth
Century Limited certainly offered golden opportunites for reporters and producers to have their say) by Louella Parsons and
told her a blatant lie: "I haven't seen a Triangle picture in
four months. I have never produced a Fine Arts production,
and the words 'supervised by David W. Griffith' were put on
the screen without my knowledge. My time has been spent
making Intolerance which has occupied all my waking hours."
It did not seem to concern Griffith that this statement was
in direct contradiction to earlier remarks he had made concerning Fine Arts, and, if true, would have branded him a
liar and an opportunist as far as his association with Fine
Arts and Triangle was concerned. Further, it should be
pointed out that extant prints of Fine Arts productions do
not contain titles stating, "Supervised by David W. Griffith."
The director was equally outspoken in Motion Picture News
(October 28, 1916), "I know very little about the Triangle,
for I have only made two pictures, and they have been my
own. The Fine Arts studio will continue making Triangle
pictures, but with that I have personally nothing to do."

However, Griffith was still very much concerned with the
running of Fine Arts--his published pronouncements not with-
standing--and on November 14, 1916, he telegraphed Harry
Aitken, tersely referring to Fine Arts players as Majestic
players:

> I have a wire from Mr. Woods in reference to
> using stars in the Majestic pictures. I had told
> you and the other Triangle crowd last fall repeatedly
> that Mae Marsh was receiving offers from other
> companies from $1,000 to $2,000 a week, and that
> she and other stars that I had selected were being
> slighted for Talmadge and others. We had been
> repeatedly told that Mae Marsh had no drawing
> power from the Triangle offices, and we naturally
> could not expect her to work and take second place
> to tenth rate people for the rest of her life as far
> as these new names suggested by Mr. Woods for

> stars, any street-car conductor would draw just as
> much money. I would suggest that you attend to
> managing the Triangle which is conceded to be the
> worst managed business in Film History and let
> Mr. Woods alone in handling the Majestic, the Ma-
> jestic stars being considered everywhere the best
> in Moving Pictures with the exception of Mary Pick-
> ford and Marguerite Clark. I insist that none of
> these fake stars be put on through the Fine Arts
> Co. I insist on this in the interest of the debt due
> me in every direction from the Triangle Company,
> after putting over such samples of lemons as two
> or three we had last year, leave this line alone.
> I would advise using your efforts while they are
> very much needed in the advertising and manager-
> ial offices of the Triangle

At Fine Arts, Griffith did utilize the company to pro-
mote his stand against censorship which had begun with the
adverse critical and public reaction to The Birth of a Nation
from certain quarters. From the spring of 1916, every Fine
Arts film contained an opening title stating: "Every state,
city, or town, has laws for the arrest and trial of those
responsible for immoral exhibitions or publications, and this
includes motion pictures. Therefore, why censorship?"

The spring of 1916, of course, also saw publication
of Griffith's pamphlet on The Rise and Fall of Free Speech
in America. Epes Winthrop Sargent reviewed the publication
in The Moving Picture World (May 20, 1916) and was critical that Griffith approached his subject from the viewpoint
of the producer of The Birth of a Nation rather than as "an
artist pleading for the salvation of his art." "In a word,"
Sargent wrote,

> Mr. Griffith approaches his subject with too strong
> a bias of personal animosity. His individual re-
> sentment shows too strongly to permit any of his
> arguments to have weight with the reader who has
> no personal interest either in or against the cen-
> sorship. He is writing because his own ox is
> gored; not because his impersonal sense of fair
> play is outraged, but herein he differs not at all
> from a host of other writers on either side. He
> views his subject too large. He makes the wrong
> approach. His arguments are, for the greater
> part, not upheld by facts. It is his book, published

at his own expense, and therein he is at liberty to
say what he will, since free speech is not yet dead,
but it is not a book that will bring conviction to
the unprejudiced mind; least of all to those newspaper publishers whom he repeatedly threatens with
a like annoyance if film censorship continues.

Conflicting anecdotes and reports aside, certain things
are very clear. The majority of the Fine Arts players and
directors were schooled in the Griffith tradition (and there
could be no better schooling for film makers in the Teens)
and whether Griffith was a large or a shadowy presence on
the sets of their films, those films do bear the Griffith im-
print, be they supervised or not by the master. One need
only take a look at The Little Yank, to understand how much
its director, George Siegmann, must have learned from Griffith as an assistant director on The Birth of a Nation; study
The Children Pay with its simple, uncluttered story and its
appeal for love and tolerance, which compares most favorably
with Griffith's True Heart Susie or A Romance of Happy Valley. Take a took at Let Katy Do It, whose editing, construction, storyline, and direction heavily show the influence of
The Birth of a Nation.

Chapter 3

THE FILMS OF 1915

In 1914, D. W. Griffith first came to the studios at 4500 Sunset Boulevard, on the south side of the street at its junction with Hollywood Boulevard, to put the finishing touches to The Escape. At that time the studios were called the Reliance-Majestic Studios; with the formation of Triangle they became the Fine Arts Studios. On the grounds of the Fine Arts Studios were filmed much of The Birth of a Nation and Intolerance, and most of the Fine Arts productions with their familiar trademark of an artist's palette with the letters "F. A." at its center.

The studio boasted three open air stages--60 by 100 feet, 70 by 190 feet and 50 by 100 feet--plus a glass-enclosed studio, sixty feet by sixty feet and twenty feet high, lit by an electric generator. As large as a good-sized village, with 209 permanent buildings, the studio contained one hundred dressing rooms, a property room (60 by 200 feet) with literally thousands of props, a backlot with a lovers' lane, a New England village street and the lower half of a New York skyscraper. As one fan magazine noted, "The Fine Arts studio is a fitting workshop for the master, and, whether you are half a mile away, in beautiful Hollywood, or three thousand miles away, along busy Broadway, you are quite likely to hear it referred to as the Griffith studio as by its other title. Here it was that David Wark Griffith not only conceived but staged a great majority of his notable film achievements."[13]

With the creation of Fine Arts, new staff were soon added to the company. Magazine writer Roy Somerville joined the scenario staff, which was under the direct supervision of long-time Griffith associate Frank Woods, who held the title of Manager of Production. It was a vague title, but there was no question as to Woods' power. When Grif-

fith was away, Frank Woods ran the studio, and as Bessie
Love recalled, "You might even go through Mr. Griffith to
get to Mr. Woods." J. A. Raynes joined Fine Arts in November 1915 to aid in the preparation of incidental music
for the films. He was to help Joseph Carl Breil, responsible
for the scores of many early Fine Arts films, including The
Lamb, Old Heidelberg, Martyrs of the Alamo, and The Lily
and the Rose. (Ince boasted four composers under contract
at this time: Louis Gottschalk, Edward Foot, Victor Schertzinger, and Joseph E. Nurnberger.) R. Ellis Wales, author
of an early Fine Arts feature, The Penitentes, joined the
studio as its librarian, supposedly the first motion picture
librarian on record. "He is an authority on the history of
decoration and part of his work is to insure correctness of
detail in the plays that touch the arts, habits and costumes
of the past," commented The Triangle (November 27, 1915).

     By the end of 1915 more than sixty actors and actress-
es were under contract, including Mary Alden, Josephine
Crowell, Dorothy and Lillian Gish, Olga Grey, Jennie Lee,
Alberta Lee, Mae and Marguerite Marsh, Fay Tincher, Kate
Toncray, Margery Wilson, Elmer Clifton, Max Davidson,
Howard Gaye, Robert Harron, Ralph Lewis, Wilfred Lucas,
Owen Moore, Alfred Paget, and Tom Wilson. In charge of
hiring the extras at Fine Arts was Karl Brown's mother,
Lucille. "She's not one of your hard-eyes policemen of the
properties," wrote Photoplay (April 1917), "but a real human
being with an ear for every woe, a competent and discrim-
inating eye, and an understanding heart." The photographic
department was nominally under the charge of Billy Bitzer,
who "manages to get around the plant seven or eight times
a day; carries on endless experiments of his own in his
private laboratory; supervises the completed works of every
one of his men."[13] Directors included Eddie Dillon and W.
Christy Cabanne (whose association with Griffith went back
to Biograph), Paul Powell (whose background was journalism),
Lloyd Ingraham, Jack Conway, Allan Dwan, the Franklin
Brothers, the "kid" directors, and John Emerson from the
New York stage.

     Emerson was responsible for the direction and screen-
play of the second Fine Arts production to be released, Old
Heidelberg, featuring Wallace Reid as Prince Karl and Dorothy Gish as Kathie, the innkeeper's daughter with whom he
falls in love. The film is somewhat dull and is chiefly of
interest today for the performance by Erich von Stroheim in
a major role--listed fourth in the published cast as Prince

The Fine Arts Studio at 4500 Sunset Boulevard.

Karl's valet, Lutz. Old Heidelberg received favorable reviews at its initial release. Louis Reeves Harrison in The
Moving Picture World (October 16, 1915) thought "It holds
and pleases to the end," while Peter Milne in Motion Picture
News (October 16, 1915) opined, "The story is slim and
relies altogether on the pathos of its theme for success.
And success it is.... Worthy indeed to be rated as a two-
dollar picture." Julian Johnson, writing in Photoplay (December, 1915), commented, "Emerson has thrown superb
atmosphere into this play. It is a triumph of accuracy, even
as it is a triumph of scene and accessory. It is only marred
by peace propaganda weak as wet gunpowder, a very burles-
quey monarch, and a pictorial implication that Teutonic people
are, naturally, averse to the present war." Contemporary publicity indicated that Griffith was perhaps involved in the direction
of some of the film's second-rate battle scenes.

There is an interesting anecdote concerning Old Heidelberg in Howard Gaye's unpublished autobiography, So This
Was Hollywood: "One day, John Emerson was directing a
scene in Old Heidelberg and the correct arrangements of the
orders on the uniforms came under discussion. In despair
he turned to anyone who could help him, and was told that
there was a supposed Austrian officer in the extras' compound
who might be able to set matters right. Accordingly Von
Stroheim was brought in and offered twenty dollars a week
to stand by and act as adviser."

Old Heidelberg was followed by Martyrs of the Alamo,
which was, without question, the most important Fine Arts
production of 1915. The story of the hopeless stand by a
small band of Texans against Santa Anna and his Mexican
army was masterfully directed by W. Christy Cabanne, with
Griffith's supervision very much in evidence. All the historical characters were represented in the drama: Santa
Anna, played by Walter Long; James Bowie, played by Alfred Paget; Davy Crockett, played by A. D. Sears; and Sam
Houston, played by Tom Wilson. Although the female members of the cast--Ora Carew as Mrs. Dickinson and Juanita
Hansen--were identified in contemporary publicity material,
the film itself adopts an oddly sexist attitude and identifies
none of the female players.

Subtitled "The Birth of Texas"--a title which appears
in bigger lettering than Martyrs of the Alamo on extant prints
--the film opens with a title proclaiming, "An historical
drama suggested by the crisis in Mexico, 1835 to 1836, and

The company and crew gather on one of the stages for an unidentified meeting.

Augustus Carney, Juanita Hansen and Sam DeGrasse in
Martyrs of the Alamo.

the immortal fall of the Alamo, which ultimately resulted in
Texas becoming an independent republic and later the largest
state of our union." The hero of the production is "Silent"
Smith (played by Sam De Grasse), who takes the lead in the
defense of the Alamo and who successfully slips through the
Mexican lines to warn Sam Houston. Walter Long is perfectly cast as the cruel, villainous and cowardly Mexican
dictator, and the film also holds interest as the first screen
appearance by Julia Faye in an unidentified "bit" part.

Dorothy Gish and Wallace Reid in Old Heidelberg.

There are obvious parallels between Martyrs of the
Alamo and The Birth of a Nation, with the Mexicans substituting for the liberated southern Negroes.   Just as Silas
Lynch had informed the Little Colonel that the sidewalk belonged to black as well as white Southerners, so do the Mexicans assert their prior rights over the Texan Americans to
walk the streets.   Shots of the dead of the Alamo instantly
bring to mind the title "War's Peace" from The Birth.   Patriotism is the key word, with references to "liberty-loving
Americans" and "the undaunted valor of the hardy American
pioneers of that age," and a statement that "the honor and
life of American womanhood was held in contempt" by the
Mexicans.   Apart from the acting of some of the minor players being overly melodramatic, Christy Cabanne seems to
have a surprisingly assured directorial touch in this production, with the battle scenes generally well handled and the
historical accuracy assured.   In a final blaze of patriotism,
the film ends with the evolution of the Texas flag from the
Mexican flag, through the Confederate flag, to the Stars and
Stripes.

Reviews were overwhelmingly favorable.   William
Ressman Andrews in Motion Picture News (November 6, 1915)
wrote, "Those who had read accounts of the American border
and its wild uncertain ways by such men as Cyrus Townsend
Brady naturally look forward to a thrilling picture in The
Martyrs of the Alamo.   But it is safe to say that the most
imaginative reader, full of frontier life from his border historians, could not have visualized one-tenth the action, the
local color, the characterization of types peculiar to Texas
in 1836, he might see in this Griffith masterpiece."   In The
Moving Picture World (November 6, 1915), Louis Reeves
Harrison commented,

> A veritable historical drama of tremendous action
> and of high added value in its elaborate subtitles,
> The Martyrs of the Alamo follows closely the best
> previous idealization of the same story with super-
> ior care as to detail and greater intensity during
> the supreme moments of struggle.   Most sublime
> sacrifice of American blood for the cause of liberty,
> the defense of the Alamo needs much adequate pic-
> turing lest we forget how the broad sweep of fair
> country we enjoy in peace was wrung from the
> hearts of those who made it what it is.   We do
> forget.   The warm hearthstone does not foster no-
> bility of character.   We become completely engrossed

in absorbing, existing, recreating and dying, like
so many vegetables. We lack the stimulus of some
great cause to fight for and lapse into so many
turnips or orchids, according to social station, except when some epic like the Alamo stirs the sap
in our veins until it feels like the red blood of
our hard-fighting ancestors.
    The accurate picturing of those ancestors, their
dress, their crudities, their strategems in warfare, their remarkable combination of cunning,
self-control and stubborn courage, is an education
in itself, but it is the great stimulus of this story
that has the highest value. It quickens our pulses,
gives new life to stagnant blood of overfed prosper-
ity. The Martyrs of the Alamo is an admirable
presentation from every point of view and should
prove a winner wherever it is shown.

    It should not be assumed that all Fine Arts productions
took place in Los Angeles. The company rented the Willat
Studios in Fort Lee, New Jersey, which had formerly been
leased to Fox. In addition, it took over the Reliance Studios
at 537 Riverdale Avenue in Yonkers. These studios were
formerly the Clara Morris estate and overlooked the Hudson
River. After the demise of Triangle, they became the Whitman Bennett Studios and were used for a series of First National features starring Lionel Barrymore. They were ad-
vertised in the 1921 Motion Picture Studio Directory as "con-
ceded to be one of the most efficient single unit producing
plants in America."

    Among the early Fine Arts productions shot at least
partially at the Riverdale studios were His Picture in the
Papers and Jordan Is a Hard Road. The latter, directed by
Allan Dwan and starring Dorothy Gish and Owen Moore, was
described by The Moving Picture World (November 20, 1915)
as "a labored and loosely made adaptation from a novel [by
Gilbert Parker], containing some bright spots and fair acting,
but so badly put together that it drags along like a two-reel
play stretched to five. The least interesting Triangle yet
shown." However, Julian Johnson in Photoplay (February
1916) thought it "an exquisite Fine Arts idyll." In an interview with Peter Bogdanovich, Allan Dwan recalled the film
being made in Hollywood and stated that Billy Sunday acted
as a technical advisor on the production, teaching Frank
Campeau how to play an evangelist. [8]

Other 1915 Triangle-Fine Arts releases included The
Sable Lorcha, directed by Lloyd Ingraham and featuring Tully
Marshall, which The Moving Picture World (October 30, 1915)
found "a story that is far from being a suitable vehicle for
its talented cast," and The Lily and the Rose, directed by
Paul Powell and based on a story by Griffith. Written somewhat in the spirit of A Fool There Was, it concerned a simple country girl (played by Lillian Gish) who marries a city
gentleman (Wilfred Lucas), who in time tires of her and devotes himself to a professional dancer (played by Rozsika
Dolly, one half of the Dolly Sisters). When she tires of him,
the husband shoots himself. "A newspaper story," commented
Julian Johnson (Photoplay, January, 1916), "but done from
start to finish with that fine imaginative sense, tenderness
of feeling and technical perfection which makes us all hope
for the ultimate wonders in camera craft."

Wynn in Variety (November 12, 1915) noted that, "it
earned a hand at the finale, something unusual under any
circumstances." He continued, "Rozsika Dolly as the dancer
was acceptable, although much of her personality was lost."
For her work in The Lily and the Rose--which boasted chor-
eography by both Ruth St. Denis and Ted Shawn--Miss Dolly
received $750 a week, the same salary that Fine Arts lead-
ing man Orrin Johnson warranted.

The Lily and the Rose was part of the sixth Triangle
program at the Knickerbocker Theatre, screened with Ince's
Aloha Oe, starring Willard Mack and Enid Markey, and two
Keystone comedies, A Janitor's Wife's Temptation, with Fred
Mace, and The Village Scandal, with Raymond Hitchcock and
"Fatty" Arbuckle.   Of the evening's entertainment, Peter
Milne wrote in Motion Picture News (November 20, 1915),
"In general this program is a collection of averagely good
pictures. The casts are the strong points in every instance,
the work of all the principals being unusual enough to warrant
a warm reception at the pictures."

On the surface, The Penitentes, the last Triangle-
Fine Arts release of 1915, directed by Jack Conway and starring Orrin Johnson and Seena Owen, would not appear to be
a particularly important production. It was the first Fine
Arts production to star Johnson (his second Fine Arts feature,
The Price of Power, filmed in October 1915, was also directed by Jack Conway), but Johnson is hardly remembered
today as an important leading man. However, Seymour Stern

Wilfred Lucas and Lillian Gish in The Lily and the Rose.

devotes considerable space to the production in An Index to
the Creative Work of David Wark Griffith* and some of his
comments are worth repeating.

Stern claims this was the first film to introduce the
Penitentes--a secret order of Franciscans who practiced
flagellation and crucifixion--to the screen. Supposedly, "doc-
umentary" footage of the Penitentes was actually photographed
in Northern New Mexico, in the mountain wilderness com-
monly known as the Penitente Country, but rejected by Griffith and Conway as unsatisfactory. Instead, the ceremonial
and ritual-murder sequences were filmed in the Sierra Madre
foothills of Los Angeles, using a small group of fanatics.
In addition, Stern claims that Griffith employed as advisors
on the film Father Eugene Sugranes, pastor of the "Old Plaza

---

*Part II, The Art Triumphant, (b) The Triangle Productions
1915-1916, published by the British Film Institute as a Special Supplement to Sight and Sound (August 1946).

Church in Los Angeles and a scholar in flagellant ritualism
in the New World" and Charles F. Lummis, one of the leading historians of the American Southwest and "the only person who had succeeded both in photographing a Penitente
crucifixion and returning to civilization alive with the photograph. "

   Seymour Stern also singles out for attention, although
nowhere does he indicate that he had actually seen the film,
Griffith's direction of Jack Conway's direction and the performances of Seena Owen and Josephine Crowell.   The first
item is reinforced by Peter Milne in his review of The Penitentes in Motion Picture News (December 4, 1915): "Several
real thrills are provided by battle scenes in which the camera
has swept great reaches of country; by cavalry dashes which
remind one continually that the supervising hand of D. W.
Griffith is stretched over the production. "

Chapter 4

DEWOLF HOPPER

"It is an interesting question whether 'legitimate' stars or the so-called 'stock stars' of film organizations will prove the more serviceable in making the highest quality of pictures. We are now experimenting at the Triangle Fine Arts studios along both lines. Each kind of service has certain elements in its favor," wrote D. W. Griffith in Variety. He continued, "The legitimate star brings to the studio not only the well-deserved reputation of a great name in old line theatricals, but also usually an enormous amount of material in the way of scripts, characters and 'business.' He has been associated with the traditions but it depends upon himself chiefly whether he shall prove adaptable to the new conditions."[24]

Sir Herbert Beerbohm Tree failed to adapt, but a stage actor who made an easy transition to films was DeWolf Hopper, who joined Fine Arts in the fall of 1915 at a yearly salary of $125,000. He brought with him his young wife, actress and gossip columnist-to-be Hedda Hopper, plus his nine-month-old son, DeWolf Hopper, Jr., who was to gain fame in films and television as William Hopper and who made his screen debut in his father's feature Sunshine Dad.

DeWolf Hopper had made his first appearance on stage on November 4, 1878, in New Haven, Connecticut; he made his New York debut less than a year later. For many years he appeared at Wallack's Theatre in New York, and his first starring role was as Filacoudre in Castles in the Air at New York's Broadway Theatre on May 5, 1890. In 1911, he portrayed Dick Deadeye in Gilbert and Sullivan's H. M. S. Pinafore, and soon became known as this country's leading exponent of Gilbert and Sullivan comic opera, playing the Police Sergeant in The Pirates of Penzance, John Wellington Wells in The Sorcerer and Ko-Ko in The Mikado.

DeWolf Hopper

It was announced that perhaps Hopper would play Mr.
Pickwick in The Pickwick Papers--a role in which he had
toured for three years--or Micawber in David Copperfield,
but instead he was assigned the title role in the first screen
version of Cervantes' classic, Don Quixote. As he read the
book for the first time, DeWolf Hopper recalled, "I thought
I saw before me an opportunity to create an immortal character of fiction in a fashion impossible to my own stage.
But my new enthusiasm wilted progressively, once the camera
began to grind."33

Hopper was not an easy convert to the motion picture;
he found problems with shooting the film out of sequence.
The inconsistencies and the incontinuities were at first be-
wildering to him. He did not understand why the script was
changed to have Don Quixote shot instead of dying of brain
fever as in the novel. It took time for Hopper and his director, Edward Dillon, to become accustomed to each other's
working methods, although Griffith was quoted in The Moving
Picture World (December 25, 1915) as saying "Don Quixote
was one of the best productions recently made by any of his
sub-directors and he paid a high compliment to Edward Dillon who had charge of it."

Chester Withey, who also appeared in the production
as Don Fernando, was responsible for the screenplay and apparently, aside from Don Quixote's death, was fairly faithful to the original work. Monte Blue doubled for DeWolf
Hopper in all the strenuous scenes, a chore he was also to
undertake for Sir Herbert Beerbohm Tree in Macbeth. (In
his autobiography, Hopper recalls that George Walsh was required, at his suggestion, to try to commit suicide in the
Cleopatra manner: with a live snake. A rattlesnake was
sent for which promptly really did bite Walsh.)

The actor claims that the film was not a box-office
success and that this was a fate which all his Fine Arts
productions suffered, but there seems to be some dispute as
to this. As late as 1919, he was interviewed by Motion Picture Classic, and when he modestly asserted, "I never felt
that I made a real success in pictures," his interviewer in-
terrupted with, "But the public did." Certainly the reviews
for Don Quixote were mixed. Naturally the trade papers
tried to be as polite as possible, but it is obvious from how
much space they allotted the feature that they had mixed
feelings about it. Harvey F. Thew in Motion Picture News
(January 1, 1916) used almost an entire page to review the

DeWolf Hopper in Don Quixote.

twelfth Triangle program at the Knickerbocker Theatre, a
program which consisted of a Keystone comedy, The Hunt,
an Ince feature, The Despoilers, starring Frank Keenan and
Enid Markey, and Don Quixote. The first two subjects
warranted sixteen paragraphs, while Don Quixote received
only four. The first sentence speaks volumes: "Don Quixote
frankly is not the work of D. W. Griffith...." Louis Reeves
Harrison in The Moving Picture World (December 25, 1915)
was more responsive, calling the film "a production of the
highest order.... DeWolf Hopper is amazing. All that he
has done on the stage will die with him, but his impersonation of Don Quixote in the Fine Arts film will assure his

immortality--it is a performance without a flaw, an ideal."
(It is ironic that critics and others back then did not realize
the fragility of nitrate film, and Don Quixote has apparently not
survived.   Like Hopper's stage work, it has died with him.)

　　　　Harrison singled out Fay Tincher as Dulcinea for
particular praise, calling her a born comedienne.   Julian
Johnson in Photoplay (March 1916), despite reservations as
to the characterization, likewise was impressed.   "Here
Dulcinea is made into a female Charley Chaplin, when she
should have resembled Lady Godiva.   The comedy as a
whole is not so much reminiscent of Cervantes as of Mutt
and Jeff.   For Dulcinea herself, I have nothing but praise;
Fay Tincher's performance is little short of wonderful.   All
things considered, she surpasses Hopper."   He returned to
Fay Tincher's performance when he gave his yearly overview of the new films in the September 1916 issue of Photoplay:

> From this welter of keystonery by an undertakers'
> convention, Fay Tincher's Dulcinea shines like a
> starbeam from anothery century.   The thing should
> live for this jewel of impersonation alone.   Fay
> Tincher visualized Cervantes.   She became the lit-
> tle serving maid of the dying Middle Ages; in her
> eyes was humble wonder, and when the senile knight
> caressed her cotton stocking with his lips it was
> as though repentant Kundry had seen The Grail glow
> crimson.

　　　　While dismissing Don Quixote as "the greatest disappointment" produced by the Fine Arts studios, Julian Johnson did hail DeWolf Hopper, noting "Never, for the Don, will
there be a man more perfectly endowed by nature and acquire-
ments than DeWolf Hopper.   His own performance is all that
his direction permits--even more.   Consider the pathos of
the death scene."

　　　　Don Quixote was originally intended for release as a
seven-reel production, but because of poor critical response
and disappointment with it at the studio, the film was cut to
five reels.   The Moving Picture World (January 1, 1916)
found it "runs with greater snap and vigor, a decided improvement on the version orginally presented."

　　　　Happily, DeWolf Hopper's next feature, Sunshine Dad,
has survived, and a true delight it proves to be.   It has a

Carl Stockdale and DeWolf Hopper in Don Quixote.

pleasant comedic style, for which much credit must go to
director Edward Dillon and writers Chester Withey and Tod
Browning, and Hopper gives a jaunty performance--which
reminds one immediately of Sidney Drew--and which seems
to indicate that he is getting as much enjoyment from playing
the role as is the audience from watching. His particular

brand of theatrics was ideally suited to this type of light-
hearted farce, which could have been played just as well,
with dialogue, on stage.

As Oscar Cooper noted in Motion Picture News (April
8, 1916), "Here he is seen as a gay old bird, who spends
his time flitting ponderously around cafes, paying court to a
young widow, and dodging a crowd of Hindoos, who are attempting to recover a diamond band stolen from the shrine
of the great god Jujab. As Alonzo Evergreen, Hopper is
called upon to perform all sorts of capers, and his performance lacks nothing of the strenuous. He relies to a large
extent upon the sort of 'business' for which he was famous
on the legitimate stage. "

Playing "the retired Thespian who still persists in
playing the juvenile," Hopper is aided immeasurably by a
cast which includes Max Davidson as a Hindoo Seer, glower-
ing at everyone; Raymond Wells as a Hindoo Doer; Eugene
Pallette as Hopper's son, Alfred; Jewel Carmen as his son's
fiancée; Fay Tincher as the widow Marrimore; and Chester
Withey as the thief of the band of diamonds, pearls and rubies,
Count Kottschkojff. The title introducing the last reads,
"Note to those in the audience who read titles out loud. Here's
where we've got you. You can't pronounce the Count's name,
you can only think it. " The titles also make ready use of
such slang as "gink" and "kick in with the goods," usually
spoken by the Hindoos.

There are some wonderful moments, such as when
Pallette discovers his father, Hopper, looking at Jewel Carmen's legs as she stands on a table holding up her dress
and worrying about an imaginary mouse, invented by Hopper.
(A risque element is added to the farce by having the stolen
band be used as a woman's garter, and thus requiring Hopper
and Withey to examine assorted ladies' legs.) The final
sequence in which a lion, borrowed from the E & R Jungle
Film Company, runs amok in the hotel is surely borrowed
from Mack Sennett, who borrowed it back for The Extra Girl
(1923). This is the lion with which D. W. Griffith was photographed for stills that are often reproduced supposedly to
illustrate the director's rapport with animals.

The only major negative review of Sunshine Dad came
from Variety, whose critic Fred wrote (April 21, 1916),
"There are two things about this Triangle-Fine Arts five-reel
comedy that prove to be its saviour. One is the remarkably

trained lion present in the last reel and the other is the
corking manner in which the leaders are written. If it
weren't for these two features this DeWolf Hopper comedy
would be an altogether sorry affair.... Mr. Hopper is a
distinct disappointment as a picture comedian and it remained
for Fay Tincher to do the best work of the production."

Variety was equally disappointed with DeWolf Hopper's
next feature, Mr. Goode, the Samaritan. Its critic, Jolo
wrote (May 26, 1916), "Somehow or other DeWolf Hopper
just misses as a picture star. He seems adaptable enough,
his work has individuality, and yet there is something lacking." The film boasted much the same personnel as Sunshine Dad, director Edward Dillon and writer Chester Withey,
both of whom also doubled as actors, along with Fay Tincher
and Max Davidson.

DeWolf Hopper first recited "Casey at the Bat" on
May 13, 1888, at Wallack's Theatre in New York. "The
outlook wasn't brilliant for the Mudville nine that day," and
the following lines of the poem became Hopper's trademark.
Jokes were made as to how many times he had given the
recitation, and so it was only natural that he should star in
a film version. With the California town of Lankershim
standing in for Mudville, Hopper apparently had the time of
his life playing the title role and told The Moving Picture
World (May 20, 1916) that so overjoyed was he at actually
playing baseball that he was now capable of reciting "Casey
at the Bat" a further eight thousand times. One of those
times is worth recording. To publicize the film, it was arranged that he would give his recitation by telephone from
the Fine Arts studios in Los Angeles to a newspaper conven-
tion in New York. It established a record for long-distance
"piece speaking."

The film, unhappily, set no records as far as De-
Wolf Hopper's screen career was concerned. Variety was
again negative, Fred reporting (June 23, 1916), "Here is
another DeWolf Hopper feature. To the exhibitor who has
played Hopper features in the past a word to the wise is
sufficient--to those who have not played any of them one
needs but to say that this Triangle-Fine Arts feature is just
another example of a good idea gone wrong. 'Casey at the
Bat' has been a standby of Mr. Hopper's in recitative form
for many years. It should have made a corking subject for
a comedy picture, but William Everett Wing, who adapted
the scenario, saw fit to make a cheap, mushy heart thriller

DeWolf Hopper in <u>Casey at the Bat</u>.

of the story and the result was that the take, coupled with
Mr. Hopper, who fails utterly to look the part, and who acted
it extremely badly, did not turn out at all in the manner that
one assumed it would from the title.   As a feature film
Casey at the Bat will fall short of expectations, although the
title will attract money."

    Louis Reeves Harrison in The Moving Picture World
(July 1, 1916) was kinder:

> Suggested by the famous poem, "Casey at the Bat,"
> tells of Casey's downfall during a final test of
> strength between the ball nine of Mudville and Frog-
> town and gives Mr. Hopper opportunity for one of
> those humanizing performances which seem to fit
> him almost as well as he fits them, and that is
> saying a great deal.   The story fits him in another
> respect--he has been The Fan, of all baseball fans,
> during a large part of his varied career, and every
> move he makes on the field is filled with that sub-
> tlety of performance which only such capable actors
> seem to understand.   He plays the role for all it
> is worth without obtruding DeWolf Hopper any more
> than one of his size and striking personality can
> help.
> Though Casey is the one man on whom the Mud-
> ville ball nine can depend to win a game in a tight
> place, a local hero as long as he is of use, he is
> nothing but a grocer's clerk in private life, and
> Hopper never loses sight of the fact.   He commands
> attention by a marvelously intelligent interpretation
> rather than by thrusting himself into the foreground,
> a great relief in these days of camera-made stars
> of the closeup variety.   Casey loses the final game
> through intense anxiety about a tiny tot of a little
> girl playmate who has been severely injured and
> becomes an object of general disfavor where he has
> really been the cause of readjusting a wrong done
> the mother of the tiny tot and leaves town on foot,
> his famous homemade bat in hand, at the end for
> what is hoped to be a happier career.   Mr. Hopper
> gives the role so much artistry that the story is
> made delightful through his adequate interpretation.

    Oscar Cooper in Motion Picture News (July 1, 1916)
thought, "Mr. Hopper's work is a little more effective here,
because he is not called upon to carry the whole burden.

Some of the scenes have considerable heart interest, notably
those depicting Casey's love of children, and his kindly good-
nature toward the villagers.   Mr. Hopper seems to fit the
atmosphere of this subject better than he fitted the atmosphere
of some other pieces in which he has appeared."

Lloyd Ingraham, who directed Casey at the Bat, also
directed Hopper's next feature, Stranded, in which he played
an elderly actor stranded while on tour.   The film's leading
lady, Bessie Love, recalled, "Tall Mr. Hopper had no hair
on the top of his head--or indeed anywhere else on his head.
I used to think he must be wearing a wig; when I think of it
now, it was quite obvious.   He had an expression which Mr.
Ingraham used to call 'peeling his eyeballs' to express sur-
prise or shock, like Frankie Howard (a popular British television comedian) with his sudden scared-horse expression.
In the middle of a take Mr. Ingraham would say to him, 'Now
peel the eyeballs!'   Mr. Hopper would, and it was very funny."42

DeWolf Hopper's Fine Arts career ended with what
was probably the company's first two-reel production, Puppets, directed and possibly written by Tod Browning.   It was
an unusual film in that it was presented as a pantomime, a
story of how a young man cures his uncle of the idea of
marrying a young girl.   In his review, Peter Milne, in Motion Picture News (September 23, 1916), explained, "The
settings, everyone of them, are designed in black and white
while, as might be guessed from the title, the characters
are clothed as per puppets, in pantaloons, pierrot costumes,
ballet effects and tights.   The story is founded on a familiar
French pantomime, although it is modernized for the occasion
and changed to suit the cast."   In The Moving Picture World
(September 23, 1916), Louis Reeves Harrison, however, was
not excited by the idea or its realization:

> This two-reel Triangle-Fine Arts reverts to the
> pantomime and illustrates as well as anything re-
> cently shown how bare of human interest is any
> screen play given over almost entirely to move-
> ment without psychology.   The faint revelations of
> mind and heart are so weak that there might as
> well be none at all.   The actors merely pantomime,
> all save DeWolf Hopper, and are as devoid of char-
> acter as so many marionettes.   The release is
> glaringly black and white, designedly so, with an
> occasional relief of bright subtitle.

After Puppets, DeWolf Hopper left Fine Arts and the cinema. He returned to the New York stage to star in The Passing Show of 1917, which he followed with a touring version of The Better 'Ole. Hopper came back to California in 1929 in an abortive attempt to return to films. On arrival in Los Angeles, he made a typical Hopper comment: "The city seems to have more climate than ever, and less Californians." DeWolf Hopper died, at the age of seventy-seven, on September 23, 1935.

Perhaps the last word on DeWolf Hopper should be left to Julian Johnson, who summed him up thusly, and perhaps somewhat unfairly, in Photoplay (September 1916), "And last of all: that delightful gentleman, grand curtain-speaker, and footlight veteran--also that celluloid lemon and shadow ruin--DeWolf Hopper. Let us forbear."

Chapter 5

DOUGLAS FAIRBANKS: THE EVOLUTION OF A
SCREEN LEGEND

In the films in which he starred at Fine Arts, Douglas
Fairbanks developed a screen character which typified his
Teens films and which remained as much a part of him as
his natural leaps and bounds long after he left the studio.
In fact, Fairbanks never really strayed from the types of
roles he had adopted at Fine Arts until 1920, when The Mark
of Zorro perhaps more than any film created a new screen
persona, a persona which carried the star through the Twenties in films such as The Three Musketeers (1921), Robin
Hood (1921), and The Thief of Bagdad (1923), reached its
zenith with Don Q, Son of Zorro (1925), and remained with
him through the end and The Private Life of Don Juan, a
noble parting from the screen for a noble actor of the screen.

In two books published in the late Teens, Laugh and
Live (Britton, 1917) and Making Life Worth While (Britton,
1918), Fairbanks wrote about his philosophy of life: "Great
trials are strengthening to character.... Recreation, a good
appetite, a healthy body, and the proper amount of sleep
are positive requirements in making life worthwhile.... A
healthy, clean body and a trained, clean mind.... Out of
energy and enthusiasm comes something that must not be
neglected ... laughter.... The ability to look the other fellow in the eye is as necessary to character as the foundation
is to a house." This philosophy is a constant presence in
his Fine Arts productions. In fact, in this age of the committed film maker, it is more than a little satisfying to find
an actor from an earlier era who carried his personal be-
liefs--two divorces notwithstanding--into his films.

At Fine Arts, in a period of little more than a year,
Douglas Fairbanks starred in twelve features plus one short,

44

Douglas Fairbanks during his Fine Arts period.

The Mystery of the Leaping Fish, which was not officially
designated a Fine Arts production. It was a phenomenal
number of films indicating not only Fairbanks' incredible
popularity but also his energy. Later, he slowed down,
spending greater time on planning and production. Between
his departure from Fine Arts and the end of 1920, he made
only seventeen features. Between 1921 and 1931, he averaged
only one film per year.

     According to Booton Herndon's definitive volume, Mary
Pickford and Douglas Fairbanks, [31] the actor met Harry Aitken at the Algonquin Hotel. Aitken offered Fairbanks an initial contract, which he declined to accept, feeling that films
would damage his stage image. Eventually, the actor agreed
to a three-year contract, which promised him that Griffith
would personally direct his Fine Arts productions and that
his commencing salary would be $2,000 a week. Fairbanks
turned his back on a tremendously successful stage career
--He Come Up Smiling, The New Henrietta and Hawthorne of
the U.S.A. , etc.--and set out for California, which for him
at least proved to be the land of opportunity. As early as
September 1915, D. W. Griffith was writing that "Douglas
Fairbanks has already proven himself of such great worth in
pictures that we have engaged him for an exclusive three
years' contract and he has definitely abandoned his old as-
sociations for that time at least."[24]

     Griffith did not direct the actor's first film, The
Lamb, nor was he to direct any of Fairbanks' other Fine
Arts features, but instead the production was assigned to
Christy Cabanne. To what extent Griffith was involved in
its production, it is impossible at this point in time to say.
D. W. Griffith certainly wrote the story for Fairbanks, and
in a 1933 radio series, D. W. Griffith's Hollywood, the di-
rector--on program no. 22, broadcast on March 22--talked
about rehearsing the actor on the set and helping him over
his initial nervousness at acting in front of the camera. The
only problem with Griffith's remembrances is that he states
Chester Withey was the director!

     Many stories have been published stating that Griffith
was uncomfortable with Fairbanks' comic antics and felt he
had no future in films--a belief squashed by Griffith's own
article in Variety. DeWolf Hopper gives Griffith credit for
directing The Lamb, but then continues, "I have been told
that when the film was finished he said to the actor, 'You'd
better take your monkey shines to Sennett: they're more in

his line. ' "33   But, of course, DeWolf Hopper was not at the
studio when The Lamb was filmed.

One thing is very clear. Harry Aitken felt so strongly
about the commercial possibilities of The Lamb that he decided it should be the opening attraction for Triangle, over
Martyrs of the Alamo and Old Heidelberg, both of which were
completed and could easily have been screened on that opening night program. In The Lamb, Fairbanks plays Gerald,
"Son of the Rich," who loses his girl when she believes him
to be a coward. He takes a course in physical training, is
kidnapped by crooks, left for dead in the desert, captured
by Indians, is involved in a fight between the Yaquis Indians
and Mexican soldiers, and eventually rescues the girl from
the wretched Indians. Exteriors were shot in the Mojave
Desert and the San Fernando Valley, probably out near Chats-
worth where portions of The Birth of a Nation were shot.
Despite its convoluted plot, The Lamb was basically the story
of a boob who becomes a true red-blooded American. Quite
frankly, when viewed today, The Lamb is a tedious melodrama
which makes one wonder why Fairbanks was ever allowed to
make another film. Its chief redeeming qualities are amusing subtitles, such as "Blood will speak--Though society may
drown the conversation," after which Anita Loos seems to
have modelled her work, and a fine performance by Alfred
Paget as "The Cactus-Fed Goat from Arizona."

Contemporary critics, however, were unanimous in
their praise. Harvey F. Thew in Motion Picture News (October 9, 1915) described Fairbanks as "an excellent actor of
the stage [who], transplanted to the screen ... becomes a
delight to the eye. " Jolo in Variety (October 1, 1915) wrote,
"It is no wonder the Triangle people signed up Fairbanks for
a period of three years at any salary within reason. They
would even have been justified in stretching a point to secure
Douglas. He 'registers' on the screen as well as any regular
film actor that has ever appeared in pictures and more strongly
than most.... Columns of praise would not do complete
justice to The Lamb. It is the classiest kind of melodramatic comedy, wonderfully staged, brilliantly acted and humorously captioned. " The Moving Picture World (October
9, 1915) commented,

> A new star has appeared in the motion-picture con-
> stellation, a comedian who wins through interesting
> personality and delightful characterization, a de-
> cided relief from the raw crudities of acrobatic

clowns. Whether or not he will continue to shine
as he does in The Lamb, Douglas Fairbanks has
scored one decided hit--he suits the role quite as
well as the role suits him and it seems to have
been especially created to display advantageously
his striking peculiarities. He holds the eye so
strongly, and without apparent effort, that he is
the whole play from beginning to end. This is not
to the detriment of the story. It is a snappy and
highly finished product--the Griffith supervision as-
sures that--it has an appetizing dash of bitters
from Christy Cabanne, and the subtitles are mar-
vels--they sound very much like the scintillations
of a certain photoplaywright who graduated from the
highest ranks of criticism.

The entire product is the result of a unified effort by many bright minds, a product trimmed
smooth in careful revision. It scores with the
audience as soon as it is under way and grows in
strength until it approaches intense drama, but it
is always delightful comedy, clean, wholesome,
not catering to low tastes at the risk of nauseating
minds, not primitive. There is nothing that could
be called startling about The Lamb, but it has a
quiet strength all its own, a certain humanness that
warms one to the story and to its leading character.
It belongs to a class of moving pictures which
firmly established the new art in popular favor, a
story to charm all who watch it unfold on the
screen.

Julian Johnson in Photoplay (December, 1915) was a
little more cautious than his fellow critics:

Typewriter drivers should be licensed, like chauf-
feurs [he declared]. One reckless unlicensee declared that the cavalry charge in The Lamb--fea-
ture offering of the first Triangle bill--surpassed
the terrific ride of the clans, in The Birth of a
Nation. Others acclaimed the play a worthy second
to the Griffith drama. Here's what The Lamb
really is, it seems to me: a rollicking, typically
American melodrama, presenting Douglas Fairbanks,
one of America's best known, best liked and most
continually agreeable stage personalities. Improb-
able--quite, and to one who knows the desert, just
a little bit absurd when one is asked to believe it.

Comparing The Birth of a Nation and The Lamb is
like comparing Balzac and one of our popular story-
writers of today; it's so unfair to today's man.
Gatling-gun fire is not the essence of thrill, any
more than gunfire on the bassdrum is the essence
of dramatic emotion.

Even before the premiere of The Lamb, Fairbanks
was at work on his second Fine Arts feature, Double Trouble,
again directed by Christy Cabanne, from a popular novel concerning dual personality by Herbert Quick.   The company
took over the town of Santa Ana, California, for one of the
scenes, using 4,000 extras, the Mayor, the Municipal Band,
the polling booth, and the police and fire departments.   This
time the critics were more subdued in their praise.   "There
is a depth of meaning to the screen version, and it affords
Douglas Fairbanks abundant opportunity to display his versa-
tile talents," wrote Louis Reeves Harrison in The Moving
Picture World (November 13, 1915), "but there is a tendency
to drag at times and more than one incongruity that could
have been completely eliminated where the main purpose is
so obviously that of light and amusing entertainment."   In
Motion Picture News (November 13, 1915), Peter Milne commented, "Here again as in The Lamb, these titles are mind-
ful of George Ade and consequently very humorous.   No
strong dramatic situations arise, partly because of the character of the titles, but the picture is quite novel in development and interesting."

Fairbanks' leading lady in Double Trouble was Margery
Wilson, who will have everlasting fame as Brown Eyes in
the French Story from Intolerance.   She was under contract
to Griffith, and Fine Arts, but apart from this one film
she spent her entire time on loan out to Ince, working with
Charles Ray, William S. Hart, and others.   It is unfortunate
that she did not make any other Fine Arts features, for as
Julian Johnson noted in Photoplay (September 1916), she was
"an ingenue who combines real girlishness with splendid
emotion."

Of working with Fairbanks, Margery Wilson recalls

He was a man of such terrific, explosive energy.
He had a way of pacing the floor and talking with
great enthusiasm.   He would drive one fist into
the other and exclaim, "Isn't that corking," which
was his favorite expression.   I always remember

Margery Wilson.

he used to say, "If any fence you see doesn't challenge you to jump it, you're getting old." He was very witty, like a grown-up boy, and I was so dreadfully thin then. My maid was always trying to force me to eat chocolate and cake and so forth. And I remember one day, he came in to my dressing room and said, "There's a policeman outside looking for you," and I got very worried and said, "Why, what have I done?" And he said, "He says you have no visible means of support."

People think it was Mary Pickford who broke up his marriage, but that is not true. There was no marriage to break up. We spent about two weeks down in Santa Ana, doing small-town scenes, and Beth Sully would drive down in a limousine and sit

and wait. And they hated each other so. You could
just feel the hate between them in their teeth-grit-
ting politeness. If they hadn't been a lady and a
gentleman, I think they would have come to blows.

For his third film, Fairbanks decided to return to
New York; perhaps because he was unhappy with the atmosphere on the Fine Arts lot and Griffith's supposed dislike of
him, perhaps because he had a yearning to return to his old
haunts, or perhaps simply because Harry Aitken was anxious
to utilize the Yonkers studios rather than have them stand
idle. Accompanying Fairbanks was his family, together with
director John Emerson, who had come from the New York
stage and with whom Fairbanks presumably felt comfortable,
and Anita Loos, who had been assigned to script the new
Fairbanks production, His Picture in the Papers. (Miss
Loos claims it was Emerson who asked for her, being impressed by some of her screenplays on file at the studio. *)
Fairbanks arrived in New York on October 2, 1915, having
already been signed--Anita Loos' statements to the contrary
--to a three-year contract by Harry Aitken, and already an
acclaimed film actor--Miss Loos' reminiscences again not-
withstanding--thanks to his performance in The Lamb.

The trio were to spend three months on production
of His Picture in the Papers, and the film was to cost approximately $40,000, which was average for Fairbanks' fea-
tures at this time. For the prize fight sequence, the Sharkey
Athletic Club in New York was utilized, and watching Fairbanks win the fight were such distinguished theatrical figures
as Nat Goodwin and George Beban. Publicity issued by

---

*As this is supposedly a serious study of the Fine Arts Company,
no reference will be made to the fanciful story concerning His
Picture in the Papers published in Anita Loos' autobiography,
Kiss Hollywood Good-Bye (The Viking Press, 1974). The recognition of such fantasy is left to "historians" of the calibre of
Richard Schickel. Any careful reading of the trade papers of
the period will indicate that Fairbanks had already established
himself by the time of His Picture in the Papers, had already
signed a three-year contract with Triangle, and that the film
was long in Triangle's release schedule and did not appear on
the screen at the Knickerbocker Theatre simply because that
week's feature had failed to arrive on time. Whatever were
Griffith's and Aitken's failings, film-making and film distribution in 1916 was not a haphazard operation.

Anita Loos and John Emerson, editing a film negative.

Triangle made great play of Fairbanks' performing his own
stunts, including jumping from an Ocean liner into the sea
off Atlantic City. The Triangle reported, "Each morning
Emerson says: 'Now, Doug, the scerario calls for this,
that or the other. It can't be done.' 'I can do it,' replies
the actor. 'Bet you $5 on each stunt.' And at night Emer-
son usually owes his star $10 or $15."48

His Picture in the Papers, the story of a young man's
endeavors to get his picture on the front page of every New
York newspaper in order to win the girl (played by Loretta
Blake, an Ince contract actress), opened at the Knickerbocker
Theatre on February 10, 1916, to enthusiastic notices. In
Variety (February 4, 1916), Fred wrote, "Douglas Fairbanks
again forcibly brings to mind that he is destined to be one of
the greatest favorites with the film seeing public. The manner in which he works in this picture will surely endear him
to those who have already seen him in pictures and those

Douglas Fairbanks in His Picture in the Papers.

that are seeing him for the first time in this film comedy
will immediately become boosters for him in the future....
Incidentally this feature is one of the first that has been
produced by the Fine Arts people in New York and it shows
that little old Gotham is just as capable of being the scene
of good comedy pictures as any picture city on the west
coast." Peter Milne in Motion Picture News (February 12,
1916) commented, "Douglas Fairbanks has risen to the ranks
of undisputed film favorites that is clearly evident from the
applause which heralds his appearance in a picture.... He
reaches his audience at the start, and before he is through
he is on intimate terms, so it seems, with every member
of it. Such is the mark of a good player, and Doug's personality is consequently one of his most valuable possessions. His Picture in the Papers was obviously molded specially for its star. It gives him a likable role, for he is
the only normal member of the family of Proteus Prindle,
a manufacturer of meatless foods, such as Predigested Prunes
and Dessicated Doughnuts or some other alliterate combination."

In Photoplay (May 1916), Julian Johnson noted that
"Mr. Fairbanks cuts a second and a half off his speed record
in every minute of the picture." In a statement that could
well have offended D. W. Griffith, Johnson also commented
that "A series of these would put Fine Arts into the keystone
class as a ruiner of solemnities." The Moving Picture World
(March 11, 1916) reported that after the Knickerbocker screening of His Picture in the Papers, Fairbanks received con-
gratulatory telegrams from Rex Beach, John Barrymore,
Billie Burke, Elsie Janis, Irving Berlin, George M. Cohan,
and Irvin S. Cobb, among others.

Anita Loos was not responsible for Fairbanks' next
five features, but returned to writing for the actor with The
Half-Breed; at Fine Arts, she also scripted American Aristocracy, The Americano and possibly Manhattan Madness for
Fairbanks. Only weeks before Fairbanks left Fine Arts for
good, The Moving Picture World on December 2, 1916, announced that Fairbanks had requested Anita Loos to write the
sub-titles (not the stories) for all films in which he was to
star. The actor was quoted, "Time and again, I have sat
through plays by Miss Loos and have heard the audience ap-
plaud her sub-titles as heartily as the liveliest scenes. There
have even been cases I could mention where her comments
outshone the scenes themselves. This has convinced me of
the great value of the kind of work she does." Anita Loos
scripted four further features for Fairbanks after his departure from Fine Arts: In Again, Out Again, Wild and Woolly,
Down to Earth and Reaching for the Moon, all released in 1917.

A one-page article in Photoplay for March, 1917,
features a photograph of Fairbanks, Emerson and Loos filming The Americano; the caption reads, "This isn't a black-
banged China doll under the camera. It's an author--honest!"
The article is of particular interest because it touches upon
a subject which has never been fully investigated, and that is
who was responsible for the sub-titles in Intolerance. Anita
Loos has claimed she wrote them, whereas most Griffith
scholars believe the director himself was responsible. Photoplay perhaps sets the record straight by stating that Anita
Loos "wrote most of the humorous sub-titles in Intolerance."
Certainly "ditto geese" reads like a Loos sub-title!

For Fairbanks' next film, The Habit of Happiness,
also filmed in the East but possibly at Fort Lee rather than
Yonkers, the actor was assigned Allan Dwan as his director,
beginning a long-term relationship between the two men.

Douglas Fairbanks in The Half-Breed.

Dwan directed three further Fairbanks features at Fine Arts,
and went on to direct the actor in six more features: A
Modern Musketeer (1918), Mr. Fix-It (1918), Bound in Morocco (1918), He Comes Up Smiling (1918), Robin Hood (1922),
and The Iron Mask (1929). Based on an idea by D. W. Griffith, The Habit of Happiness is a perfect vehicle for Douglas
Fairbanks, who, as Sunny Wiggins, practices the "brother-
hood of man" theory, spreading sunshine and happiness in
true Fairbanksian fashion. Fairbanks is even able to ponder,
at the end of reel one, "Gee, I wonder if I acted like a
boob?" a classic Fairbanks thought. Even though they were
not written by Anita Loos, the sub-titles are witty and amusing, with the first setting the mood for the film: "Our first
scene is at the home of the Wigginses, a family of climbers,
who have spent years in mounting to the point where they can
be snubbed by the best people in town." In many respects,
The Habit of Happiness is better than The Lamb and many
of Fairbanks' later Fine Arts productions; it certainly begins
very well compared to Flirting with Fate, for example. However, Louis Reeves Harrison in The Moving Picture World
(March 25, 1916) thought, "It is thrust upon the audience that
the presentation is really a vehicle especially created for the
talented star, a common enough fault, but one to be avoided
where there is so much good material as in this release."

Allan Dwan directed Fairbanks' next feature, The
Good Bad Man, which was chosen as the opening film for
Roxy's Rialto Theatre, and which introduced Bessie Love as
Fairbanks' new leading lady. She remembers Fairbanks as
"a very important person at the studio," and recalls that it
was the actor's wife, Beth Sully, who chose her as his leading lady: "It was no secret she was not exactly wearing the
pants, but the manager. She was a little bit stern, a little
bit the manageress. But, never mind, she was a good one."
The story of a "Robin Hood of the West" was also written
by Fairbanks, and the first in a long line of films either
written or based on ideas by the actor. In providing the
screenplay, Fairbanks was proving how easily and quickly he
had adapted to the new nedium. As Fred in Variety (April
14, 1916) noted, "In his writting for the screen Mr. Fairbanks discloses a fine sense of what the public wants in pictures and he gives it to them."

In the summer of 1916, Dwan was to direct two further
Fairbanks productions, The Half-Breed and Manhattan Madness. The former was based on a story by Bret Harte and
is interesting in that it allowed Fairbanks to appear in a

straight drama concerning the barriers that exist between
the American Indian and the White Man.   Fairbanks plays
the title role of a half-breed son of an Indian girl betrayed
by a young white settler.   Dwan recalled that Mrs. Fairbanks was not pleased with the thought of her husband running
around as a dirty and filthy character--unconsciously display-
ing the bigotry with which the story was concerned--and to
allay her concerns, the director arranged that in the opening scene, Fairbanks would be seen almost naked, swimming
in a river, to prove that he took a bath. [8]   Oscar Cooper in
Motion Picture News (July 22, 1916) wrote,

> Those who look for stirring fights in every Fair-
> banks picture will find none of them in this.   His
> athletic prowess is demonstrated in other milder
> ways, and flashes out of the picture at intervals
> as a relief offsetting the heavier scenes.   There
> is also less than the usual footage given the star.
> But it seems to us that Fairbanks is just as "sure-
> fire" as ever, although the part itself does not give
> him the opportunities afforded by such vehicles as
> The Habit of Happiness and The Good Bad Man.
> As to direction, no exhibitor need have any mis-
> givings about this picture.   The reputation which
> the Fine Arts staff has for care and distinction is
> fully maintained by Allan Dwan.   There are splendid
> panoramas, colorful scenes of frontier life in two
> small villages, and, particularly, locations among
> the giant redwood trees, which are both beautiful
> and impressive.   Finally, a forest fire is staged,
> and it is excellent in realism.   Some remarkable
> night photography is also presented.

Manhattan Madness, Allan Dwan recalls, was supposed
to be a Western, but he and Fairbanks wanted to work in
New York, so it became a Western set in New York.   It is
an amusing tale of a young westerner who comes to the effete
East and is immediately bored by his surroundings.   His
friends plan a few surprises for him, however, and in the
end he is forced to admit that New York can also hold some
excitement.   The plot gave Fairbanks ample opportunity to
indulge in unlimited stunts and, as Julian Johnson noted in
Photoplay (December, 1916), "It is a huge, roistering joke
of a good time, with Douglas Fairbanks as head joker."
Peter Milne in Motion Picture News (September 30, 1916)
began his review, "Douglas Fairbanks in another winner,"
and continued,

which short statement ought to suffice for a review
of Manhattan Madness. In fact it is, but merely
because such a small collection of words might be
lost in the shuffle it remains for more to be written. We can tell you that Douglas Fairbanks has
the sunniest and most contagious personality that
ever flickered across the screen, that as an all-
round athlete Douglas Fairbanks puts Jim Thorpe
way back stage, that Douglas Fairbanks is the best
actor of the silent drama, that the Fine Arts producers know just how to present Douglas Fairbanks
to the public; but then we can also tell you that
water is usually wet, that babies aren't given a
diet of absinthe, that the picture business is beyond
its infancy, and a lot of other things that you know
as well as we do. The thing is that Douglas Fairbanks in Manhattan Madness is a winner, as we
remarked before.

Motion Picture News (June 24, 1916) reported that
while working on Manhattan Madness, Fairbanks stayed at
Pelham, where he kept his yacht, on which he would sail
every morning through the Harlem River, over into the Hudson River, and across to Fort Lee and the Fine Arts studios.
"Why use an automobile, taxi or even a street car," Fairbanks asked, "when you can have a yacht?"[19]

Christy Cabanne returned to direct Fairbanks in Reggie
Mixes In, which followed The Good Bad Man into release.
Bessie Love played a girl "who dances in a dive," with whom
the wealthy young idler, played by Fairbanks, falls in love.
The film offered Fairbanks several opportunities to display
his pugilistic talents, causing Jolo in Variety (June 2, 1916)
to note that "Jess Willard has nothin' on him." Fairbanks
recalled for The Moving Picture World,

We had some professional "pugs" in the making of
that picture. Griffith was opposed to their employ-
ment through fear of my getting hurt, but I told
him I would take chances. I told the boys in the
beginning it was going to be real fighting, nothing
easy about it at all. Nor was there. I got a bit
gouged up myself. I've been told there were one
or two fellows really looking for me since, too,
but I guess that's not so. Do you know in the picture business money comes in from all directions.
I've collected $1,800 in accident insurance since I

went to the Coast.   But it's great, though.   I've
been working outdoors for four months.   I can
hardly walk in ordinary shoes, these low-heeled
affairs.   I feel as if I was going to fall backward.
I was just getting used to the big, high-heeled sort.
No more for me the old days in New York--get up
late in the morning, a stroll around to the Lambs,
a ride in the park, a nap in the afternoon, then
the theater and supper afterward.   Now I am called
at 5 o-clock, see the doctor and get bandaged up;
then out on location.   If by luck we escape the
doctor and the ambulance it is dinner between 5
and 6 and then to bed. [7]

Writing in Photoplay (September 1916), Julian Johnson
said, "Speaking of comedy: the dumb stage has never had
so quick, big and wholesome a triumph as that of Douglas
Fairbanks.   And that without especially good vehicles.   Fairbanks' success has been in the assumption of brash American
boys who were blind to obstacles, deaf to the quavering voice
of fear, ready with the left hook, strong for chicken garnished
with marriage license, and constantly, completely ablink in
dazzling smiles."   Nothing better answers Johnson's description than the actor's next film, Flirting with Fate, again
directed by Christy Cabanne, which introduced a new leading
lady in the delightful form of Jewel Carmen.

Fairbanks play Augustus Holliday ("long on tempera-
ment and short on funds.   He can draw everything except a
salary"), whose name allows for such endless sub-title jokes
as "the last of August," "August lingers on" and "Cheer up
August, let September mourn."   "Augy" Ainsworth is a pen-
niless young artist, in love with Gladys Kingsley (Jewel Carmen), whose aunt believes she should marry wealthy Roland
Dabney (Howard Gaye), a suggestion which Gladys agrees to
after mistakenly assuming Augy to be unfaithful.   In despair
Augy hires Automatic Joe (George "Andre" Beranger in the
best and biggest role he had had up to that time), a paid
killer, to murder him.   However, Gladys discovers the truth
and Augy conveniently inherits a million dollars.   In disguise,
Augy tries to elude Automatic Joe, who has, in turn, been
"saved" by the Salvation Army and only wishes to break his
agreement with Augy.   When Joe turns up at Augy's wedding,
the latter leaves his bride and runs for his life.

The film is slow in getting started and does not really
become interesting or give any indication as to where it is

Douglas Fairbanks and Jewel Carmen in Flirting with Fate.

leading until the third reel. From then on, Flirting with Fate is little more than a gigantic chase, with Fairbanks running away from imaginary Automatic Joes and the detective he has hired to protect him. The chase provides Fairbanks with endless opportunities to leap on and off buildings, scramble up fire escapes and leap down drain pipes. The use of the element of fear upon which to build comedy is skillfully handled by Fairbanks, and the hide-and-seek antics between star and assassin are a delight. Mention should also be made of an actress named Dorothy Haydel, who portrays Gladys' chum Phyllis. She is one of the most beautiful girls ever to appear in silent films, with a "modern" face, much like the one Miriam Cooper had.

Reviews of Flirting with Fate were mixed. Fred in Variety (June 30, 1916) thought that "the feature isn't by any means as strong as the preceding Fairbanks releases have been." Louis Reeves Harrison in The Moving Picture World (July 8, 1916) said exactly the opposite:

Superior in many respects to any vehicle Fairbanks

has had, Flirting with Fate introduces a comical
element of fear which would enable the story to
stand on its own merits in open competition, whether
interpreted by Mr. Fairbanks or not. Of course, he
brings to it an element of intense personality which
materially helps where there is structural strength
and enlivens in moments of weakness, but Flirting
with Fate comes nearer being a true story than
any of those in which he has recently appeared,
and it contains opportunity for other members of
his company, those who ordinarily support him as
merely negative members of a chorus with one
active principal. This greater story breadth is of
high value in sustaining interest.

John Emerson returned to direct Fairbanks in a two-
reel short, The Mystery of the Leaping Fish, released on
June 11, 1916. A silly story involving opium smuggling, the
film has taken on mammoth proportions in recent years as
a cult movie because of its drug-related plot and because
Fairbanks plays a character named Coke Ennyday. Griffith
wrote the story and even allowed Fairbanks to end the film
with his discussing the plot with the scenario editor who,
believing Fairbanks to be the author, tells him to stick to
acting and give up trying to be a scenario writer. Oscar
Cooper in Motion Picture News (July 15, 1916) wrote, "It
is near-slapstick, without a trace of the heart interest which
Fairbanks handles with such distinction, and in fact is a
burlesque of Fairbanks' own style of acting."

Bessie Love, who had a small part in The Mystery
of the Leaping Fish, recalls that Fairbanks had talked of
taking her, and his family, to South America to produce
films, and this is backed up by a story in the June 24, 1916,
issue of Motion Picture News. "When the fall comes," he
said, "I want to go down to South America and make a few
pictures there, and then when that's over and if the war
stops, I want to tour all Europe with a company and make
pictures wherever we stop. We'll be able to get variety that
way and there's no one in the company that will object. Why
should they? They'll have a nice trip, see the world and
get the work in en route."[19]

Instead, the fall of 1916 saw Fairbanks in New York
at work on American Aristocracy under the direction of Lloyd
Ingraham. The film was also shot in part in Watch Hill,
Rhode Island, a fashionable New England resort, where a

group of "society girls" plus Truman Newberry, former
United States Secretary of the Navy, appeared in some scenes
The critics noticed two things: Fairbanks' stunts and Anita
Loos' sub-titles. Of the latter, Julian Johnson wrote in
Photoplay (February 1917),

> Is Mr. Fairbanks the star of this picture? Seems
> to me Miss Anita Loos, who wrote the quaint little
> burlesque on our bear-can nobility, and the odd
> little type-phrases which join the illustrations, is
> the real luminary. Miss Loos was short on plot,
> but long on laughs. Here melodrama is that of
> an old-fashioned motion picture; her satire is worthy
> of Irvin Cobb.

In Motion Picture News (November 4, 1916), Peter Milne
wrote,

> It is hardly necessary to dwell on the merit of the
> subtitles written by Anita Loos. Written in a free,
> easy and highly humorous style they are responsible
> for almost as many laughs as the comedian him-
> self--perhaps more in the case of the present pic-
> ture. Miss Loos also wrote the scenario for Amer-
> ican Aristocracy, and while she has not done as
> good work in this line, judging it from a construc-
> tive viewpoint as she has in the matter of the sub-
> titles, hers is on the whole no ordinary or mean
> piece of work.

Of Fairbanks' stunting, Milne said, "In American Aristocracy, he does a lot of amazing stunts such as vaulting a
fence as high as his head, riding aloft an automobile and
jumping off to land on a wire and flying in a 'hydro.' Aside
from that he uncovers a plot to furnish gunpowder to Mexico
by packing it in Malted Milk bottles." "Mr. Fairbanks is
being completely eaten up by his jumping ability," wrote Julian Johnson. "He leaps into chairs, over his motors, onto
his horses, out of his difficulties, like a godson of St. Vitus.
Acrobatics and agility are good, but in this picture they are
driven into the ground, to the exclusion of much better stuff
of which he is entirely capable." Louis Reeves Harrison in
The Moving Picture World (November 4, 1916) agreed, urging
that Fairbanks be given more opportunity as an actor and
less as an acrobat and complaining that American Aristocracy
at times took on the appearance of a Keystone comedy.

For his next feature, The Matrimaniac, Fairbanks had
a new director, Paul Powell, and a new leading lady, Constance Talmadge. However, the film is chiefly of interest
because it introduced the work of the noted humor writer,
Octavus Roy Cohen, to the screen. The story of Fairbanks'
attempts to reach the town where the girl with whom he had
eloped was waiting for him and the minister was criticized
for its slowness and its padding. Variety (December 8, 1916),
noting that it ran a mere fifty-three minutes, felt it would
have been better produced as a two-reel Keystone comedy,
but continued, "The picture will get the money." Peter Milne
in Motion Picture News (December 16, 1916) assumed the
sub-titles were the work of Anita Loos; "at any rate they
read like hers." Simultaneous with the release of the film,
the story was published as a four-part novel in the All-Story
Magazine.

John Emerson had been on loan-out from Fine Arts
to Famous Players, but he was hastily recalled in October of
1916 after Fairbanks had cabled Harry Aitken that he wanted
him to direct his next feature and that he wanted Anita Loos
to write the sub-titles for all his future films. (Because
Fairbanks' request for Loos came while The Matrimaniac was
still in production, it is highly probable that Loos did indeed
supply the sub-titles for that feature. She was certainly at
the Fine Arts studio in Los Angeles at that time, having
returned from a brief vacation in New York.)

The tri-star combination, as Motion Picture News
called them, were soon at work on The Americano, which
saw Fairbanks at large in a tottering South American Republic and in love with the president's daughter, played by
Alma Rubens. Jolo in Variety (December 29, 1916) thought
Fine Arts "has one of its biggest winners" in the film. In
Motion Picture News (January 13, 1917), Peter Milne wrote,

> Fairbanks brings his store of athletic stunts into
> play once again. When a high wall is shown and
> you see Fairbanks approaching you know very well
> he is going over it, probably in one spring. It
> makes you marvel every time. He does other things
> in The Americano. One of his feats is to jump from
> a high balcony to a tree not so conveniently near
> and slide down it. He makes his fights original
> to a degree. Not content with the usual method
> of getting a stranglehold on his opponent, he takes

Carl Stockdale, Spottiswoode Aitken, Alma Rubens, and Douglas Fairbanks in The Americano.

to using his feet and legs as hands and arms. And
through it all runs his sunny disposition. Fairbanks
never seriously frowns. One of his biggest assets
lies in the lack of the frown, just as another lies
in his smile.

Seymour Stern, questionably, called The Americano simply
the best of the Griffith-supervised Douglas Fairbanks series.
It was also to be the last.

On December 18, 1916, even before The Americano
was released, Fairbanks left California for New York. Something of his popularity may be deduced from the fact that
Mayor Woodman of Los Angeles entrusted him with a letter
of greetings to the Mayor and citizens of New York. It was
as if everyone at Triangle knew he was leaving the company
for good. A few days before leaving, on December 14, the
actor visited the Ince studios at Culver City, and The Moving
Picture World reported,

> Though he did not entirely demoralize the four
> hundred and fifty employees of the plant, he brought
> about a partial suspension of activities during his
> visit, while the Thomas H. Ince forces watched
> and admired, it is said, the dexterity and ease
> with which he performed--impromptu--many of the
> inimitable "Fairbanks" stunts. Doug's entrance to
> the studios was nothing if not spectacular. Not
> waiting for "John Law" to open the gates, he vaulted
> this fifteen-foot obstacle, grasping the hands of
> Producer Ince and Bill Hart, who were waiting for
> him, as he alighted. After being formerly pre-
> sented to Ince, and doing an Indian war-dance with
> Hart, he found himself hemmed in by William Des-
> mond, Dorothy Dalton, Margery Wilson, Director
> Walter Edwards and several other Ince players, all
> of whom were his personal friends. After a few min-
> utes chat be began a tour of the studios, accompanied
> by Ince, Hart and Desmond. The Four forgot the
> cares and worries of everyday life and frolicked,
> it is said, like boys just let out of school. Fair-
> banks discovered a lariat in the prop room, and
> he lassoed everyone and everything in sight. Then
> he and Bill Hart engaged in many feats of strength,
> after which Desmond boxed with him. The party
> eventually wound up on the lawn, facing the Ward-
> robe Building, and before the performance of the

final stunt all were minus hats, coats and vests,
while Fairbanks and Hart had even discarded their
shoes in a moment of athletic enthusiasm.   Long
after the noon hour, the "Big Four" adjourned to
the commissary, and everyone enjoyed a hearty
lunch.   So hearty, in fact, that the chef was later
heard in telephone communication with a Los Angeles
market, ordering relays of steaks and chops.   A
parting toast was drunk to Fairbanks, coupled with
hearty wishes for a pleasant journey.[76]

It is curious there is no mention of Fairbanks' saying farewell at Fine Arts, perhaps an indication of personal problems
with the company.   Indeed, in the December 30, 1916, issue
of The Moving Picture World, Fine Arts denied Fairbanks
was leaving the company.

On January 12, 1917, Variety published a front-page
story that Douglas Fairbanks was the highest paid film star
in the industry, earning $15,000 a week--a huge jump from
$2,000 a week with which he commenced his Triangle con-
tract--and that his gross annual salary was $780,000.   Va-
riety also reported that "Fairbanks is dissatisfied with [his
contract] through Griffith having failed to give the Fairbanks
feature productions the personal attention promised by the
director.   One story is that Griffith has given no further
attention to any Fairbanks release and never looked at one
of the Fairbanks films before release excepting the first,
when Griffith remained one day at the studio."   Fairbanks
also complained that Fine Arts had used his films to build
up contract actresses and "establish their names for value."

A lengthy statement from Fairbanks appeared in Motion Picture News:

In my contract with the Majestic Motion Picture
Company there was inserted the following provision:
"Said corporation agrees that the motion picture or
pictures that said Mr. Fairbanks is to render services in the making shall be supervised by Mr.
David Griffith, General Manager and Chief Director
of said corporation, and in the event of said Mr.
Griffith severing his connections with the company,
or discontinuing the active management of the same,
the said Mr. Fairbanks may at his option withdraw
from the employ of said corporation, but said action
on the part of said Mr. Fairbanks shall not prejudice

his rights to said compensation already earned by said Mr. Fairbanks.... Said corporation shall give or cause to be given the name of Douglas Fairbanks chief prominence, and by 'chief prominence' is meant that his name shall appear in larger type than any other part of the subject matter in which his name appears on all positive films, and in all advertising and literature used in connection with the motion pictures in which he appears, and shall not specially feature any other person in the cast representing any motion picture in which Mr. Fairbanks' written consent first had been obtained.''

Relative to the provision concerning Mr. Griffith, I demanded that the same be put in my contract, because I had great faith in Mr. Griffith, and desired the benefit of his superior ability and judgment as supervisor and general director in the motion picture company with which I was to be connected.

At the time of the making of my contract, the promoters of the Triangle Film Corporation were conducting a most extensive campaign for the sale of its stock of a tremendous capitalization, based primarily upon the good will of Mr. David Griffith, who had come into great prominence in the motion picture world on account of The Birth of a Nation and of Thomas Ince and Mack Sennett, the title of the corporation being suggested by this triangle of names.

It was my opinion that if Mr. Griffith devoted his entire time and attention to the manufacturing of motion picture films for this corporation, it would aid greatly in its success, and that if the corporation were over-capitalized, or if its capital were issued for a consideration other than money, and resulted in a financial failure, Mr. Griffith would no doubt cease to be active in the making of pictures, and that would enable me to withdraw from any connection with the enterprise, and prevent my pictures from being hypothecated as security for loans, and subsequently marketed so as to upset the standard of value that my pictures ought to bring.

When Mr. Griffith ceased to be active in the studio of the company, I made every effort to ascertain the true status of Mr. Griffith with the company, but every avenue of information was closed to me.

As regards the provision in my contract regulat-
ing the method of advertising of my pictures, the
exhibitors and the public through the United States
have seen the effort made by the Majestic Motion
Picture Company to establish a value to the names
of actresses by connecting them with mine, in vio-
lation of my contract.

Immediately upon my becoming assured of the
true situation, I elected to stand upon my legal
and moral rights, and severed my connection with
the company.

I have come to no conclusion relative to my
future plans in the motion picture business. [16]

However, within days, in fact on February 6, 1917,
Fairbanks announced formation of his own company, to release its productions through Adolph Zukor's Artcraft Pictures Corporation. "John Emerson who has directed several
of my most successful pictures will have entire charge of
production and scenarios will be written by Miss Anita Loos,
who is responsible for most of the best stories I have had
in the past," said the actor. Also joining Fairbanks from
Fine Arts were cutter Bill Shay, assistant director Jack
Scott, technical director R. W. Nichols, master of properties
James P. Hogan, and Erich von Stroheim, who was identified as location scout. In May 1917, Fairbanks also hired
Joseph Henabery and Sam De Grasse away from an ailing
Fine Arts.

In the meantime, Fairbanks had to resolve an injunction brought against him by Triangle, in which the company
claimed that it was the actor who had asked for John Emerson to direct his films rather than Griffith; a statement to
which there would appear to be a certain amount of truth.
A settlement was eventually reached late in February 1917
whereby Fairbanks agreed to pay Triangle an unspecified sum
of money to have the injunction vacated.

Douglas Fairbanks was on his way. Fine Arts had,
as in so many cases, proved a trusted training ground at
which the actor had created and evolved a screen persona
which was to see him in good stead in the years ahead. A
film star had been made and a legend had begun to evolve.

Chapter 6

THE FILMS OF 1916

The Fine Arts Company reached its zenith in 1916.
In January of that year, The Moving Picture World reported
that ten companies were at work on the lot. Robert Harron
proudly told Motion Picture News (January 22, 1916) that
production at the Griffith studio was now at its busiest, noting
that the sets for the Griffith twelve-reeler formerly called
The Mother and the Law occupied buildings covering several
city blocks. Fine Arts even boasted seven still photogra-
phers: J. Townsend, E. Ross, P. W. Saunders, H. Dingman,
J. E. Woodbury, C. S. Warrington, and W. S. Wright.

Norma and Constance Talmadge joined the company
and, with their mother, leased Anna Pavlova's Hollywood
home, within walking distance of the Fine Arts studio. Norma
made her Fine Arts debut in The Missing Links, in which a
missing cuff link leads to the discovery of a murderer. The
Triangle described it as "a definitive picture of everyday
American existence done with all the Griffith feeling for values
and care of detail. Here are the home folks most of us
grew up with, simple, kindly, well-intentioned people seen
just as we knew them in home, in church and on Main Street.
The potent but unassuming realism of the picture is startling."

Louis Reeves Harrison in The Moving Picture World
(December 18, 1915) thought that "In its attenuated five-reel
form, in spite of good acting, good directing and fine scien-
tific work, it is not up to the standard set by earlier Fine
Arts films." However, Julian Johnson, writing in Photoplay
(March 1916), was very impressed: "In its fidelity to fact, in
its detailed comments upon the very unsimple phases of the so-
called simple life, this photoplay was much less a motion-pic-
ture than contemporary literature. It exemplified to the top
notch the Fine Arts reputation for painstaking perfection of detail.

D. W. Griffith was riding high; in January 1916 he
attended the annual dinner of the Merchants' and Manufacturers' Association of Los Angeles and gave a speech on "The
Film Industry in Its Relation to the Commercial Community,"
noting that twenty million dollars a year was spent by studios
and employees in Los Angeles.

> You need not be ashamed of any part of the business
> [Griffith told his audience]. There are sinners in
> it, but you will not find them any more numerous
> proportionately than in any other profession, and
> I do not even exempt the law-making and preach-
> ing professions, because I have statistics to prove
> my statement. People all over the world--in India,
> China, Australia, Germany, Russia, everywhere--
> are having Los Angeles and her imcomparable sur-
> roundings shown and translated to them by the mov-
> ing picture. And into this art there is being put
> beauty, love and, I believe, a great deal of under-
> standing.

Not even a fire on January 20 which destroyed $25,000
worth of positive and negative film could dampen the enthusiasm at Fine Arts. "D. W. Griffith and other prominent
persons entered the burning frame building and rescued reels
and cans of negatives, valuable film which had just been
finished," reported The Moving Picture World (February 5,
1916). Within fifteen minutes of the fire, work was resumed.

January 1916 saw the release of the first feature starring the Fine Arts kiddies and directed by Sidney and Chester
Franklin, Let Katy Do It (sometimes called Let Katie Do It).
The Franklin brothers had first come to Griffith's attention
in 1914 with a split-reel comedy titled The Sheriff. He signed
them to direct a series of one-reel kiddie comedies, and
gave them their first opportunity to direct a feature with Let
Katy Do It, a charming story of a group of children in Maine
who become orphaned, are adopted by their mother's unmarried sister, and move with her to Mexico, where her boyfriend and her uncle are running a mine. When the Mexicans,
led as one might expect by Walter Long, attack the mine,
the children defend the homestead and the villains are routed.

The production is remarkable in many ways, the first
of which is that it moves along at such a snappy pace, beginning in Maine and ending in Mexico, with Sunland, California, substituting for that country. There is a down-to-earth,

simplistic quality to the characters of Kate (Jane Grey) and
her boyfriend (Tully Marshall)--they seem to be real people
rather than actors portraying a role.   As Louis Reeves Harrison noted in The Moving Picture World (December 11, 1915),
"The story is that of a Cinderella sister-in-law, who takes
charge of her deceased sister's brood after spending all her
girlhood in perpetual self-sacrifice.   Her character is a
very beautiful one, and Jane Grey makes it one of strong
appeal by delicate methods."   William Ressman Andrews in
Motion Picture News (December 18, 1915) also noticed the
playing of Grey and Marshall: "A memorable episode is the
stand made by Oliver Putnam in the deserted hut where he
and his sweetheart have taken refuge from the frenzied crowd
of bandits.   A mere exchange of glances between Jane Grey
and Tully Marshall when the last cartridge was fired and the
pair was at the mercy of the yelling throngs outside impressed the spectator with swift deft touches always at the command of these players for getting big effects."   Jane Grey
attended the first night of Let Katy Do It at the Knickerbocker
Theatre on December 5, 1915, and must have felt justly
proud of her performance and the response it evoked from
the audience.

Above all, the children are superb.   They are pre-
cocious, but never once offend with their precocity.   "Not
once," wrote Andrews, "was there the slightest suggestion
of the patient coaching which must have been necessary from
the directors.   Every child acted naturally."   The editing
and direction of the scenes in which the Mexicans are re-
pulsed by the children using all manner of booby traps, racks
of firing rifles and the like are quite magnificent, and compare more than favorably with Griffith's work on The Birth
of a Nation.   In fact, historian William K. Everson noted,
"There are so many echoes of Griffith in specific shots--
ranging from his Biograph Fighting Blood to the concurrent
Birth of a Nation--that it's obvious that his 'supervision' was
more than just casual."

In Photoplay (March 1916), Julian Johnson wrote,
"Eugene Field would have enjoyed this.   He might have written it.   It is a big heroic of childhood, a nursery story about
the Trojan war, in which Ned becomes a little hero for some
Homeric lyre, and little Nellie a new Helen.... The comedy
takes on the proportions of an American Peter Pan."

An interesting article on the working methods of the
Franklin brothers appeared in the September 30, 1916, issue
of The Triangle:

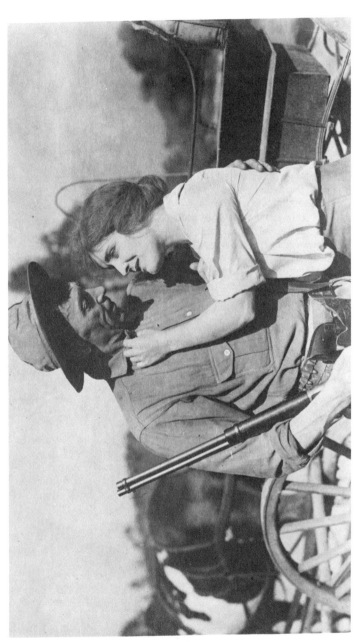

Tully Marshall and Jane Grey in Let Katy Do It.

The Brothers Franklin, makers of photoplays of
childhood for the Triangle program, are a strik-
ingly unusual and effective pair of team-mates.
Their unusualness consists partly in the perfect
harmony with which they work together. Not a
few brothers are singularly antagonistic, and very
few can work together or play together without wide
divergence of opinion and frequent wrangles. These
two, doing a highly individual job of nerve-strain-
ing creative artistry, fit together like the prover-
bial two thieves in a dark closet. Not that these
two artists do not have differences of opinion in
regard to details of the work; but when they do,
they go over to a quiet corner and calmly talk each
other into a complete understanding and agreement.
"Now, Syd, seems to me it will be more preferable
if--" "Yes; but, Chet, she is supposed to have--"
In a few minutes they are back, the children have
been herded gently to the set and work has begun--
work that goes on hour after hour without a hitch,
without an irritating word or a raised voice. Of
course, the children adore them and they adore
the children. They cannot tell you themselves what
their secret is, but the fact remains that they can
handle a dozen jolly, irresponsible youngsters
through scene after scene with never a show of
selfconsciousness or camera-fright on a single small
face. You see, acting is play to children, and
these young directors have the gift of keeping it a
transcendental sort of game that it is a privilege
to be in.

There were seven children featured in Let Katy Do
It--Violet Radcliffe, George Stone, Carmen De Rue, Francis
Carpenter, Ninon Fovieri, Lloyd Pearl, and Beulah Burns--
of which only the first five were considered regular members
of the group that reviewers soon dubbed "The Triangle Kiddies." Francis Carpenter is the most easily identifiable,
and often made uncredited appearances in films as varied as
Intolerance and Martyrs of the Alamo. Bessie Love remembers that he would walk around the studio directing the stage
hands and was much liked by everyone on the crews. The
children attended their own, private school on the lot--at one
time there were twelve children enrolled there--which was
run by Sarah McClung. There were certain advantages attached to attending school at a film studio, such as having

Douglas Fairbanks give $100 for distribution to the children
with the highest grades at the end of the summer term.

The Franklins followed Let Katy Do It with Martha's
Vindication, which starred Norma Talmadge in a story of
religious bigotry and of "organizations which arrogate to
themselves the privilege of making a superficial examination
of the lives of members and of bringing about social destruction where social helpfulness would be more in accord with
the spirit of Christianity." Its link to the Modern Story of
Intolerance was obvious. Louis Reeves Harrison in The Moving Picture World (March 25, 1916) wrote, "The story is
far from being an easy one to tell, but its structure is without blemish, and the sparkling subtitles help every inch of
the way. The author is to be congratulated for getting away
from the beaten track into new fields without wandering off
wasting time. Interest never sags, as it does in padded
five-reel releases. Several lines of forces are in operation
during the development, but they are skilfully gathered up
and woven into a highly dramatic plan." Frank Woods' wife,
Ella, was responsible for the story. Julian Johnson in Photoplay (June 1916) described Martha's Vindication as, "One of
the finest of last month's Fine Arts' plays ... a very human
story of girl friends, kindness, and the irresistible desire
to dodge consequences if we can. The delicate handling of
the sex side of this picture, as well as artful attention to
detail, calls for enthusiastic appreciation."

Norma Talmadge was featured in the next Franklin
production, The Children in the House, which was criticized,
as were a good many of the Fine Arts features, as containing inadequate story material for a five-reel production.
Typical of the comments was Louis Reeves Harrison's in
The Moving Picture World (April 29, 1916), "The Children
in the House presents a good three-reel situation, worked
out with considerable ingenuity and amplified to five reels
by such outworn methods as the burning shack, the automobile
chase of thieves by policemen, too near the Keystone style
to have dramatic effect, and that last resort to picture-play
manufacturers, the automobile run off a cliff ... a composition below the Fine Arts standard." The next Franklin production was hardly very original in its theme, that of a reformed thief asked to break open one more safe to prevent
an old pal from revealing his past. However, as Harrison
noted, in The Moving Picture World (June 3, 1916), "Going
Straight gives opportunity for Norma Talmadge, Eugene Pallette and the Triangle children to do some fine acting, and

the story is admirably handled." The Little School Ma'am,
starring Dorothy Gish, again brought complaints of padding.
Jolo in Variety (July 7, 1916) hailed the Franklins as "mas-
ters in stretching out into full length features the slimmest
sort of scenarios." Julian Johnson in Photoplay (October
1916) described The Little School Ma'am as "a tame story,
indeed."

Following a minor production, Gretchen the Greenhorn,
again starring Dorothy Gish, the Franklins embarked on their
last film for Fine Arts, A Sister of Six, which began shooting in August 1916 on location in Sunland, California, under
the title of The Defenders. The Moving Picture World (September 30, 1916) reported that "a fully equipped nursery,
with hobby horses, dolls, wagons, Teddy bears, and all the
paraphernalia necessary in a juvenile room has been installed.... The kiddies are having the time of their lives
on the location." The mother of the film's star, Bessie
Love, was placed in charge of the children.

The story of seven orphans' fight to retain their owner-
ship of land rich in gold, set in the California of the 1860's,
provided Bessie Love with her first starring role, and she
was easily able to prove her worth and ability. While cri-
ticizing the film for limited attempt at characterization and
lack of action, save for the denouement in which the children
defend their ranch against attack--shades of Let Katy Do It--,
Louis Reeves Harrison in The Moving Picture World (October 21, 1916) noted, "Miss Love does full justice to her
role." Fred in Variety (October 13, 1916) commented, "Bessie Love has added another branch to her laurel crown by
her delightful portrayal of the role of Prudence Winthrop."

Immediately after completion of A Sister of Six, the
Franklins were approached by Winfield Sheehan, general manager of the William Fox studios, who offered them $300 a
week, their own company and their own stage, and a school-
room for the children if they would come and work for him.
According to Kevin Brownlow, "The Franklins were thrown
into a quandary. They were proud of their association with
D. W. Griffith. Yet here was a solid contract, which they
did not have at Fine Arts, and an offer of three times their
salary. They decided, with some reluctance, to accept Fox's
offer."* The Franklins' signing with Fox was announced in

---

*See "The Franklin Kid Pictures" by Kevin Brownlow in
(Cont'd on p. 76.)

The Moving Picture World for September 23, 1916. The
Triangle kiddies, led by Francis Carpenter, went along with
the Franklins, and were soon joined by others, including
Raymond Lee, Virginia Lee Corbin, and Buddy and Gertrude
Messinger. Under the guidance of Sidney and Chester Frank-
lin, they appeared in what Brownlow describes as "a remark-
able series of full-length pictures designed directly for chil-
dren," including Jack and the Beanstalk, Aladdin and His
Wonderful Lamp, Babes in the Wood, Treasure Island, and
Ali Baba and the Forty Thieves.

They easily lived up to the tribute paid to them in the
November 18, 1916, issue of Motion Picture News: "In the
ranks of the Triangle-Fine Arts players a little group of
performers stands unique, and has gained more and more
eminence throughout the year. These are the Triangle 'kiddies,' the only group of children working together continuously
in one picture after another, and showing dramatic ability as
well in their scenes with one another as when playing opposite the older actors."

On October 23, 1915, The Triangle had announced the
signing of Marie Doro from the legitimate stage. She was to
receive the princely sum of $2,500 a week. Her arrival at
the Fine Arts studio almost corresponded with the appearance
of Billie Burke, another major stage star, at the Ince studios,
where Miss Burke filmed Peggy. Marie Doro's stay with
Fine Arts was a brief one, limited to a single film, The
Wood Nymph, released in January of 1916. The story of
Daphne, a girl brought up among the California redwoods and
taught to believe in Greek mythology, was written by D. W.
Griffith and directed by Paul Powell on location in the Muir
Valley of Northern California.

According to The Triangle, Miss Doro was delighted
with the production. "Altogether, aside from my part in it,
the play is exquisite," she was quoted as saying. "I mean
for the real beauty of its pictures, its atmosphere and its
delicate fantasy. It has made me see the making of photoplays

(cont'd from page 75.) Films in Review, Vol. 23, No. 7
(August-September, 1972), pages 396-404. Surprisingly, this
piece glosses over the Franklin films at Fine Arts, mention-
ing only two very briefly: Let Katy Do It and A Sister of
Six.

from a new angle--as a fine and delicate art capable of
capturing the most elusive moods, of recording even the hid-
den stirrings of the spirit.   Everyone has an inner life of
thoughts and feelings that no one can share.   We draw tight
the curtains about our secret shrine, fearing any footstep.
Then this strange instrument is built and our soul is bared
by a little strip of photographs.   It is like a sort of pre-
mature Judgment Day, and very often it hurts.   But it means
that the demands of the photoplay upon the sincerity and the
whole character of actors, as well as upon their talent for
expression, are going to grow more and more severe as the
public insight quickens.   And that will be another wonderful
achievement for the new art. "21

       The critics did not share Miss Doro's excitement.
Julian Johnson in Photoplay (March 1916) thought the film
"a rambling, tiresome, unbelievable film story (that) did
little justice to the Fine Arts equipment or the gifts and personality of Marie Doro."   Jolo in Variety (January 7, 1916)
found it "Too long drawn out for the light weight of the story,"
but liked the tinting of the climactic forest fire which led to
Daphne being rescued from the forest, and being almost raped
by her own brother.   (In true Griffith fashion, the girl is
saved by her natural innocence.)

       Louis Reeves Harrison in The Moving Picture World
(January 8, 1916) wrote,

>   The Wood Nymph is entirely dependent upon the
> charming personality and fine acting of Marie Doro
> for interest.   Without her, or without an actress
> as attractive and capable, it would fall very flat.
> It drags as it stands except at bright moments,
> when there is promise of high comedy in its mater-
> ial.   There is a painful monotony of scene, a lack
> of characterization in all other roles save that of
> the principal, a confusing sameness of types and
> costumes among the four leading men, especially
> during the obscurity of the fire scenes, and these
> scenes, well enough done in themselves, are re-
> peated and attenuated to the limit of good-natured
> tolerance.

       Oscar Cooper in Motion Picture News (January 15,
1916) was more enthusiastic:

       It is difficult to make such a character (Daphne)

convincing, but Marie Doro did make it convincing
and more. She caught, and pressed, with fine art,
the spirit of the wild. Some of the most beautiful
scenes that have been given on the screen are found
in this picture, and Miss Doro is herself a vision
of beauty.... One of the most realistic of forest
fires occupies much of the footage, and here, as
in the other forest views, the photography is flawless. Much of the naive humour of the piece is
directly due to the skilfully written and skilfully
placed subtitles.

No sooner was The Wood Nymph completed than Marie
Doro signed a long-term contract with Famous Players-Lasky,
for whom her first feature was Diplomacy. She also married
Elliott Dexter, who had been Lillian Gish's leading man in
Daphne and the Pirate (author D. W. Griffith/Granville Warwick seemed very fond of the name Daphne) which, as Seymour Stern has pointed out, utilizes an idea used earlier by
Victor Herbert for his operetta Naughty Marietta. However,
it was the star and not the plot which the critics noticed.
Peter Milne in Motion Picture News (February 26, 1916)
wrote, "It is a Lillian Gish picture from first to last. She
has been allowed any number of closeups, and in them she
displays a varied series of realistic and telling expressions....
Anyone who denies the fact that she is a star is either out
of his mind or not capable to speak on the subject." Daphne
and the Pirate also gave Walter Long an opportunity to men-
ace Miss Gish, but unlike Mae Marsh in The Birth of a Nation she proved a lot more cool-headed.

The Moving Picture World for January 1, 1916, contained an amusing news item that "D. W. Griffith thought so
highly of this scenario by Granville Warwick that he has associated with Miss Gish and Mr. Dexter some of the very
best Fine Arts stock players" to work on Daphne and the Pirate. In fact, there is no evidence that the majority of persons at the Fine Arts studio were aware that D. W. Griffith
was also Granville Warwick, and Bessie Love maintains that
no-one there would have found this particularly funny; "It
would have been sacrilege."

On January 8, The Moving Picture World announced
that Wilfred Lucas had been promoted to stardom in recognition of his good work in The Lily and the Rose. However,
it was the Paul Powell production of Acquitted that brought
Lucas into national prominence as a major silent star of the

Mary Alden, Bessie Love, Wilfred Lucas, and Carmen De Rue in <u>Acquitted.</u>

Teens. He had first entered films for D. W. Griffith at Biograph, and if he had any shortcomings as an actor it was that he was too proficient a director to be allowed to fully exercise his acting talents, and many times acting had to take a second place. Lucas was not a typical silent leading

man, but rather he was a character actor playing leading
roles, and playing them with total proficiency and complete
attention to detail.

Acquitted is the story of the head bookkeeper with an
insurance company who is accused, but acquitted, of murder-
ing the cashier there.   However, the notoriety he has achieved
makes him unemployable, and only as he is about to take
his own life do his daughter and former employer come forward to save him--"and the end is gentle happiness." Bessie Love played the daughter, and she recalls Lucas as "such
a wonderful person," who directed her in her screen test for
Griffith.

Reviewing Acquitted in The Moving Picture World
(February 5, 1916), Louis Reeves Harrison wrote, "Wilfred
Lucas responds so fully to the requirements of his role that
one forgets the beauty of his performance in the interest he
arouses, the interpretation of an artist rather than that of
an actor." Fred in Variety (January 28, 1916) hailed the
film as "one of the best five-reel features that the Fine Arts
Company has produced in some time."

Photoplay's Julian Johnson proved to be Lucas' greatest admirer.   In the April 1916 issue of his publication, he
wrote,

> The Fine Arts studio, already noted as a foremost
> apostle of realism, hit the month's high spot, pro-
> vided the most intense and absorbing drama, and
> by far the finest piece of acting, in Acquitted, in
> which Wilfred Lucas, for sheer power and sincerity
> of impersonation, made himself the peer of any
> contemporary actor on any sort of stage.... Lu-
> cas' marvellous fidelity to type--behold his droop-
> ing moustache, his placid countenance, his obse-
> quious manner, his shuffling walk, his simple out-
> look on all problems--has never been surpassed
> in photodrama.   Here is a man you and I know.
> He belongs to every American town.   Let calamity
> hit him, and he performs according to programme.
> Otherwise, he brings up his decent, inconspicuous
> little family in a decent, inconspicuous way.   He
> never does anything worthy of note.   He gets his
> name in the local papers when he is born, when
> he is married, when his firm gives him a dinner
> or an uncomfortable watch on the twentieth anniver-

sary of his faithful service--and when he dies....
Here is an actor!

Johnson returned to Lucas' performance in his yearly overview of "The Shadow Stage" in the September 1916 issue of
Photoplay. Hailing Wilfred Lucas' work as the best male
performance of the year, Johnson noted, "You have not seen
on any silversheet a single piece of acting surpassing Wilfred
Lucas's impersonation of the persecuted bookkeeper in Acquitted."

    In an interview with John Aye in Photoplay (June 1916),
Wilfred Lucas explained his characterization of John Carter,
the bookkeeper:

> No specific person was taken for John Carter. A
> number of persons have told me they know the
> character and insist that the old bookkeeper of their
> acquaintance is John Carter. A friend said to me
> just a few days ago, "Will, I know now where you
> found John Carter. I saw him in a bank the other
> day and was so fascinated with the discovery that
> I stood watching him half the morning." He was
> mistaken, but only as to detail. In the main he
> was right. The bookkeeper he saw was John Car-
> ter, I have no doubt, although I never saw his
> bookkeeper. But I know the type. He is the crea-
> ture of a certain fixed environment. He has a
> stoop to his shoulders. He is timid. He does not
> know the world very well. He is subdued and med-
> itative and lives a good deal in dreams. And yet
> there is something deeply wise about him because
> he knows secrets, great secrets, perhaps. The
> old bookkeepers I have known had very kindly souls
> and, having been effaced, having lived in dim places
> on the tops of high stools for years--just cipher-
> makers and almost ciphers--they are capable of
> great sacrifices. To have achieved the externals
> of John Carter was not difficult; go into any bank
> or counting house and ask to see the old bookkeeper
> --there's nearly always one in any institution--and
> he will look at you over his glasses and you will
> see a man who is honest and simple. To slip over
> your personality that of another's, especially one
> who, despite his simplicity, is subtle, is much
> more difficult than to approximate the superficials
> of him. If I accomplished the substitution with any

John Emerson in The Flying Torpedo.

success it was perhaps because I have been around
a great deal. Some time ago a clergyman asked
me how I had been able to so faithfully portray a
member of his profession. I answered in the words
of a famous person whom the clergyman is trying
to put out of business--"From going to and fro in
the earth, and walking up and down in it." Now
some actors, even in character work, insist upon
maintaining their own externals. Their maxim is,
"The public must know it is I." That is not my
conception of what character acting should be. I
try to be the person I portray and to present myself to the audience, via the camera, as that person and with my own self completely submerged.

Bessie Love was also featured in The Flying Torpedo,
a film warning Americans to practice "Preparedness" for a
possible invasion, along the lines of J. Stuart Blackton's
The Battle Cry of Peace. John Emerson was the star and
also co-author of the screenplay. In her autobiography, Bessie Love states the film was based on a play by Emerson
titled Conspiracy, in which she played the lead in a 1930 re-
make, directed by Christy Cabanne, and starring Ned Sparks,
in the original Emerson role. Neither the original 1913
play nor the 1930 film had anything to do with "Preparedness."
"It was a novel and entirely appropriate idea to make an
author the hero of a story, although he is somewhat idealized,"
wrote Louis Reeves Harrison in The Moving Picture World
(March 25, 1916). "He it is who carries the whole idea of
repelling the invasion of a foreign army through an invention
which he backed financially and stole from spies by a rare
combination of courage and cunning. Almost to the last he
depends wholly on his own resources to defeat those who kill
the inventor and attempt to thwart the designs of a committee
of defence. This adds heavily to the attractiveness of the
characterization. And it is exceedingly clever to make his
chief aid a simp servant girl, most delightfully portrayed
by Bessie Love. The elaborate and costly war scenes will
bring round after round of applause at this time, and the
whole picture, deserving a high praise for the care shown
in its production, should be a big winner." Jolo in Variety
(March 17, 1916) called The Flying Torpedo, "A very pre-
tentious feature for a program, full of suspensive interest,
tremendous battle scenes, etc. One of the best Triangle
pictures thus far shown." The film's dramatic scenes were
directed by Jack O'Brien. Christy Cabanne took care of the
battle scenes, and the McCarthy Brothers were responsible
for the special effects.

The year 1916 was in many ways Bessie Love's.
Within months of joining Griffith's company, she was given
a small, but nonetheless important, role in Intolerance, that
of the Bride of Cana in the Judaean sequence, playing opposite George Walsh. She played opposite Douglas Fairbanks
and William S. Hart (in The Aryan), and she was dubbed
"Our Mary," hailed by Picture-Play Magazine (July 1916) as
"a probable second Mary Pickford." As far as Bessie Love
is concerned, there is much truth to the statement in the
December 11, 1915, issue of The Triangle: "It soon must
also be admitted that most of the dominant screen personal-
itites of the day are Triangle discoveries."

On December 11, 1915, The Moving Picture World
wrote, "There have been more inquiries as to the date of
Mae Marsh's first Triangle picture than those for any other
star with the exception of W. S. Hart, Billie Burke, Lillian
Gish and DeWolf Hopper, thereby indicating that Miss Marsh
is one of the most popular Triangle players." As has already been noted, Mae Marsh's first Fine Arts production
was Hoodoo Ann, in which D. W. Griffith took a close directorial interest, although the credited director is Lloyd Ingraham.

Hoodoo Ann features Mae Marsh in the title role as
an orphan who, thanks to the warnings of Black Cindy (the
orphanage cook played by Madame Sul-Te-Wan), believes
herself hoodooed. She blames herself for a fire which de-
stroys the orphanage, and with which she was uninvolved,
and later believes she has accidentally shot a neighbor. (In
reality, she had merely wounded the neighbor's cat.) The
film gives Mae Marsh many opportunities to display her
unique, and often misused, acting talents, particularly in
the early scenes of orphanage life where she is the outsider,
first seen scrubbing the floors. In a scene with direct links
to Intolerance, she practices a new walk, thinking, "If I
walk dignified, maybe they'll like me." They don't! She
cannot participate on the orphans' slide, but gains enjoyment
from merely touching the slide as the other children go by
and push her out of the way. When she "borrows" the best-
loved orphan's (Goldie, played by Mildred Harris) doll, her
happiness is short-lived when she accidentally breaks off its
leg, and to add to her worries, the next day she must listen
to a lecture on the famous George Washington's "Never Tell
a Lie" story.

In a delightful sequence, Mae Marsh and Robert

Mae Marsh in a scene from <u>Hoodoo Ann.</u>

Harron visit a typical movie theatre of the Teens, complete
with a diligent and hard-working pianist, and witness a Mus-
tang Charlie Western, produced by the Hoboken Film Company. A lengthy comic-melodrama spoof of silent films, the
film within a film features Carl Stockdale (a veteran Griffith actor) in the title role, which is an outrageous parody
of William S. Hart.

Many of the subtitles have the Griffith ring to them,
the ending, at which Mae Marsh and Robert Harron are married, is handled in a typically light Griffith fashion, with
Mae at the close asking Harron, "Is it over?" The ending
also contains an interesting use of screen size, with the
participants shown individually in the center of the frame
with one quarter of the frame on each side blacked out, and

then, as if to symbolize the two actors becoming one in the marriage ceremony, they are united for a shot utilizing the entire frame.

Oscar Cooper in Motion Picture News (April 15, 1916) commented, "Here is Mae Marsh in her first Triangle play, fully justifying all predictions of her eminent fitness to be starred in pictures. She has been provided with a typical Fine Arts story, a first rate supporting cast, and superior direction. Even if Miss Marsh were not surrounded with these, we believe she could not fail to gain a personal success. For, without shadow of a doubt, she was born to the camera." Jolo in Variety (April 7, 1916) was less impressed: "A lot of good travesty melodrama is introduced, without which the picture would hardly be worthwhile. Usual excellent Fine Arts photography and direction." Although somewhat outrageous, there is a certain truth to James Card's comment in Image (September 1958): "If the ability to understand its own weaknesses and laugh at its own faults is an indication of the cinema's maturity, then Hoodoo Ann marks 1916 as the year the American film grew up even more so than did Intolerance."

Mae Marsh followed Hoodoo Ann with A Child of the Paris Streets, a ridiculous and extremely dull story of Parisien Apache life, in which she wore a blonde wig. It is hard to understand the enthusiasm of some of the critics, particularly Motion Picture News' Oscar Cooper who described it (May 27, 1916) as "a reel photoplay," although one can endorse Cooper's praise of Jennie Lee in the role of the "mother" Apache.

Other Mae Marsh features included The Marriage of Molly O', filmed in part in Santa Barbara as a substitute for Ireland. "The picture is not up to the Triangle Fine Arts standard," commented Fred in Variety (July 21, 1916). The Wild Girl of the Sierras was described by Vachel Lindsay in The Art of the Moving Picture as "one of the loveliest bits of poetry ever put into screen or fable." The Wharf Rat was praised for its screenplay by Anita Loos (see more about her in Chapter 5 on Douglas Fairbanks) of which Peter Milne wrote in Motion Picture News (December 9, 1916), "Comedy is its major element; much of it comes as a result of the subtitles written by Miss Loos. We agree with Douglas Fairbanks that she is supreme in this line. The humor and satire that she pens is far and above her plots." In all her Fine Arts features, Mae Marsh was partnered by Robert

Tully Marshall and Mae Marsh in A Child of the Paris Streets.

Harron, and a totally satisfying, almost unsurpassed in the
history of the cinema, teaming it was.

Of course Lillian Gish was also making her mark at
Fine Arts.   D. W. Griffith wrote An Innocent Magdalene and
Diane of the Follies for her, plus the already discussed
Daphne and the Pirate.   Sold for Marriage is an interesting
story of a Russian family emigrating to the United States and
attempting to sell their daughter (Lillian Gish) to a wealthy,
elderly suitor.   The first two reels, set in the Russian steppes,
are impressive in their detail, and in these reels there
is at times a comic vein apparent, particularly in the titles
and in Miss Gish's looking her ugly and old suitor up and
down before exclaiming, "Marry that beast!"   Throughout
much of the film, the actress has a pouting look on her face,
but there is fine acting in the scene in which she grabs a
pair of scissors and considers killing the suitor to whom she

has been sold. Despite some beautiful early scenes in the
snow and one brief shot of Lillian's lover, Jim, played by
Frank Bennett, on a train speeding from San Francisco to
Los Angeles, Sold for Marriage is not a great film. Julian
Johnson, writing in Photoplay (June, 1916) gives an accurate
appraisal: "Lillian Gish puts a convincing touch on a play
of Russian life which is not convincing in itself." Oscar
Cooper in Motion Picture News (April 15, 1916) also endorsed
Miss Gish's performance, noting "Her work here, as always,
gives the impression that she is one of the very few who can
justly be called screen stars."

Far more impressive is The Children Pay, directed
by Lloyd Ingraham and scripted by Frank Woods. It is a
simple story, told in that simple, straightforward fashion
which Griffith had perfected at Biograph, and was to use to
advantage later in True Heart Susie and A Romance of Happy
Valley. The early scenes give Lillian Gish a superb opportunity to play a tomboy, firing a catapult, driving a soap
box derby-type car and fighting with a boy outside the church
and thus breaking up the service. In all this, she is aided
and abelled by the delightful Violet Wilkey, who played Mae
Marsh as a child in The Birth of a Nation.

Of The Children Pay, Julian Johnson wrote in Photoplay (February 1917),

> Here is the sanest, most humanly interesting five-
> reeler of the month, although in most of its epi-
> sodes decidedly undramatic. It is such a story of
> drifting parents, an ever-widening domestic gulf,
> and the keen sorrows and quaint joys of a pair of
> little girls as you might expect from the pen of a
> young William Dean Howells. As a matter of fact,
> Frank E. Woods of Fine Arts wrote it, and there
> are deployed in its unrolling such redoubtable char-
> acter persons as Ralph Lewis, Jennie Lee, Loyola
> O'Connor and Carl Stockdale. Miss O'Connor, as
> the demi-artist mother, provides a remarkable ex-
> hibit of self-satisfied selfishness, wholly different
> from the usual sympathetic vehicle accorded her.
> Lillian Gish plays Millicent, the oldest girl who is
> the focal center of all the activity. I have never
> seen Miss Gish draw a more real, interesting and
> believable young woman. She has literal pep and
> actual punch--two qualities which tradition says
> are extremely ungishy. There are those who say

the final legal situation is impossible. I don't
know that the body of the play is a page of life,
of which the screen shows far too little.

A House Built upon Sand is noteworthy for Lillian
Gish's wearing $6,000 worth of gowns. As the shallow wife
who learns to respect and obey her husband, Lillian Gish
was praised by the critics. In Motion Picture News (January 6, 1917), Peter Milne wrote, "She plays well. Her
forte is comedy and in it a certain theatrical tone in her
work, which is apt to be taken for insincerity, is more appropriate. Hers is in general a fetching performance."

To play opposite Lillian Gish in The House Built upon
Sand, Fine Arts brought in Roy Stuart, who had made his
mark in Lois Weber productions at Universal, and who, as
The Moving Picture World (December 23, 1916) noted, "physically is one of the largest screen heroes to gain attention,
standing some 6 feet 3 inches in height and weighing 210
pounds." In other words, he looked bulky, middle-aged and
somewhat unattractive.

Norma Talmadge was also proving her worth at Fine
Arts, following her role in The Missing Links with a series
of fine dramatic performances, of which she had already
shown herself capable at Vitagraph. In The Devil's Needle,
the first film to be directed by Chester Withey, Talmadge
played an artist's model addicted to drugs, who persuades
the artist, Tully Marshall, to partake and then kicks the
habit and tries to save him from the addiction. She panto-
mimes giving the injection and the effects on the mind to
Tully Marshall as she first suggests he should try the needle.
The actress makes expressive use of her hands to indicate
everything from sorrow to the need for another fix, but as
Motion Picture News (August 5, 1916) noted it was a part
unworthy of her talents, and the film, without question, belongs to Tully Marshall.

Marshall had already portrayed a drug addict in Clyde
Fitch's play The City, and matched his performance there
with the one in The Devil's Needle. In one scene, he sits
holding the needle in his mouth, seeing the images of his
paintings in the flames of the fire. In another, he throws
his fiancée, played by Marguerite Marsh, out of the room
and grabs the cocaine from Talmadge's hands, licking the
drug from the paper as he falls to the floor. "Mr. Marshall's
work is superb and uncanny and terrible, and for 'family

groups,' as the National Board would say, there is just a
little too much of it," commented Peter Milne in Motion Picture News (August 5, 1916). Julian Johnson in Photoplay
(October 1916) hailed Tully Marshall as "our most prominent
mimic dopester."

As Marshall is cured, with fresh air and country
living, there are a couple of beautiful rural shots of him
with a horse-drawn plough, welcome dramatic relief from
the earlier scenes of his degradation. However, as Variety
(July 28, 1916) pointed out, "If it's true that hard manual
labor will kill the taste for drugs, Chester Withey and Roy
Somerville, who wrote this story, deserve to have a niche
in the film discovery hall."

The Social Secretary was filmed by director John
Emerson, assisted by Erich von Stroheim who also plays a
small part, at Fine Arts' Yonkers studio. A silly and tedious story of a girl who is unable to hold a job because her
male employers keep making advances received highly favorable reviews. "Norma Talmadge adds much in the way of
ability and beauty to the title role," wrote Peter Milne in
Motion Picture News (September 16, 1916), while Fred in
Variety (September 15, 1916) commented, "The Social Secretary is a comedy drama that gives Miss Talmadge a role
she can play to perfection and the feature is one that will
hold any audience from start to finish."

In between screen roles, Norma Talmadge, along with
Seena Owen, found time to host matinee teas at Hamburger's
Cafe Beautiful in downtown Los Angeles. Every lady who
entered the Majestic Theatre, where Fine Arts films played
in Los Angeles, was invited to attend the tea. "Tea and
photoplays!" noted The Moving Picture World (April 15, 1916).
"It is a fad which promises to be popular and D. W. Griffith, Mose Hamburger and Manager Sam Rork of the Majestic
theater say that photoplays with tea afterwards will be a
pleasing divertisement all summer."

Norma's sister Constance was also working at Fine
Arts, but not in as many features as her elder sister, probably because she was tied up with her role as the Mountain
Girl in Intolerance. One very interesting Constance Talmadge
feature, The Microscope Mystery, was directed by Paul Powell, and much liked by Julian Johnson. The Moving Picture
World (November 4, 1916) explained something of the film's
unusuality:

The latest addition to the acting forces of the Triangle-Fine Arts company are a troupe of remarkable "microbe actors" that play a prominent part
in the solution of The Microscopic Mystery [sic],
a unique comedy-drama by W. E. Wing that has
recently been completed with Wilfred Lucas and
Constance Talmadge in the leading roles.   The use
of bacilli and infinitesimal insect life in motion
pictures has been brought about by the invention of
Louis H. Tolhurst of Los Angeles, who has perfected apparatus which makes it possible to photograph the tiniest particles of sentient protoplasm.
Application has been made by Mr. Tolhurst for
patents on his invention.   Meanwhile, the original
model, used in the filming of The Microscopic
Mystery, is being carefully guarded to prevent its
secret from being learned.   In this feature they
have not been dragged into the action "by their
heels."   Mr. Wing has written a vehicle for the
microbes which bring them into the story in a perfectly logical manner.   In fact, the solution of the
mystery is solved by the leading character--and
the audience--through observing the antics of the
tiny disease germs under the microscope.   The
first four reels of the play are largely comedy,
involving a country doctor and his rivals, a firm
of quacks.   Suddenly, in the fifth reel, a revolver
shot turns the comedy into the grimmest of
dramas.   In his effort to save an innocent girl
from the charge of murder, the country doctor at
the coroner's inquest puts his microscope upon the
handle of the revolver.   The spectators look through
the lens with him, by the aid of the Tolhurst invention.   They see what he is seeing, and with
him solve the riddle of the crime.

In October 1916, Norma Talmadge left Fine Arts and
with Joseph Schenck organized the Norma Talmadge Film
Corporation, which was to release its films through Selznick.
The actress temporarily borrowed Allan Dwan from Fine
Arts to direct her first independent feature, Panthea.

Other 1916 Fine Arts productions that should be
mentioned are Cross Currents, directed by Francis J. Grandon and for which a yacht was burned off Balboa Beach; The
Price of Power, shot in part on location at a cotton mill
near Los Angeles; Betty of Greystone, which marked F. M.

Pierson's addition to the Fine Arts ranks as a screenwriter
and which was filmed at both the Yonkers and Fort Lee
Studios as well as on location in Connecticut; Atta Boy's
Last Race, the climactic race for which was to have been
filmed in Tijuana but because the Mexican atmosphere was
too strong was shot in San Francisco. Pillars of Society
was released in the summer of 1916, but according to Seymour Stern it had been shot in 1915, immediately following
production of Ghosts, but was shelved because of the poor
response to the first Ibsen adaptation starring Henry B. Walthall. Jolo in Variety (August 4, 1916) wrote, "Like all Ibsen stories, it is morbid in theme and in its psychology shows
the weakness of man. The plot is scant, having a dearth
of drama. It is, however, ingeniously handled, magnificently
acted and directed with an excellent exhibition of photography.
The feature will pass nicely on any program."

There was literally non-stop activity at the Fine Arts
studio. Madame Claire, formerly of Maison-Claire of Fifth
Avenue, New York, was named head of the costume department in April 1916. On May 20, 1916, Motion Picture News
announced that a series of two-reelers for Triangle release
would be produced at the Griffith studio; these would be light
comedy dramas, beginning with The Mystery of the Leaping
Fish, directed by John Emerson and starring Douglas Fairbanks, to be followed by a Fay Tincher comedy. It was later
announced that these would be designated "Komedy Brand"--
not to be confused with the 1917 Triangle Komedies--and
that Fay Tincher would be featured. According to Motion
Picture News (June 17, 1916), "The second [short] is said
to possess all the color possible for an ordinary picture without tinting or hand coloring, as Miss Tincher has worn gloves
of such color that none is lost in the photographs."

As evidence of Fine Arts pre-eminence, its payroll
in August 1916 amounted to $45,000 a week, with a further
$30,000 paid out monthly in general expenses. Only Univer-
sal, with a payroll of $50,000 a week, was higher. The
payrolls at Ince and Sennett were $30,000 weekly, with a
similar figure for general expenses.

However, by the fall of 1916, changes were taking
place at the studio. Bennie Zeidman, who had spent two
years as Griffith's publicist, left to join Metro in September.
Christy Cabanne, who had been earning in excess of $25,000
a year at Fine Arts, also left to join Metro at the same time;
he took with him his personal staff, including assistant direc-

tor Eugene Thurston; film cutter Millie Richter; and cameraman William Fildew. Motion Picture News on October 7,
1916, announced that Cabanne shot his first Metro production,
untitled, in the remarkably short time of eight days. Not
only did he direct the film in that time, he also wrote the
story and cast the players! "The pace that the director set
proved inspiring, but nerve racking to some of the players
not used to the Cabanne method," noted the News. In December, Mae Marsh left--the greatest loss of all.

Writing in Variety on October 29, 1915, Sime (Sime
Silverman) said, "About the best way always to gauge how
a show strikes one is to notice whether time drags or whirls.
It's almost a certain index. Though the Triangle program
ran nearly three hours, it hardly seemed longer than an
ordinary five-reeler would require. If the Triangle can turn
out the programs! If!! And to back up those ifs, it has
Griffith, Ince and Sennett! If they can't, no one can, and
there's an 'if' that says something." A year later, based
on contemporary critical reviews and on a viewing of extant
Fine Arts prints, the Fine Arts side of the Triangle was
indeed turning out those programs.

In the Triangle itself much was happening. S. L.
Rothapfel (Roxy) had taken over the Knickerbocker Theatre
and began his reign on Saturday, January 15, 1916, with the
premiere of the Billie Burke vehicle, Peggy. It was Roxy
who opened the Chicago home of Triangle pictures, the Colonial, on Saturday, February 26, with Daphne and the Pirate.
It was Roxy again who closed the Knickerbocker on Saturday,
April 29, after the owners of the building objected to its use
as anything other than a legitimate theatre. In its place
he had opened on April 21, the Rialto Theatre at the corner
of 42nd Street and Seventh Avenue as the new New York
home of the Triangle program. Present for the opening
night's program, which included The Good-Bad Man with Douglas Fairbanks and The Other Man with Roscoe "Fatty" Arbuckle
were the Arbuckles, plus Daniel Frohman, David Belasco, William Fox, Irvin S. Cobb, Morris Gest, Adolph Zukor, Edwin S.
Porter, Florenz Ziegfeld, Sigmund Lubin, B. P. Schulberg, J.
and Lee Shubert, J. Stuart Blackton, A. L. Erlanger, Marc
Klaw, and Charles Pathe--in fact anyone who was anyone in
the film and theatre world. If anything, Roxy showed Harry
Aitken and D. W. Griffith what true showmanship was all
about.

On the business front, there had been talk of a merger

in spring of 1916 between Triangle and Famous Players-Lasky,
which Variety (May 5, 1916) hoped might mean D. W. Griffith would once again direct Mary Pickford "in a Lasky studio, for a feature that will bear the Triangle brand when released. " The proposal came to naught. In October, Triangle did decide to sell the interest in its twenty-one branch
exchanges across the country, presumably to bring in much-
needed capital to the company. Triangle encouraged the
setting up of smaller exchanges, thereby selling their releases almost on a states' rights basis. Ince and Sennett
expressed their approval of the new scheme; D. W. Griffith
was strangely silent.

Chapter 7

ENTER SIR HERBERT

       Sir Herbert Beerbohm Tree is one of the great names
in the British theatre. As an actor-manager he gained last-
ing fame for the productions he staged at London's Her Majesty's Theatre (later renamed His Majesty's after the death
of Queen Victoria). He played everything from Bottom in
A Midsummer Night's Dream and Falstaff in The Merry Wives
of Windsor to Fagin in Oliver Twist and Sir Peter Teazle
in The School for Scandal. Born in London on December 17,
1853, he made his first stage appearance in 1876. However,
it was not until 1879 that he achieved his first success as
Bonneteau in A Cruise to China; his first appearance in America came in January 1895, when he appeared in The Ballad
Monger and The Red Lamp at New York's Abbey's Theatre.
His biography in Who's Who in the Theatre covers almost
five pages, and yet Herbert Beerbohm Tree was never a
magnificent actor, but rather, as Variety pointed out in its
obituary (July 6, 1917), "He was considered the most artistic producer of legitimate plays of the present day."

       Although certainly still a name, and a distinguished
one at that, by the Teens Sir Herbert Beerbohm Tree was
not at the peak of his career. He had made his vaudeville
debut at London's Palace Theatre in 1912, and during the
first part of 1915 was touring the British vaudeville circuit
in a condensed version of Trilby. An offer from Harry Aitken, on behalf of Triangle and Fine Arts, to star in motion
pictures must have come as a godsend to the actor, particularly from a financial point of view considering that his salary was announced to be in excess of $100,000. The exact
terms of Tree's contract called for him to be paid $100,000
in weekly installments, and to work fifteen consecutive weeks
from November 1, 1915, to be laid off for fifteen weeks, and
then to resume work for a final sixteen consecutive weeks.

The first announcement of Tree's entry into films came in
the October 22, 1915, issue of Variety in a one paragraph
news item, stating, "Sir Herbert Tree will shortly plan a
season in New York in a repertoire of his London successes,
chiefly Shakespearian. At the conclusion of his New York
engagement, Sir Herbert will pose for a feature film in Los
Angeles."

The draft contract for Tree's Macbeth, on file in the
Griffith papers at the Museum of Modern Art, indicates that
the director was to receive twenty-five percent of the profits
from the film, and that "Mr. Griffith hereby agrees to use
his best efforts in the supervision of the production of said
motion picture by said company for the purpose of imparting
to such production artistic, dramatic and commercial value."

Although a number of stage performers were being
signed for films at this time, including Otis Skinner, Edward
H. Sothern, William Gillette, and even Ellen Terry in England, Tree's contracting with Aitken is somewhat odd, as
there was proving to be a distinct lack of interest in stage
stars by moviegoers. Variety (December 10, 1915) noted,

> the producers have been bidding against each other
> for the services of the stars and the result has
> been that several of the concerns in their haste
> to get a signature of a "name" before a competitive
> firm should secure it have made contracts with
> stage stars before they had had any knowledge how
> they would screen or what they would do in pic-
> tures, and when the final result was turned out
> the picture people have been sorely disappointed on
> more than one occasion.... One producer stated
> recently he was sure he could have "made" half a
> dozen good film stars of stable quality with the
> difference that he paid in salary to as many stage
> celebrities, if he had devoted that money for ad-
> vertising them.... A manager figured it out the
> other day that instead of placing a star under con-
> tract whose only asset was a name that she had
> developed in stage work and paying her $50,000
> annually he was going to take the possibilities in
> his employ in pictures and when there is a girl
> whose salary may be anywhere from $2,500 to
> $10,000 a year the balance between that and $50,000
> is to be spent in advertising. 58

Sir Herbert Beerbohm Tree

The signing of Sir Herbert Beerbohm Tree was clearly based
on Harry Aitken's misguided need for prestige and Griffith's
equally misguided awe of anyone who had achieved greatness
on the legitimate stage.

At the time of Tree's signing, it was also stated that
Fine Arts had signed Mary Anderson de Navarro to make her
film debut in The Garden of Allah. Hichens' novel was indeed
filmed the following year, but by Selig with Helen Ware in
the leading female role. It was also rumored that Alla Naz-
imova would follow Tree to Fine Arts, but this proved to be
incorrect.

In October 1915, it was announced that Tree's first
American film would be a screen adaptation of Shakespeare's
The Tempest, in which the actor would be supported by Lillian Gish and Mae Marsh, a fascinating proposition which
sadly came to naught. Instead, by January 1916 it was widely
known that Tree's American screen debut would be in Macbeth. (The actor had already appeared in a least one British
production.)

Sir Herbert Beerbohm Tree arrived in Los Angeles
in late December 1915, accompanied by his daughter, Iris.
He was welcomed by almost everyone in Los Angeles, from
Mayor Sebastian to D. W. Griffith, from DeWolf Hopper to
two of Fine Arts' youngest stars, George Stone and Francis
Carpenter, not to mention "a band of real western cowboys
attached to the studio, who fired a salvo from their six-
shooters."[56] In his autobiography, DeWolf Hopper recalled,
"The Los Angeles reporters met him at the station and addressed him variously as 'Sir,' 'Your Lordship' and 'Sir
Tree.' One of them sensible of the confusion said, 'May I
ask just how you would be addressed?' 'My dear boy, call
me Oscar,' Tree told him in a stage whisper. Another young
man who had been called in hurriedly from police headquarters
to catch the distinguished visitor, asked him what he did in
London, and the actor replied that he played at His Majesty's
Theatre. 'I never knew the King had a theatre,' the police
reporter exclaimed. Tree passed triumphantly through the
reception, but once in the motor car which whisked him to
Hollywood he turned to his daughter, and said, 'If I only
could capture that type for the stage, our fortune would be
made.' He had the police reporter in mind."[33]*

---

*An almost identical story is told by Howard Gaye in his
(cont'd on p. 99)

Tree's welcome to the Fine Arts Studios.

        Tree, of course, had much to say regarding the si-
lent cinema and his filming of Macbeth.   He told Motion Picture News (December 11, 1915), "The human voice can never
be superseded.   The drama of dialogue and of emotions best
expressed by words will always prevail, but the spectacular
drama of the pictures will have enormous importance." Of
Macbeth, he was quoted by The Triangle as saying, "I am
more and more convinced that the selection is an ideal one,
and I am eager to be at work on the production. Macbeth,
apart from the power and beauty of its dialogue, is a highly
pictorial narrative, its characterizations are strongly developed, and it is throughout a story of action.   It is, too, one

(cont'd from page 98.) unpublished autobiography, So This
Was Hollywood, except that he claims it was a costumier
and not a reporter involved.

of the world's great classics, and to be taking part in its
photo-dramatization is at once a responsibility and a distinguished opportunity."[56] It may be that Tree's enthusiasm
had something to do with the fee he was being paid for his
services.

To direct and adapt Macbeth, Aitken and Griffith selected John Emerson, without question the most distinguished
of the Fine Arts directors, with a lengthy career as a stage
director in his background. (There are some sources that
claim it was Emerson who suggested Macbeth as Tree's initial offering.) Constance Collier, an actress whose career
was almost as illustrious as Tree's, was already in California starring in features for Morosco-Pallas, and she was
quickly signed to portray Lady Macbeth. Other roles were
played by Spottiswoode Aitken (Duncan), Wilfred Lucas (Macduff), and Ralph Lewis (Banquo).

Tuesday, January 4, 1916, marked Tree's first day
of work on Macbeth. He told The Moving Picture World
(January 15, 1916),

> It is quite wonderful how many things can be done
> in pictures for the Shakespearian tales that cannot
> be done on the stage. With all due reverence to
> the master dramatist, it is possible to illuminate
> and accentuate many details so as to produce a
> marvelously truth-telling commentary on the text
> and at the same time heighten the dramatic values.
> That is what I have learned from my first day's
> work with Director Emerson upon the scenario.
> The pictorial possibilities of Macbeth grow, as
> one studies it in the light of this strange new art,
> into something very beautiful and wonderful--not
> precisely a play in the Shakespearian sense, per-
> haps, but a dramatic narrative of great power. I
> should like to call this series of productions "Tales
> from Shakespeare." If we can bring to the dramas
> some such reverent and illuminating interpretation
> as did Charles Lamb, I shall be happy indeed to
> have entered upon this enterprise. The motion
> picture studios are naturally strange places to me,
> but I am delighted with the kindly spirit of welcome
> and co-operation manifested and the amazing vital-
> ity of the industry. I know now that I am going
> to like it immensely.

According to DeWolf Hopper, Tree did not entirely
accept the regimentation of film making. He would not appear at the studio until noon, and would work well into the
night. Endless hours were apparently spent on research,
with R. Ellis Wales, the studio's librarian, consulting every
conceivable book and paper on Macbeth and that period of
Scottish history. Typical of the unnecessary effort that went
into detail rather than consideration of whether Macbeth was
filmable as a silent drama or if Tree was an adequate silent
film actor, is this quote from Motion Picture News: " 'One
question which came up,' Mr. Aitken adds, 'was whether there
were any mountain sheep among the Scottish hills nine or ten
centuries ago. Sir Herbert thought that it was quite probable
wild sheep and goats roamed in Britain in the early days.
He based his opinion on the fact that as far back as history
goes there have been domesticated flocks, but Emerson decided that the big horn sheep were suggestive of the California mountains. He fixed upon the antlers of the royal stag
as more in harmony with the picture. And the Fine Arts
studio scouts spent days producing the goods.' "[32]

John Emerson has left a fairly detailed account of the
filming of Macbeth in the form of an interview with Hector
Ames, published in the September 1916 issue of Motion Picture Classic, from which it is worth quoting in some detail:

> I had often thought of Macbeth as a great picture
> subject, the plot seeming to lend itself so well to
> the picture method of treatment. The supernatural
> atmosphere that pervades Macbeth, exemplified by
> the witches and the visions Macbeth sees at differ-
> ent times, is very difficult to realize on the speak-
> ing stage. The witches on the stage do not appear
> supernatural, and the desired illusion is therefore
> impossible. On the screen, with the aid of the
> camera, the witches are easily given supernatural
> quality. The same applies to Banquo's ghost, which
> has always been so hard to produce convincingly on
> the stage. You can't have a two-hundred-pound man
> seated at a table and expect an audience to accept
> him for an apparition. Sir Henry Irving discarded
> the ghost in this scene, and I believe Sir Herbert
> adopted the same course in his London production
> of the play, leaving the whole thing to the imagin-
> ation of the audience. The visionary dagger is
> also an impossibility on the stage, but on the screen

Constance Collier and Sir Herbert Beerbohm Tree in Macbeth.

we can show it in a very effective and mystical sort of way.   And don't forget that Macbeth, aside from its psychological aspects, is a rattling good melodrama.   Another big thing in the favor of the Macbeth production is that scenery can be found in California almost identical with that of Scotland. We are considering doing The Merchant of Venice, and in that case shall build Venice on the canals at Santa Monica for the exterior scenes.

I think the few attempts to date that have been made to produce Shakespeare on the screen have proven fruitless, and the only reason I can logically see for that failure is the effort to produce a play like Hamlet, with a man like Forbes Robertson, in three reels of film, which ordinarily takes about forty-five minutes to project.   You can't success- fully produce Shakespeare on a small scale; there is too much meat in his plots, so it was decided to produce Macbeth in nine reels and thereby avoid omitting any of the essentials of the play.   There is great detail accuracy in the production, due to the great deal of time I, with my assistants, spent on thorough research work and securing exactness in detail of costume and settings, in order that the production might have an educational as well as a dramatic value.

While rummaging through volumes of historical references, we discovered that the people in the eleventh century in Scotland did not sleep in night- robes. *   I had planned to introduce a scene show- ing King Duncan praying at the foot of his bed, so had to delve a bit deeper and discovered that the higher classes to which King Duncan, of course, belonged, were just beginning at this time to use night-robes.   This saved the day for me.

When it came to preparing the screen scenario for Macbeth, the task was not so difficult as I had anticipated.   In fact, it was surprisingly easy, as Shakespeare's dramatic structure is more near in form to that of the film than the modern play or novel.   Owing to the limitations of the stage, an author must seek to reduce his action to one, two, three, or, at the most, four localities, in which

---

*This fact had obviously also been uncovered by Roman Po- lanski when he filmed his 1972 version of Macbeth.

the action of the various acts takes place. And,
of course, time-lapse must correspond exactly with
lengths of acts, whereas on the screen one may
have as many different locations as desired, and
the lapses of time are more easily covered.   A
modern play is ordinarily written in three acts.
Shakespeare wrote Macbeth in twenty-eight scenes,
so you see how much nearer Shakespeare's play is
to Motion Picture construction than any of the modern plays.   This is due to the fact that in Shakespeare's time it was not necessary to move the
scenery, as they did not have any to move.   It is
practically impossible to produce Macbeth, as written, on the speaking stage.   With the change of
sets, it would at least necessitate five or six hours
for production, whereas on the screen the scene
shifts instantaneously, so we can not only do all
the scenes Shakespeare provided for us in practically the same sequence, but are able to fill in the
lapses of time by adding scenes merely described
in the lines of the play.   As, for instance, the
fight between Macbeth and Cawdor and the execution
of the latter.
    The coronation of Macbeth, which is completely
jumped over in the play, will be one of the biggest
scenes in the picture.   I employed about a thousand
supernumeraries for the coronation.   All that is
said about the coronation in Shakespeare's play is:

> Ross: Will you to Scone?
> Macduff: No, cousin; I'll to Fife.
> Ross: Well, I will thither.
> Macduff: Well, may you see things well done
>   there.   Adieu!   Lest our old robes
>   sit easier than our new!

    The stone of Scone, where all the Scottish kings
were crowned, is duplicated accurately in the picture.
    And another instance, where I elaborated on a
line in the play, is Birnam Wood, which is merely
spoken of; we show it moving toward the castle of
Macbeth.
    Our film version of Macbeth will contain approx-
imately two hundred and fifty scenes in nine reels,
which means a full evening's entertainment.
    We found it much simpler on the screen to suggest

the evil influence of the witches than on the stage.
The opening scene of the picturization presents the
witches in their cavern, where they are brewing
trouble, which is to come to Scotland through Macbeth.   In the depths of their cavern they draw forth
the fires of evil, which are thrown from their fin-
gers down into the valley of destruction, where
Macbeth and the traitor Cawdor are fighting for
supremacy.

It became necessary at times to take liberties
with the text, in order to knit the story closely
enough to be able to project it in the limits of two
hours and yet retain practically all the incidents of
the play.   While taking these liberties, we have
endeavored to show a spirit of reverence for the
text and have consulted Shakespearian authorities
for justification on every alteration we made.   One
change in particular was in the sleep-walking scene.
In the play, a gentlewoman and doctor overhear this
scene.   But, in order to knit the photoplay structure together, it was essential that Ross and Lennox overhear this scene.   We justified this change
by the statement of the gentlewoman to the doctor
that she had seen Lady Macbeth walk and talk in
this way night after night.   Why couldn't Ross and
Lennox see her one night as well as the doctor and
the lady?

With all his scenes shot and the film almost completed,
Sir Herbert Beerbohm Tree prepared to leave Los Angeles
for New York to play Cardinal Wolsey at the New Amsterdam
Theatre.   On March 24, 1916, the day before he departed,
the Fine Arts Company gave a dinner in Tree's honor at the
Alexandria Hotel.   Douglas Fairbanks acted as chairman for
the event, and also contributed a number of magic tricks,
and also present were DeWolf Hopper, Constance Collier,
William and Dustin Farnum, John Emerson, Erich von Stroheim, Kathlyn Williams, and D. W. Griffith.   The last made
a speech, which read in part, "On the eve of your departure,
Sir Herbert, I, on behalf of the studio, call you our 'friend';
with more sentiment I could say, 'love,' for, Sir Herbert,
with your great democracy, you have won the love of the
entire studio, from the executive down to the property man."

Harry Aitken, who was not present, might have echoed
Griffith's sentiments before the opening of Macbeth.   He would
not have done so after the initial critical and box-office response.

On April 29, 1916, <u>Motion Picture News</u> reported that
John Emerson had left for New York with an eight-reel version of <u>Macbeth</u>, to be shown as part of the Shakespearian
Centennial revival. Whether this screening ever took place
is doubtful, but <u>Macbeth</u> did receive its official world premiere on June 4, 1916, at the Rialto Theatre in New York
at a performance attended by Tree and Constance Collier.
The Los Angeles premiere took place at the Majestic Theatre
on June 6. The film was screened in two parts, with the
first act closing with MacDuff's decision to drive Macbeth
from the throne. After the first day at the Rialto, the management added a one-reel comedy, "as the heavy tragedy of
Avan d'Bard [sic] seemed a little too indigestible for the film
patrons of the house," according to <u>Variety</u>.

Reviews were generally lukewarm. Lynde Denig in
<u>The Moving Picture World</u> (June 24, 1916) wrote,

> In constructing a photoplay of this type the art of
> a director is manifested in the scenes he chooses
> to visualize, scenes that cannot be shown on the
> stage, but the meaning of which is communicated
> to the audience through subsequent dialogue. When
> such additions are made it is not altering the orig-
> inal, rather expressing the same things in the lan-
> guage Mr. Emerson utilizes with fine effect to
> realize the true spirit of <u>Macbeth</u>. The murder of
> the king is visualized, as are many other happen-
> ings left to the imagination in stage performances,
> but never once is anything foreign to Shakespeare's
> tragedy allowed to intrude. When speech is neces-
> sary, lines from the play are invariably used, and
> the arrangement of the scenario necessitates few
> explanatory leaders. It is a treat, indeed, to read
> so much of Shakespeare on the screen, even if
> some familiar quotations are slightly altered.
>   Sir Herbert is a virile, compelling Macbeth,
> possessed of the rare art that makes possible the
> communication of emotional states. Characteriza-
> tion with a psychological background is possible
> where such an actor is concerned. We see the
> birth of ambition after the prophesy of the witches
> and feel the irresistible force of temptation as Lady
> Macbeth urges courage that his deeds may fulfill
> his hopes. There is infinite variety and subtle
> shading in the portrayal, as Macbeth, suffering
> from the conscience that "makes cowards of us all,"

shrinks before the phantom dagger or the pursuing
ghost of Banquo. Judiciously used close-ups of
his wonderfully mobile features enable Sir Herbert
to reveal the ever-increasing mental torture that
eats into the soul of the usurper.

The Lady Macbeth of Miss Collier is no less
impressive, for she, too, possesses a rich personality perfectly suited to Shakespearian tragedy. She
uses natural advantages of face and figure with un-
failing intelligence to indicate emotional feeling and
the hard cruelty of the relentlessly ambitious woman.
In the sleep walking scene and the scenes preceding
the tragic death of Lady Macbeth, Miss Collier
reaches the high moments of a superb performance.

But it must not be gathered that the picture depends entirely upon these two characterizations.
Other roles are properly presented and in the con-
cluding reel, bringing the attack on Macbeth's castle, there is a stirring spectacular conflict handled
on a large scale. From first to last the production, 7,500 feet in length, is marked by artistic
lighting, tinting and appropriate settings."

Peter Milne in Motion Picture News (June 17, 1916)
commented,

Shakespeare's Macbeth has received what may be
summed up as excellent treatment in its migration
to the motion picture. The passages have been
changed a little bit here, enlarged upon slightly
there and scenes have been added that were merely
suggested at in the play and some that are products
of the present producer's imagination have been
inserted to meet the demands of the camera....
John Emerson is credited with shaping the play for
the screen and the directing. Mr. Emerson, perhaps because he was dealing with Macbeth, has
adhered more or less rigidly to stage production.
In close-ups his characters deliver what seem to
be speeches from the play directly into the lens.
Talking, however, seems in no wise to hinder fa-
cial expression, and so the point may be disposed
of lightly.

In respect to his scenario Mr. Emerson has done
excellently. The bits of action that up to this time
have been foreign to Shakespeare, inserted by Mr.
Emerson, bear out the suggestions of the play to

a degree of perfection.   Battle scenes, for instance,
the sight of MacDuff at home with his wife and
child, the final storming of Macbeth's castle and
other incidents create a strong impression entirely
in keeping with the original play.

Likewise in the matter of production has Mr.
Emerson carried out his scenario to a perfect degree.   The costuming, the settings and the handling
of the hordes of extras in the battle scenes could
not be improved upon.   And besides, there are the
three witches and Banquo's ghost introduced as only
the films can properly introduce them; by use of
double exposure.   In smaller but no less important
instances has Mr. Emerson taken advantage of the
power of the camera.   In that most crucial point
in the play when Macbeth, after he has murdered
Duncan, is brooding over his deed and of future
glories prophesied to follow he is awakened from
his lethargy by the knocking of Macduff at the castle door.   Again calling the double exposure into
play, a mailed fist is seen knocking on Macbeth's
heart.   There are other bits of equal significance.

In fact from first to last, the picture Macbeth
is a powerful tragedy.   There was opportunity,
plenty of opportunity to visualize it as violent melodrama because the various murders done and caused
by Macbeth are all pictured in this production.   Happily, however, the play is worthy to be called a
tragedy, for it depicts with great intensity the down-
fall and ruination of an overly ambitious man,
spurred on to murder by an even more ambitious
wife.

It is a picture which will provide amply for the
entertainment of those who have before considered
Shakespeare to be beyond their scope of conception,
while it is also a production that will in no wise
offend the sensibilities and the traditions held by
the student.

Fred in Variety (June 9, 1916) provided a more down-
to-earth viewpoint:

> To the student of Shakespeare the picturization of
> his greatest tragedy will be most interesting, but
> it is doubtful if the regular film patron will care
> to witness the production.   Of course there will
> be a certain amount of box office draught to the

name of Sir Herbert Tree in the small towns, but
judging from the manner of reception which the offering has been received to date, it is safe to assume that Shakespeare on the screen will never
have any great vogue.

Julian Johnson in Photoplay (August, 1916) was perhaps the
most critical:

> The picture fails of greatness because it relied
> upon stellar acting, and after the first few episodes,
> this acting consisted, on the part of Sir Herbert,
> of staring and wobbling, and the staring eye when
> translated into black and white, becomes extremely
> monotonous.   Miss Collier was more versatile in
> her moods, and her sleepwalking scene was decid-
> edly eerie.   Doubtless, to the millions who have
> never seen Sothern as the arch murderer, and
> some actress of the caliber of the late Helen Mod-
> jeska as his temptress, particularly to the millions
> who never even have read the classic, this film
> will be a revelation of thrills.   To us who have
> been reading and seeing the play for more years
> than we care to admit, it brings little of interest.
> But for one thing at least, many thanks--the Re-
> liance folks were able to find material for their
> captions in the lines of the play itself, for the most
> part, even though there does seem to be a differ-
> ence of opinion as to the spelling of the word
> "weird."

Macbeth opened in London at Tree's own theatre, His
Majesty's, on June 28.   It was received without enthusiasm
by press and public--aside from the usual deference due the
Tree name--and was taken off on July 6.   To add to Triangle's problems, the Big A Film Corporation simultaneously
released a British film version of Macbeth featuring Arthur
Bouchier.

In July 1916 Sir Herbert Beerbohm Tree returned to
Los Angeles and Fine Arts supposedly to appear in a series
of filmed Shakesperian plays.   Chester Withey was selected
as director, replacing John Emerson who had by this time
left Fine Arts.   Tree announced that he would spend three
months in Los Angeles and pontificated on the motion picture
as "a tremendous educational force in civilization" and as
"a big factor in advancement of the arts."   However, by this

time Harry Aitken had decided that Shakesperian productions
were no way to keep Triangle and Fine Arts solvent, particularly if those productions starred Sir Herbert Beerbohm Tree.
Although it is hard to believe that Griffith went along with
this, Aitken's solution was to star Tree in an American rural
drama, in which he was totally miscast, in the hope that the
actor would cancel his lucrative contract and return to England. He did.

In fact, the film, The Old Folks at Home, was apparently
not that bad. It told of a country boy (Elmer Clifton) who goes
to the city with sudden wealth, commits a murder and is shielded
by his parents, one of whom (Tree) is a Senator. Acting honors
went to Josephine Crowell as the mother who breaks down
on the witness stand and begs the jury to free her guilty
son. "A splendid characterwoman, this lady!" noted Julian
Johnson in Photoplay (December 1916). He found Tree "con-
foundedly miscast." Peter Milne in Motion Picture News
(October 21, 1916) thought that Sir Herbert "plays the part
for what it is worth, no more, no less." Variety (October
6, 1916) thought, "From an exhibitor's standpoint the picture
is a good feature, for it has a name that is in the first rank
of the theatre's realm of stardom, and in this particular case
there is a mighty good story by an author as well known in
this country as the star himself."

Author Rupert Hughes claimed in a Saturday Evening
Post article in the Thirties that Tree was threatened with
being cast in blackface unless he cancelled his contract. The
only contemporary evidence for this is a gossip item in the
November 1916 issue of Photoplay, which reads, "Sir Herbert
Beerbohm Tree is through celluloiding and is once more on
British soil. His parting with Fine Arts is said to have been
hastened by a directorial desire to have the distinguished
actor appear in blackface. The desire, it is said, was in-
spired by the discovery that the limited success of Sir Herbert's filmed Macbeth did not justify his large salary." Amusing as this story is, it is hard to accept, particularly in
view of Griffith's total adulation of the legitimate stage which
Tree represented and in that Tree's departure from Los Angeles was on the surface amicable with his attending a farewell dinner hosted by his director, Chester Withey.

Sir Herbert Beerbohm Tree died at his London home
on July 2, 1917, following an operation. Robert Hamilton
Ball in his definitive volume on Shakespeare on Silent Film

provides a perfect quote from Tree as to his reasons for entering the film medium: "Well, you see, I thought I had reached the time of my life when I ought to be seen--and not heard."5

Chapter 8

FINE ARTS' FINAL MONTHS, 1917

"A year ago," mused Julian Johnson in Photoplay
(February 1917), "the Fine Arts studio, treading with minc-
ing condescension, began to dispense culture to a crude,
crude people.... And Mr. Griffith, suave and mysterious,
reigned on a throne so glittering that no other producer dared
turn his eyes that way." Now, however, in the final months
of Fine Arts, the critic had mixed reactions to the studio's
product, ranging from "Well done, but by no means notable"
for A Sister of Six to "Quite impossible" for The Wharf Rat.
But as far as D. W. Griffith was concerned, Julian Johnson's
opinion had not changed: "As for that crown, Griffith still
wears it. Intolerance is a tremendous, stupendous study
which fails to advance its maker. It is a museum of anti-
quity and a modern picture gallery, but it lacks a story. Mr.
Griffith can tell great stories with the simplicity of greatness.
He is at the zenith of his powers, and he had better be about
his producing, handing his impressarioship to those who have
smaller imagination and larger adding machines."

It was as if Johnson was urging the director to renew
his interest in the "small" five-reel Fine Arts productions,
and, for the time being at least, forget about the multi-reel
spectacles, which the critic felt were overwhelming the cinema
and its audiences, from Cecil B. DeMille's Joan the Woman
to Thomas H. Ince's Civilization. However, as if in answer
to Julian Johnson, Photoplay in that same issue contained a
news item that stated that "the exact status of David Wark
Griffith with respect to his former affiliations is a thing of
mystery. Since the premiere of Intolerance, he has stead-
fastly reiterated that he has nothing to do with Triangle. In
effect, he has disowned all Fine Arts productions since the
formation of that company."

Yet, as if to prove that Fine Arts was still at the top of its form, the company's first release for 1917, The Little Yank is one of its best extant productions. A civil war drama, featuring Dorothy Gish, Frank Bennett, Robert Burns, and A. D. Sears, The Little Yank was directed by George Siegmann, whose training is more than apparent in this production. An opening title explains that the story by Roy Somerville was "based upon actual occurrences in the Civil War, as related and vouched for in the autobiography of Captain John T. Wickersham of the Confederate Army." Basically, it tells of a Northern girl living in the town of Hayward near the border line between North and South who, in crossing into enemy territory to aid her wounded brother, falls in love with a Confederate soldier, Captain Johnny.

The Little Yank features a touching performance by Dorothy Gish as she turns down Captain Johnny's affection for her because he is an enemy of her flag. She is a woman torn between love and duty to the Union cause, meeting her Captain Johnny beside an old cannon, a trysting place that plays an important part in the story, for it is here that the little Yank's Union lover lures Captain Johnny to accuse him falsely of spying. There are obvious similarities to The Birth of a Nation, but here it is a Negro servant, played by Hal Wilson in blackface, who helps Union soldiers, and the Yankee heroine proudly replies, "It was a salute, Sir, to the Union," when asked by the Confederate soldiers to explain why she fired gunshots to allow the Union soldiers to escape. The battle scenes, although small in scope, are well directed and photographed. And there is even a Confederate soldier who looks at Dorothy Gish and gives a passable imitation of the "mooning soldier" from The Birth of a Nation. Griffith must have felt pride with Siegmann's work, particularly one beautiful shot inside a tent, in which we see sunlight streaming through the canvas and casting shadows of the trees and the marching soldiers outside.

Particular praise should go to Frank Bennett as Captain Johnny, one of the forgotten leading men of the Griffith-Fine Arts Company. His sensitive features make him an ideal Griffith hero in the Robert Harron manner: young and boyish but with an inner maturity. Born in Bakersfield, California, on September 15, 1890, Bennett was educated at Frohman Dramatic School in New York, and had entered films with Vitagraph in 1913. Photoplay (October 1914) described him as "One of Reliance's leading character actors," and he

played Charles IX in the French story from Intolerance. After the demise of Fine Arts, he moved on first to Metro and
then to Paramount. By 1921 he had ceased acting on the
screen and what happened to him remains a mystery.

    At the time of its initial release, The Little Yank
was not highly regarded.   Julian Johnson in Photoplay (April
1917) described it and Nina, the Flower Girl as "two Fine
Arts productions which by no means approach Fine Arts
standard. Both of them seem to be the result of a day in
which a release was needed and the hypo of inspiration was
not to be found." Louis Reeves Harrison in The Moving Picture World (January 13, 1917) was struck by the ludicrous
nature of the story:

> The Little Yank is not intended to be comical, but
> it is unconsciously so at times. Dorothy Gish is
> the "Little Yank" who lives with other ladies in
> hoopskirts near the scene of our civil war. They
> decide to send some supplies to the Union Army,
> and a wagon load of creature comforts is escorted
> by Dorothy in a carriage. At a fork in the road,
> the wagon goes to the right and lands comfortably
> in the Union ranks. The carriage goes to the left
> and encounters a detachment of Confederates. They
> politely indicate the right course. It is thus made
> obvious that going from one army to the other is
> not a matter of great difficulty, not particularly
> logical, but accepted as possible. Dorothy finds
> that her brother is a wounded prisoner in the hands
> of the enemy. She politely requests the Union Gen-
> eral to stop a terrific engagement then in progress
> --she wishes to visit her brother, and why should
> she go back to the convenient fork in the road.
> Two great battle lines are in the midst of a life
> and death struggle, when the Union General sends a
> flag of truce asking the enemy to stop firing while
> a lady crosses over to see her brother. Both
> armies rest, while Miss Dotty crosses the battle-
> field with her man servant, and she is spared the
> annoyance of driving a few miles to the fork in the
> road. She gets back to the Union lines without any
> particular trouble. Moral--Place aux dames. Of-
> ficers and troops have really nothing at stake when
> the author is directing the battle from both sides
> at the same time. When an author intervenes to
> command the sun to stand still, the story fails in

Bessie Love [center] and Elmer Clifton [far right] in Nina,
The Flower Girl.

adherence to the inevitable--it lacks all the charm
and illusion of abiding veracity.

There were no outward signs that the death knell was
sounding at Fine Arts. Elmer Clifton was promoted to director with Her Official Father, co-directed with Joseph Henabery, being his initial endeavor. Kenneth Harlan was signed
from the legitimate stage and vaudeville as a new leading
man, and according to Motion Picture News (February 10,
1917) spent his first day at the studio discussing his future
with the management. In fact, he made only one film at
Fine Arts, Betsy's Burglar, in which he was co-starred opposite Constance Talmadge, but he did achieve some fame
as a vapid leading man in dozens of forgettable Twenties
features.

On the negative side, the studio lost Robert Harron
when he followed Mae Marsh briefly to Goldwyn. Despite
his integral leading role in Intolerance, Triangle and Fine
Arts had not actually named him as a star until January
1917 when he was co-starred opposite Mildred Harris in The
Bad Boy, the story of "a misunderstood American lad of
weak will but good intent." Harron followed The Bad Boy
with An Old Fashioned Young Man, under the directorship of
Lloyd Ingraham, in which his leading lady was Colleen Moore,
who had a "bit" part in the previous film. Miss Moore recalls, "I hardly knew how to put on makeup.... What I
remember most about the picture is that I wore my first
pair of high heels and I kept stumbling all over the set. Mr.
Ingraham suggested that at night I practice walking around the
block in the high heels so as to become accustomed to them.
By the time the picture was finished I could have walked on
stilts. I remember the picture took about two or three weeks
to shoot as they were done quickly with few retakes."

On January 27, 1917, The Moving Picture World announced that Triangle had a series of one-reel "Komedies"
ready for immediate release. No players or directors were
mentioned, nor was there any indication as to which of the
three Triangle producers was responsible for them. It seems
pretty clear that they were not Mack Sennett productions, as
there can be no question that his name would have been used
as a selling point for them if at all possible. The following
are the titles of these shorts, with their respective release
dates: Love Under Cover and The Pipe of Discontent (January 14), A Noble Fraud and Honest Thieves (January 21),
Heart Strategy and A Grab Bag Bride (January 28), The Male
Governess and The Road Agent (February 4), Won by a Foot
and His Deadly Undertaking (February 11), The Telephone
Belle and When Hearts Collide (February 18). The Moving
Picture World explained, "The demand for single-reel comedies has been insistent since the beginning of the motion picture industry, and will undoubtedly continue as long as pictures retain their universal appeal. The Triangle has utilized
its best resources in putting on these short laugh-makers
and this assurance should be enough to stimulate the interest
of exhibitors generally."

A second Dorothy Gish Fine Arts feature from 1917
has survived and that is Stage Struck, directed by Edward
Morrissey, and featuring Frank Bennett, Jennie Lee and
Spottiswoode Aitken. A comedy of theatrical life, Stage Struck
features Dorothy as Penelope, a simple country girl who is

duped of her savings by a fake drama school, Schneider's
College of Dramatic Art (complete with a slogan on its wall
announcing "Richard Mansfield says Schneider's leads them
all"). Along the way, she meets and marries Jack Martin
(Bennett), who comes from a wealthy family and has similar
theatrical ambitions to her own. Jennie Lee as Mrs. Tweedle,
referred to in the sub-titles as "Big Heart," gives a suitably
sympathetic performance as the kindly proprietor of a theatrical boarding house.

The screenplay by Roy Somerville contains endless
references to birds, from "fly the coop" through "the groom
hustled up a nook for a nest" to "picking the last pin-feathers
of his flock." Julian Johnson in Photoplay (May 1917) considered Stage Struck, "a light fabric wrapped about slender
Dorothy Gish." Louis Reeves Harrison in The Moving Picture World (March 3, 1917) found the comedy lacking dramatic depth, and continued, "There are some amusing sub-
titles and a generally good performance on the part of a well
balanced company. Miss Dorothy has little to do, and does
it well. The whole effect is pleasing, but the story is rob-
bed of its possibilities by lack of mature grasp of its own
merits, such as would fasten attention upon developing its
most interesting situations."

One other Fine Arts production of 1917 should be mentioned, and that is Jim Bludso, co-directed by Wilfred Lucas
and Tod Browning and based on John Hay's Pike County ballad. It was the last Fine Arts film to receive a warm review from Julian Johnson, an avid admirer of Wilfred Lucas'
talent. Johnson wrote in Photoplay (April 1917),

> Peace hath her heroes, as well as her victories,
> and of these Jim Bludso, a Mississippi river en-
> gineer, who, with his craft in flames, held her
> nozzle agin the bank till the last galoot got ashore,
> is in the front rank. Mr. Bludso was renowned
> in the poetry of a generation or two behind Edgar
> Lee Masters--probably Mr. Masters would pour
> vinegar into the milk of renown by proving that
> our hero never sent money home to his folks, or
> heaved firewood at his old man--and has been warmed
> over in various dishes of art. Now comes the
> thoroughly applaudable Fine Arts vision, with our
> champion character-maker, Wilfred Lucas, as the
> engineer. In the slightly shifted story Olga Grey
> is the wife, George Stone is "Little Breeches,"

and James O'Shea is Banty Tim. The suspense is
excellent and the burning of "The Prairie Belle" a
scenic spectacle.   There are many fine touches of
detail in properties and people.

Although obviously expected for some time, the bomb
fell in March 1917 when Griffith's departure from Fine Arts
was made public. Variety carried the first story on March
16, reporting,

> R. W. France, General Manager of the Triangle
> Distributing Corp. on Wednesday confirmed the
> withdrawal of Griffith, but denied emphatically there
> was any ill-feeling.   He got in communication by
> phone with Mr. Griffith who stated: "Our relations
> are quite friendly.   I simply severed connections
> with Triangle for business reasons and have no
> definite plans for the future, though I have several
> things under consideration. "   The opinion is preva-
> lent in New York that the reason for the denials
> up to the present time of the Griffith-Triangle sev-
> erance of relations was founded on the expectation
> that a new alliance would be made between the two
> and the apparently cordial relations still existing
> leads to the belief that such a contingency is not
> yet altogether unlikely.

Such a contingency, of course, did not occur. Instead, on March 17, Griffith announced in The New York
Times that he planned to sail to Europe to make a film for
the allies, which was to be Hearts of the World. The following day he set sail on the S. S. Baltic. On March 31, 1917,
the trade papers announced that the director had "sold out"
his stock in the Triangle Film Corporation and had signed a
long-term contract with the Artcraft Pictures Corporation.
The following statement by Griffith appeared in The Moving
Picture World:

> The demand on the part of the exhibitors and public
> throughout the world for a series of productions
> along the lines I traced in The Birth of a Nation
> and Intolerance had become so insistent that I would
> feel almost remiss in duty if I did not pay it heed.
> In determining upon the purpose of producing such
> an annual schedule of important cinema offerings,
> the essential consideration was the choice of dis-
> tribution which would in the greatest degree respond

to this demand. After a very careful analysis of
the various distributing organizations operating in
the film industry, I came to the conclusion that
Artcraft, because of the exalted standard of the
productions it has already offered the public, because of its tremendous source of distribution and
its equitable and comprehensive policies, was the
one organization through which to circulate my productions through the world. I am convinced that
I have never had such an opportunity to reach the
great heart of mankind with my screen messages.
I feel that the degree of success which has been
meted out to The Birth of a Nation and Intolerance
placed me in the debt of the public which can only
be equalized by bending every effort to surpass all
my former efforts. 28

Naturally Griffith left undiscussed the sordid question of how
much money Adolph Zukor had offered him to join Artcraft.

Artcraft issued a similar, shorter statement: "Mr.
Griffith intends to concentrate his time and energy in such
a manner as to create a number of subjects of wide dramatic
and scenic scope in order to comply with the insistent public
demand for more Griffith productions. Mr. Griffith's producing force will operate wherever necessary to obtain the
startling realism for which this noted director is famous. "26

With Griffith's departure from Fine Arts, Frank Woods
tendered his resignation as did Edward Dillon. Lillian Gish,
Robert Harron and Lloyd Ingraham were under personal contract to D. W. Griffith and also left. Alma Rubens' Fine
Arts contract was taken over by Ince. Bernard McConville
signed a contract with Fox, and two other Fine Arts screenwriters, Mary H. O'Connor and Roy Somerville, resigned.

It was announced that Thomas Ince would produce all
future Fine Arts films at his Culver City studios. Triangle
hastily issued a statement,

According to the most carefully compiled reports
of unprejudiced film critics Triangle releases, produced under the supervision of Thomas H. Ince,
have been the best box-office attractions of any
program releases produced during the part year.
This fact confirms the claim of Ince adherents that
the presiding genius of Culver City is perhaps the

greatest supervising director that the motion picture industry has yet produced, that it is a noteworthy fact that Ince had outdistanced all competitors in his ability to keep his organization running
at the top notch of efficiency month in and month
out. No other producer can be called to mind with
a list of successes equally imposing, turned out in
the regular course of events. Ince is not only a
director of the highest quality himself, but he possesses the much rarer accomplishments of being
able to stimulate his subordinates to their best
endeavors under all circumstances.

How soon did Triangle choose to forget Griffith's contribution
to its fame!

Triangle also announced changes in its production
schedule. Effective from the beginning of June 1917, the
company would release only special productions, to be known
as Super-Triangles, "featuring the biggest and best stars
obtainable regardless of cost" or "unusual productions by
such master-directors as Thomas H. Ince, Mack Sennett,
Allan Dwan and others" or "productions having extraordinary
drawing power because of special publicity or advertising."
Exhibitors could book one of the special features, reject the
special feature and rebook any Triangle subject which they
had already screened at half-price or reject Triangle altogether and book a film on the open market. "The purpose
of this plan we are frank to say," announced Triangle, "is
to supply to our exhibitors a type of production which we
cannot afford to give them for the moderate sum paid for
our regular program service, and we believe our course
will be appreciated."

Allan Dwan was named supervising director at Fine
Arts' Yonkers studios, with two new directors, Arthur Rosson and Albert Parker, under his direct control. Players
based at Yonkers included Wilfred Lucas, Hedda Hopper and
Joseph Kilgore. "We are going to make serious pictures
here," said Dwan, "pictures that pulse with the problems of
today. We are going to accentuate the value of ideals in
industry and business, to attemp to show how men and women
may be honest and highly successful, too. The tendency in
business today is toward the idealistic, and we are going to
try to do what we can to help it along."[2]

The first of these "serious" pictures was <u>Her Father's</u>

Keeper, starring Irene Howley, Jack Devereux and Frank
Currier. Miss Howley played the daughter of a rich Wall
Street merchant who, against her father's objections, sets out
to find herself a husband and to do something in the world
other than be a dilettante daughter of a wealthy father. William J. McGrath in Motion Picture News (March 31, 1917)
described it as "a picture that happily combines drama and
comedy in a manner that is refreshing and pleasing."

Allan Dwan supervised production of several further
Triangle releases in 1917 at the Yonkers studios: The Man
Who Made Good (directed by Albert Rosson), American--
That's All (directed by Rosson), A Successful Failure (di-
rected by Albert Parker), Grafters (directed by Rosson), The
Haunted House (directed by Parker), Cassidy (directed by
Rosson), and The Man Hater (directed by Parker).

However, all was not well with Triangle. W. W.
Hodkinson was no sooner named president of the company
than he resigned, to be replaced by S. A. Lynch. H. O.
Davis, formerly general manager of Universal City, was
brought in as Triangle's general manager and as a member
of its board of directors. Davis soon had plenty to do when,
in June 1917, Ince announced that he was withdrawing from
Triangle, and that Sennett would follow. Davis told Motion
Picture News,

> This separation between Mr. Ince and Triangle
> has been made with the best of feelings on each
> side. It is simply a parting of the ways, conceived
> and followed out in the best interests, we all be-
> lieve, of all concerned. It is a matter purely of
> policy in production and distribution.... Organi-
> zation is always greater than any man in it. This
> is the rule of modern business. It makes for suc-
> cess and makes a successful product. To make
> good pictures requires a good organization. Many
> important factors are involved; all must be balanced
> and each one right. The mechanical novelty era
> of the picture is entirely gone. Pictures must be
> made so well today that the audience for the time
> being forgets it is seeing a motion picture at all.
> Reliance upon a star, or indeed upon any one fac-
> tor, in a picture is, in my opinion, a confession
> of weakness. The picture itself is what counts....
> The first step is unity of organization. The suc-
> cessful manufacturer today in any line is the man

> who makes his dealers succeed. He fixes prices
> and policies, and makes the public buy. That is
> the aim of our service policy--to fill the exhibitors'
> seats at a profit to the exhibitors. This also can
> be done. We realize that the exhibitor today is
> looking for service--for a surety that he can sell
> profitably to the public. We will give him such
> service. It will be our business to see that the
> exhibitors make money to the end that we may.
> The dealers' success must be in direct proportion
> to our own.... We are in business for the future.
> We can wait. [69]

Ince was apparently paid three quarters of a million
dollars for his stock in Triangle and the New York Motion
Picture Corporation. With his passing, Hart also resigned,
claiming that his contract with Triangle demanded that Ince
and no one else could personally supervise his productions.
C. Gardner Sullivan was to stay on as scenario editor and
Jack Conway was named to be manager of the Culver City
studios.

The last film to be made at Fine Arts under the Griffith banner was Madame Bo-peep, directed by Chester Withey,
whose contract with Triangle did not expire until June, and
starring Seena Owen. Louis Reeves Harrison in The Moving
Picture World (May 26, 1917) was scathing in his criticism:

> Madame Bo-Peep is the story of a young woman
> who acts with so little intelligence that she might
> be suspected of feeble-mindedness when she is
> persuaded to marry a distasteful old man for the
> money she might get by taking a life partner from
> among men whom she could tolerate with a sem-
> blance of self-respect. She lacks sufficient strength
> of mind to do anything on her own account, is pushed
> into an undesirable alliance by the recommendation
> of acquaintances. The only property the supposed
> wealthy husband leaves is a sheep ranch in charge
> of young suitor. When she goes there all interest
> in her career, if any has been aroused, comes to
> an end. It is easily foreseen that she will wed the
> young man, and the rest is mere padding with only
> one bright spot, where the heroine does some good
> riding, but the entire composition is lacking in the
> main and guiding principles of a five-reel screen
> story, cuff-made and unworthy of being classed
> with other Ince productions.

Peter Milne in Motion Picture News (June 2, 1917) described
it merely as "an average picture."

Plans were announced in June 1917 to reopen the Fine
Arts studios "on a large scale." Instead, by 1921, the studios had become the Arthur H. Gooden rental studios. A
Fine Arts Pictures Company was established in Jacksonville,
Florida, with no connection to the Griffith company, and Independent Distributors of America was formed to take over
the Triangle releases.

Today, nothing is left of the Fine Arts studios on
Sunset Boulevard. The gigantic Intolerance sets had been
dismantled by the Twenties, and the Fine Arts Company was
scattered. The studios, during the Forties and Fifties, were
used as annex studios by Columbia, chiefly for the production
of its "B" pictures, although one or two major features, including Anna Lucasta and Autumn Leaves, were filmed there.
Yet Fine Arts lives on in proud memory as a unique experiment in film production by a very unique film maker. As
a dream it had possibilities, and in reality it lived up to
many of those possibilities. D. W. Griffith had nothing of
which to be ashamed in the work of his company of players
and directors. Nor, for that matter, had Harry Aitken and
Triangle anything to excuse; two features a week produced
and released on time between 1915 and 1917 is a fine record.

APPENDIXES

Appendix A

A FINE ARTS WHO'S WHO

(Biographies have been kept deliberately short
for those Fine Arts Personnel, such as D. W.
Griffith and Lillian Gish, whose careers have
been adequately covered elsewhere.)

DAVID ABEL

Born, Amsterdam, circa December 15, 1884. Died,
Los Angeles, November 12, 1973. Studio directories from
the Teens indicate that Abel was born in Russia on December
10, 1884, but he told this writer he was born in Amsterdam
of Russian parents, and that he always celebrated his birthday on the date given here. David Abel became a cinematographer in 1913 and was active through the mid-Forties; he
deserves particular credit for his photography of most of the
Fred Astaire-Ginger Rogers features in the Thirties.

At Fine Arts, he photographed many films, including
A Sister of Six (1916), The Heiress at Coffee Dan's (1916)
and The Bad Boy (1917). His other films include Thais (1917),
The Splendid Sinner (1918), The Way of a Woman (1919),
Babbitt (1924), Beau Brummell (1924), Craig's Wife (1928),
Grumpy (1930), The Gay Divorcee (1934), Top Hat (1935),
Follow the Fleet (1936), Shall We Dance (1937), Holiday Inn
(1942), and The Affairs of Susan (1945). He claimed (in a
1922 interview) to have photographed Constance Talmadge in
the Babylonian sequences of Intolerance, but there is no doc-
umentary proof of this and it could be that what he photographed were the additional scenes for Griffith's 1919 release
of The Fall of Babylon.

In 1972, this writer taped an oral history with David
Abel on behalf of the American Society of Cinematographers,
and this tape is available for study at the A.S.C.

GEORGE (ANDRE) BERANGER

Born, Sydney, Australia, March 27, 1895. Reported to have died in 1973, but no confirmation is available. A personable, attractive actor, who worked with Griffith for many years (from American Biograph), acting as an assistant to the master and becoming a director himself for a short period in the late Teens. He directed Uncle Sam of Freedom Ridge, among others, in 1920. Beranger made his stage debut at the age of sixteen in an Australian repertory company production of Othello. He appeared, usually uncredited, in many Fine Arts productions, including Let Katy Do It (1916), The Good-Bad Man (1916), Flirting with Fate (1916), The Half-Breed (1916), Pillars of Society (1916), Manhattan Madness (1916), A Love Sublime (1917), and A Daughter of the Poor (1917).

His other films include The Bright Shawl (1923), Beau Brummell (1924), Confessions of a Queen (1925), Are Parents People? (1925), The Grand Duchess and the Waiter (1926), The Bat (1926), Lilies of the Field (1930), Annabelle's Affairs (1931), Surrender (1931), Ladies of the Jury (1932), Mama Loves Papa (1933), Young and Beautiful (1934), Love before Breakfast (1936), Hot Money (1936), Beauty for the Asking (1939), Over My Dead Body (1942), and Road House (1948). He is best remembered for his role as Alfred in Ernst Lubitsch's production of So This Is Paris (1926). Aside from his work as an actor and director, Beranger was famous in Hollywood for his collection of early films on 28mm, which he screened often at parties during the Twenties.

MONTE BLUE

Born, Indianapolis, January 11, 1890. Died, Milwaukee, February 18, 1963. A leading man of the silent screen, noted for his slightly plump features. Monte Blue began in the film industry in 1914 as an extra, stuntman and assistant with D. W. Griffith. He appeared in many, many films, including The Man from Painted Post (1917), M'Liss (1918), The Squaw Man (1918), The Affairs of Anatol (1921), Orphans of the Storm (1921), The Marriage Circle (1924), So This Is Paris (1926), White Shadows in the South Seas (1928), The Show of Shows (1929), The Thundering Herd (1934), Lives of a Bengal Lancer (1935), Mary of Scotland (1936), Juarez (1939), Mission to Moscow (1943), Life with Father (1947), Key Largo (1948), and Apache (1954). In a way his screen career may be

said to have come full circle, for he started as an extra and
ended his career in the same capacity. His Fine Arts films,
and he was uncredited in many of them, include Martyrs of the
Alamo (1915) , Sold for Marriage (1916), Jim Bludso (1917), and
Betsy's Burglar (1917).

For more information, see "The Man Who Found Himself" by Jim Tully in Photoplay (February 1925), pages 42 and
131-134; a letter from Bert Gray in Films in Review (May 1963),
pages 313-314, and a letter from Kenneth W. Scott in Films in
Review (October 1963), pages 508-509.

KARL BROWN

Born in Pennsylvania, date unknown. Thanks largely
to his resurrection by Kevin Brownlow, Karl Brown has become one of the great names of the silent screen. Brown's
book, Adventures with D. W. Griffith (Farrar, Straus and
Giroux, 1973) is without question, one of the finest volumes
ever written on D. W. Griffith. Karl Brown entered the film
industry in 1913 as a laboratory assistant with Kinemacolor.
In the same year, he joined D. W. Griffith's company as an
assistant to Billy Bitzer, and it was while working at Fine
Arts, in the spring of 1917, that he became a full-fledged
cameraman. "It is claimed he is the youngest cameraman
in the film industry," commented The Moving Picture World
(March 10, 1917).

From Griffith, Karl Brown joined Famous Players-
Lasky, and his photographic credits with that company include
Brewster's Millions (1921), The Covered Wagon (1923), Rug-
gles of Red Gap (1923), Merton of the Movies (1924), Beg-
gar on Horseback (1925), and The Pony Express (1925). He
became a director with Stark Love (1927), a drama shot on
location in the Great Smoky Mountains of North Carolina,
which Brown produced, directed and scripted. During the
Thirties and early Forties, he was director and/or screenwriter on many "B" pictures.

On February 1, 1922, American Cinematographer made
the following comment, "Karl Brown, A.S.C., is a student
with a passion to learn. He wants to know what there is apper-
taining to his profession believing that the only way to beat
a game is to know all there is about it." Brown's work as
both a cinematographer and a director testify to that approach.

Brown's mother, Lucille also worked at the Griffith

studios, often in the capacity of a chaperone. She played
one of the Uplifters in the Modern Story of Intolerance.

TOD BROWNING

Born, Louisville, Kentucky, July 12, 1882. Died,
Hollywood, California, October 6, 1962. A director whose
name will forever be associated with the horror genre, but
who was a director of more talent than his sobriquet, "the
Edgar Allan Poe of the Cinema," might lead one to believe.
He entered films with D. W. Griffith, who cannot have been
entirely uninfluenced by Browning's birthplace, and appeared
as an actor in Intolerance, among others. Browning directed
his first feature, Jim Bludso, for Fine Arts in 1917. Other
films include The Virgin of Stamboul (1920), Outside the Law
(1921), Under Two Flags (1922), The Unholy Three (1925),
The Road to Mandalay (1926), London After Midnight (1927),
The Unknown (1927), Where East Is East (1929), Dracula
(1931), Freaks (1932), and The Devil-Doll (1936). He retired from the film industry in 1939.

For more information, see "Tod Browning" by George
Geltzer in Films in Review (October 1953), pages 410-416;
and Tod Browning/Don Siegel by Stuart Rosenthal and Judith
M. Kass (Volume 4 in the Hollywood Professionals series,
A. S. Barnes, 1975).

WILLIAM CHRISTY CABANNE

Born, St. Louis, Missouri, April 16, 1888. Died,
Philadelphia, October 15, 1950. Regarded, perhaps wrongly,
as a major directing talent in the Teens, Cabanne's name
today is usually associated with "B" pictures of the Thirties
and Forties for studios such as Monogram and P. R. C. He
had a naval career prior to making his stage debut with Laura
Nelson Hall in Salvation Nell in 1908. He joined American
Biograph in 1910 as an actor and assistant to D. W. Griffith,
and was supposedly the Biograph employee who invited the
Gish sisters to work as extras in films when they came to
the studio to visit Mary Pickford.

He remained with Griffith through 1916, and directed
the following films for Fine Arts: The Lamb (1915), Martyrs
of the Alamo (1915), Double Trouble (1915), Daphne and the
Pirate (1916), The Flying Torpedo (1916, co-director), Sold

William Christy Cabanne

for Marriage (1916), Reggie Mixes In (1916), Flirting with
Fate (1916), and Diane of the Follies (1916). K. Owen in
Photoplay (March 1916) wrote, "Cabanne has the reputation
of coming nearer the Griffith technique and methods than any
other director." The Moving Picture World of August 26,
1916, indicated that his salary at Fine Arts was in excess
of $25,000 a year, and when he left Fine Arts to join Metro
in the summer of 1916, it was reported that his salary there
was to be $900 a week for fifty-two weeks a year.

Cabanne joined Metro initially as Frances X. Bushman's
and Beverly Bayne's director, and he directed their first
serial, The Great Secret (1917). An article, "A Busy Day
in Mr. Bushman's Business," published in Photoplay (April
1917), pages 120-121 provides an interesting series of photographs of Cabanne at work.

Among the director's more than 150 films are The
Great Leap (1914), The Outlaw's Revenge (1914), Enoch Arden (1915), The Lost House (1915), Miss Robinson Crusoe
(1917), The Slacker (1917), The Pest (1919), The Beloved
Cheater (1920), Beyond the Rainbow (1922), Lend Me Your
Husband (1924), The Masked Bride (1925), Monte Carlo (1926),
Restless Youth (1928), Convicted (1931), Hearts of Humanity
(1932), Jane Eyre (1934), Keeper of the Bees (1935), The
Last Outlaw (1936), The Outcasts of Poker Flats (1937), Legion of Lost Flyers (1939), Alias the Deacon (1940), Melody
and Moonlight (1940), The Mummy's Hand (1940), Scatter-
good Baines (1941), Cinderella Swings It (1943), Robin Hood
of Monterey (1947), King of the Bandits (1947), and Silver
Trails (1948). At the time of his death, he was negotiating
a television contract.

JEWEL CARMEN

Born, Danville, Kentucky, 1897. No information as
to present whereabouts or whether living or dead. A beautiful, blonde actress first glimpsed in Intolerance (as one of
the favorites of the harem), who was supposedly discovered
by Douglas Fairbanks and became his leading lady in four
Fine Arts productions, all released in 1916: Manhattan Madness, American Aristocracy, The Half Breed, and Flirting
with Fate. The Moving Picture World (November 25, 1916)
described her as "one of the prettiest and most capable actresses in motion pictures," while Motion Picture Magazine
(March 1918) thought she was "agile as a squirrel, blonde as

a Valkyrie, sure of herself as a Browning machine-gun."
Jewel Carmen is the subject of a vicious character assassin-
ation by Anita Loos in her book, The Talmadge Girls.

Jewel Carmen left Fine Arts to become a Fox contract
star, and her later films included A Tale of Two Cities (1917),
Les Miserables (1917), The Kingdom of Love (1918), The
Bride of Fear (1918), Confession (1918), Nobody (1921), and
The Silver Lining (1921). She retired from the screen apparently in 1921, but returned in 1926 to star in her hus-
hand, Roland West's, production of The Bat.

For more information, see "A Queen of Blondes" by
Cal York in Photoplay (July 1917), pages 108-109 and "Found
--by 'D. W.'--a Jewel" by Elizabeth Peltret in Motion Picture Magazine (November 1918), pages 68-69 and 123.

EDWARD (EDDIE) DILLON

Born, New York City, 1873. Died, Hollywood, California, July 11, 1933. A comedy performer who became a
director, primarily of comedies, and finished his screen
career as a "bit" player. After an early career as a jockey
and a lengthy stage career, including appearances in The
Sporting Duchess, In Old Kentucky, with Ada Rehan in Shakespeare, and with Rose Melville in Sis Hopkins, Dillon joined
the American Biograph Company in 1908. Eddie Dillon directed many of Fay Tincher's comedies, at which time he
gained the nickname "Komic." At Fine Arts, he directed
Don Quixote (1916), Sunshine Dad (1916), Mr. Goode, the
Samaritan (1916), The Heiress at Coffee Dan's (1916), and
A Daughter of the Poor (1917). Bessie Love recalls him as
being "an awfully good comedy director."

Edward Dillon's other films as director include The
Antics of Ann (1917), Luck and Pluck (1919), Putting One
Over (1919), Never Say Quit (1919), The Winning Stroke
(1919), The Education of Elizabeth (1921), A Heart to Let
(1921), Sheltered Daughters (1921), The Beauty Shop (1922),
Women Men Marry (1922), Broadway Gold (1923), The Drums
of Jeopardy (1923), The Danger Girl (1926), Bred in Old Kentucky (1926), Flame in the Argentine (1926), and The Dice
Woman (1927). As an actor, Dillon's films include The Sky-
rocket (1926, as a comedy director), Lilac Time (1928), Hot
for Paris (1929), Broadway Melody (1929), The Locked Door
(1929), Caught Short (1930), Sob Sister (1931), Iron Man

(1931), The Trial of Vivienne Ware (1932), Sherlock Holmes
(1932), The Golden West (1932), and While Paris Sleeps
(1932).

ALLAN DWAN

     Born, Joseph Aloysius Dwan, Toronto, Canada, April
3, 1885. An American director whose career spans the
years from 1911 through 61, and whose films are of variable
quality, ranging from the excellence of Robin Hood (1922)
and Manhandled (1924) through such obvious low-budget pro-
grammers as Up in Mabel's Room (1944) and Calendar Girl
(1947). He entered the film industry with the Essanay Company in 1909, and began directing two years later with the
American Flying A Company. Major films include Panthea
(1917), Heidi (1937), Rebecca of Sunnybrook Farm (1938),
Suez (1938), The Three Musketeers (1939), Rise and Shine
(1941), and Sands of Iwo Jima (1949). He directed four of
Douglas Fairbanks' Fine Arts features--The Habit of Happiness, The Good Bad Man, The Half-Breed, and Manhattan
Madness, all released in 1916--and went on to direct Fairbanks in six further features.

     For more information, see Allan Dwan: The Last
Pioneer by Peter Bogdanovich (Praeger, 1971).

JOHN EMERSON

     Born, Sandusky, Ohio, May 28, 1874. Died, Pasa-
dena, California, March 8, 1956. A prominent stage director who made an easy transition to films, as a director and
screenwriter in the Teens. Thanks largely to the writings
of his wife, Anita Loos (whom he married in 1919), his con-
tributions to the screen have been denigrated. Emerson attended Oberlin College, Heidelberg University and the University of Chicago, and was educated for the Episcopalian
ministry. He made his stage debut at the Savoy Theatre,
New York, on April 25, 1904, with Bessie Tyree in Tit for
Tat. From 1908 through 1911, he was stage director for the
Shuberts and from 1911 through 1915, general stage director
for Charles Frohman. (For more information on Emerson's
stage career, see Who Was Who in the Theatre.)

     He entered films with D. W. Griffith, and his Fine
Arts productions are Old Heidelberg (1915, director and

screenplay), His Picture in the Papers (1916, director and
co-screenplay), The Social Secretary (1916, director), Macbeth (1916, director and screenplay), and The Americano
(1917, director and co-screenplay). He left Fine Arts briefly
in the summer of 1916 to direct Mary Pickford in what is
generally considered to have been her worst film, Less Than
the Dust. When Fairbanks left Fine Arts for Artcraft, Emerson joined him, and directed the actor in the following
films, all released in 1917: In Again, Out Again, Wild and
Woolly, Down to Earth, and Reaching for the Moon (also co-
screenplay).

        John Emerson's other films as a director include
Come on In (1918), Oh, You Women! (1919), A Temperamental Wife (1919), A Virtuous Vamp (1919), In Search of a Sinner (1920), and Polly of the Follies (1922). Emerson retired
from directing with Polly of the Follies, but continued to
write stories and screenplays with Anita Loos, including Red
Hot Romance (1922), Dulcy (1923), Three Miles Out (1924),
Learning to Love (1925), Gentlemen Prefer Blondes (1928),
The Fall of Eve (1929), The Struggle (1931), The Social Reg-
ister (1931), and The Girl from Missouri (1934). He is
credited as co-producer on San Francisco (1936).

        With Anita Loos, he co-authored two books, How to
Write Photoplays (The James A. McCann Company, 1920)
and Breaking into the Movies (The James A. McCann Company, 1921). For more information, see "His Job: Directing Mary Pickford" by J. A. Kent in Photoplay (November
1916), pages 50-51; "The Play's the Thing!" by Lillian Mon-
tanye in Motion Picture Magazine (April 1918), pages 67-68
and 123; " 'I Do,' said Anita" by Agnes Smith in Picture Play
Magazine (October 1919), pages 49-51 and 80; "The One-Man
Movie" by Isador M. Stern in Motion Picture Magazine (April-
May 1920), pages 36-37, 103 and 109; and "John Interviews
Anita" in Photoplay (June 1921), pages 62 and 107-108.

C. M. (CHESTER) FRANKLIN

        Born, San Francisco, September 1, 1890. Died, Los
Angeles, March 12, 1954. A far less distinguished director
than his brother, Chester Franklin has the dubious distinction
of being noted as a director of animal pictures, having been
responsible for one of the first Rin-Tin-Tin films, Where the
North Begins (1923), Sequoia (1935) and the animal sequences
in The Yearling (1946). It should also be noted that he di-

rected one of the first Technicolor features, The Toll of the
Sea (1922).

For more information, see the entry on his brother,
S. A. (Sidney) Franklin.

S. A. (SIDNEY) FRANKLIN

Born, San Francisco, March 21, 1893. Died, Santa
Monica, May 18, 1972. He entered the film industry in
1913 with the Selig Company; in 1914, according to Kevin
Brownlow, he and his brother, C. M. (Chester) Franklin,
independently produced a split-reel comedy, The Sheriff,
which they were able to sell to D. W. Griffith. Griffith had
the brothers produce a series of one-reel children's comedies
for Reliance-Majectic. They directed their first feature, Let
Katy Do It, for Fine Arts in 1915. Their other Fine Arts
productions were Martha's Vindication, The Children in the
House, Going Straight, The Little School Ma'am, Gretchen
the Greenhorn, and A Sister of Six, all released in 1916.
From Fine Arts, the brothers moved to Fox, and Franklin
became a solo director in 1917 with Babes in the Wood. His
other films as director include The Hoodlum (1919), The
Guardsman (1931), The Barretts of Wimpole Street (1934),
and The Good Earth (1937). He became a producer in 1938
with On Borrowed Time, and his other films as producer include Waterloo Bridge (1940), Mrs. Miniver (1942), Random
Harvest (1942), and The Yearling (1946).

A literate and sensitive director and producer, Franklin is best known for the films he directed and produced at
Metro-Goldwyn-Mayer, which he joined in 1927 until his re-
tirement in 1957. His maxim was, "You can say important
things in books without boring people, so why be afraid to
try it in pictures?"

For more information, see "Nearly a Bean Magnate"
by Alfred A. Cohn in Photoplay (January 1920), pages 51
and 125; "The Modest Pioneer" by Kevin Brownlow in Focus
on Film (Summer 1972), pages 30-41; and "The Franklin Kid
Pictures" by Kevin Brownlow in Films in Review (August-
September 1972), pages 396-404.

DOROTHY GISH

Born, Dayton, Ohio, March 11, 1898. Died, Rapallo,

Dorothy Gish

Italy, June 4, 1968. This talented comedienne of silent films, whose career was eclipsed by that of her sister, made her stage debut in 1902 and her film debut in 1912 with the American Biograph Company under the direction of D. W. Griffith. Dorothy Gish's major films include Old Heidelberg (1915), Hearts of the World (1918), Remodeling Her Husband (1920), Orphans of the Storm (1922), The Bright Shawl (1923), Romola (1924), and Nell Gwyn (1926). She made her final screen appearance in The Cardinal (1964). Not without reason did Julian Johnson write in Photoplay (September 1916), "At Fine Arts ... Lillian Gish has been completely outclassed by her roguish little sister Dorothy."

For more information, see Dorothy and Lillian Gish by Lillian Gish (Charles Scribner's Sons, 1973), and "Dorothy Gish" by DeWitt Bodeen in Films in Review (August-September 1968), pages 393-414.

LILLIAN GISH

Born, Springfield, Ohio, October 14, 1896. One of the greatest of silent dramatic actresses, and a legend in her own lifetime, Lillian Gish's career has embraced all areas of entertainment, including the legitimate stage, television and the sound film. Like her sister, Dorothy, she made her screen debut with the American Biograph Company, under the direction of D. W. Griffith, in 1912. Her principal films include The Birth of a Nation (1915), Hearts of the World (1918), True Heart Susie (1919), Broken Blossoms (1919), Way Down East (1920), Orphans of the Storm (1922), The White Sister (1923), La Boheme (1926), The Scarlet Letter (1926), The Wind (1928), His Double Life (1933), The Night of the Hunter (1955), and A Wedding (1978). In 1920, she directed her sister in Remodeling Her Husband.

For more information, see Life and Lillian Gish by Albert Bigelow Paine (Macmillan, 1932), The Movies, Mr. Griffith and Me by Lillian Gish (Prentice-Hall, 1969) and Dorothy and Lillian Gish by Lillian Gish (Charles Scribner's Sons, 1973).

FRANK B. (BUTCHER) GOOD

Born, Columbus, Ohio, October 3, 1884. Died, Los Angeles, May 31, 1939. Noted as a cinematographer of

Lillian Gish

Westerns.   He spent six years in vaudeville, performing a
"loop the loop" and "mechanical doll" act, and from 1906
through 1912 was an automobile racing driver.   He entered
films as an actor in 1912 with Ford Sterling, and in the
same year became a cameraman with the Sterling Motion
Picture Company.   He photographed many films for Tom
Mix, including The Cyclone (1920), Desert Love (1920), The
Terror (1920), Three Gold Coins (1920), The Untamed (1920),
and The Road Demon (1921), and many films for Buck Jones,
including The Big Punch, Get Your Man, The One-Man Trail,
Straight from the Shoulder, and To a Finish (all 1921).   His
other films include The Wizard of Oz (1925), The California
Mail (1929), When a Man's a Man (1935), The Cowboy Million-
aire (1935), and The Mine with the Iron Door (1937).

Frank Good's Fine Arts films include: Let Katy Do
It, The Price of Power, Martha's Vindication, The Children
in the House, and Going Straight, all released in 1916.

FRANCIS J. GRANDON

Born, Chicago, 1879. Died, Los Angeles, July 11,
1929. Also known as Frank Grandon, and also often mistakenly identified in early films as Francis Grandin. He
began his career in the theatre, prior to entering films with
the American Biograph Company (he was an actor in films
there as early as 1910). Later he worked for the Lubin and
Selig Companies, directing the serial, The Adventures of
Kathlyn, for the latter. The Moving Picture World (January
22, 1916) described Grandon as "One of the foremost directors in the country." According to his obituary in the New
York Times, Grandon was known as the "father of the serial
motion picture." In 1925, he disappeared, but was found in
Portland, Oregon, a victim of a paralytic stroke. Grandon's
films include The Dummy (1917), Heart's Desire (1917), The
Little Boy Scout (1917), Conquered Hearts (1918), Wild Honey
(1918), The Lamb and the Lion (1919), Lotus Blossom (1921),
Barb Wire (1922), Phantom Shadows (1925), and Scarlet and
Gold (1925). He directed one Fine Arts production, Cross
Currents, released in 1916.

JANE GREY

Born, Middlebury, Vermont, May 22, 1883. Died,
New York City, November 9, 1944. A prominent stage
actress of her day, Jane Grey had an extensive theatrical
career, making her Broadway debut in Is Matrimony a Failure? (1909), before making her screen debut in Famous Players' 1914 production of the Channing Pollock play, The Little
Gray Lady. Jane Grey's last Broadway appearance was in
1935, in A Lady Detained.

She starred in only one Fine Arts production, Let
Katy Do It (1916), but is simply superb in her underplaying
and unassuming, natural charm, and deserves recognition as
a member, albeit briefly, of the Fine Arts Company. Jane
Grey's other films include Her Fighting Chance (1917), When
My Ship Comes In (1919), The Governor's Lady (1923), and
The Love Wager (1927). Reviewing her first film after leav-
ing Fine Arts, Man and His Angel, Peter Milne wrote in

Motion Picture News (March 25, 1916), "Jane Grey steps into
Equitable stardom by way of this picture. Miss Grey is
plainly a star--there is no denying that. She is expressive
without being too emotional and the utmost significance marks
her histrionic endeavors. She has mastered the art of pantomime and besides her prettiness and charm will undoubtedly
arouse a feeling of admiration."

OLGA GREY

        Born, Anushka Zacsek, Budapest, Hungary, date un-
known. Died, Los Angeles, April 25, 1973. According to
Griffith's one-time publicist, Bennie Zeidman, in an article
on the extras at the Griffith studios, published in the December 1916 issue of Motion Picture Magazine, "Olga Grey, while
touring California, with her father, visited the Griffith studio.
That night she informed her father that she would enjoy working in a film studio. He consented, and bright and early
the next morning Miss Grey arrived at the studio. She being
of the foreign type was given a place in the mob of exotic-
looking supernumeraries. A few days later she was given a
small part; as the days passed, her parts became better."
She was an extra in The Birth of a Nation, and played Mary
Magdalene in Intolerance. Olga Grey's other films include
His Lesson (1915), The Failure (1915), The Woman God Forgot (1917), The Ghost House (1917), Fanatics (1917), Trixie
from Broadway (1919), and When a Man Rides Alone (1919).
She retired from the screen in 1920.

        Olga Grey was featured in the following Fine Arts
productions: Double Trouble (1915), Sold for Marriage (1916),
The Wild Girl of the Sierras (1916), and The Little Liar
(1916). The only article on her which appeared in the fan
magazines appears to have been a one-page piece, "A Vamp
with a Goulash Name," in Photoplay (February 1917), page
73.

D. W. GRIFFITH

        Born, Crestwood, Kentucky, January 22, 1875. Died,
Los Angeles, California, July 23, 1948. Generally considered
the greatest of all film directors, and the one man most responsible for the emergence of film as an art form. Griffith directed his first film, The Adventures of Dollie, for the
American Biograph Company in 1908, and his last film, The

Struggle, for his own company in 1931. His major productions
include The Birth of a Nation (1915), Intolerance (1916),
Hearts of the World (1918), Way Down East (1920), Orphans
of the Storm (1921), and Isn't Life Wonderful (1924). Under
the pseudonym of Granville Warwick, he wrote a number of
stories from which the following Fine Arts productions were
adapted: The Lamb (1915), The Lily and the Rose (1915),
Let Katy Do It (1916), The Missing Links (1916), The Wood
Nymph (1916), Daphne and the Pirate (1916), Hoodoo Ann (1916),
and Diane of the Follies (1916).

      For more information, see When The Movies Were Young
by Mrs. D. W. Griffith (Dutton, 1925; Dover Books, 1969), D.
W. Griffith: American Film Master by Iris Barry and Eileen
Bowser (The Museum of Modern Art-Doubleday, 1965) and The
Films of D. W. Griffith by Edward Wagenknecht and Anthony
Slide (Crown, 1975), etc.

ROBERT HARRON

      Born, New York City, April 24 1896.   Died, New York
City, September 5, 1920. One of the American cinema's finest
actors from the Teens, Robert Harron was equally at home in
both comedy and drama. In films such as The Birth of a Nation.
Intolerance and True Heart Susie, he showed a remarkable ability to mature, in his roles, from young boy to manhood. Harron entered films in 1907 with the American Biograph Company,
where Griffith first teamed him with Mae Marsh and
the two made a perfect romantic couple. His principal
films are A Misunderstood Boy (1913), Fate (1913), Home,
Sweet Home (1914), The Birth of a Nation (1915), Intolerance (1916), Hearts of the World (1918), A Romance of Happy
Valley (1918), and True Heart Susie (1919). Among his Fine
Arts productions were Hoodoo Ann (1916), The Wharf Rat (1916),
Bad Boy (1917), and An Old-Fashioned Young Man (1917). During Harron's Fine Arts contract, tragedy struck with the death
of his brother, Charles (who also worked for the studio), in a
car accident on December 24, 1915.

      Harron's death, as a result of a gunshot wound, is
shrouded in mystery, but the evidence in hand seems to point
to its being an accident.   For more information on Harron's
career, see "Bobby Harron" by Harold Dunham in Films in
Review (December 1963), pages 607-618, and "Mae Marsh,
Robert Harron and D. W. Griffith" by Harold Dunham in The
Silent Picture (Autumn 1969), pages 10-17.

Lloyd Ingraham as a "bit" player in 1937.

LLOYD INGRAHAM

Born, Rochelle, Illinois, 1874.   Died, Woodland Hills,
California, April 4, 1956.   A prolific director at Fine Arts,
whose work is acceptable if uninspiring.   After a stage career as a stock director for Oliver Morosco, among others,
Ingraham entered films in 1912 with Reliance-Majestic.   At
Fine Arts, he directed the following films: The Sable Lorcha
(1915), The Missing Links (1916), Hoodoo Ann (1916), A Child
of the Paris Streets (1916), Casey at the Bat (1916), Stranded
(1916), The Little Liar (1916), American Aristocracy (1916),
The Children Pay (1916), Nina, the Flower Girl (1917), and
An Old Fashioned Young Man (1917).   Ingraham's assistant
director at Fine Arts was Bert Hadley.

From Fine Arts, he went to the American Flying A
Company, where he was one of Mary Miles Minter's directors.   His other films include Charity Castle (1917), Her
Country's Call (1917), Peggy Leads the Way (1917), The Eyes
of Julia Deep (1918), What's Your Husband Doing? (1919),
Mary's Ankle (1920), Twin Beds (1920), The Girl in the Taxi
(1921), Marry the Poor Girl (1921), My Lady Friends (1921),
Second Hand Rose (1922), The Wise Virgin (1924), Hearts
and Fists (1926), Arizona Nights (1927), The Pioneer Scout
(1928, co-director), Kit Carson (1928, co-director), and The
Sunset Legion (1928, co-director).   With the coming of sound,
he retired from directing and became a small-time actor--
although he had acted in films as early as Rex Ingram's production of Scaramouche in 1923--and continued to act until
1946.

The final comment should be left to Bessie Love, who
remarked, "If Ingraham could think of a four letter word, he
would use it."

RALPH LEWIS

Born, Chicago, October 28, 1872.   Died, Los Angeles,
December 6, 1937.   A fine character actor who will always
be remembered for his portrayal of Austin Stoneman in The
Birth of a Nation.   "The massive and powerful portrayal of
Stoneman by Ralph Lewis established for decades to come a
high watermark and yardstick for screen character roles,"
wrote Seymour Stern in Film Culture (Spring/Summer 1965).
His wife, Vera Lewis, was also a prominent supporting actress both in silent and sound productions.   Lewis spent

twenty years on the stage, playing with Julia Marlowe, Margaret Anglin and Wilton Lackaye among others, before entering films with D. W. Griffith in 1914. Ralph Lewis appeared frequently on the screen through the mid-Thirties, and his films include The Great Leap (1914), Jack and the Beanstalk (1917), The Hoodlum (1919), Eyes of Youth (1920), Outside the Law (1921), The Conquering Power (1921), The Third Alarm (1922), Dante's Inferno (1924), and Abraham Lincoln (1930). He was in the following Fine Arts productions: Jordan Is a Hard Road (1915), Let Katy Do It (1916), Martha's Vindication (1916), Going Straight (1916), and The Children Pay (1916).

For more information, see "A Hundred Times a Father" by Margaret Mack in Motion Picture Magazine (March, 1922), pages 68 and 113.

WALTER LONG

Born, Milford, New Hampshire, March 5, 1888. Died, Los Angeles, July 4, 1952. The classic screen villain, who will always be remembered for his portrayal of the Negro renegade, Gus, in The Birth of a Nation. Walter Long made his screen debut with the Essanay Company in 1909 after many years on the stage and in vaudeville. His films include The Little American (1917), Scarlet Days (1919), The Sheik (1921), Moran of the Lady Letty (1922), The Road to Yesterday (1925), The Yankee Clipper (1927), Moby Dick (1930), Pardon Us (1931), Operator 13 (1933), Naughty Marietta (1935), and Wabash Avenue (1950).

Walter Long appeared in the following Fine Arts productions: Martyrs of the Alamo (1915), Let Katy Do It (1916), Daphne and the Pirate (1916), Sold for Marriage (1916), The Children in the House (1916), and The Marriage of Molly O' (1916).

ANITA LOOS

Born, Sisson, California, April 26, 1893. One of the few screenwriters who have been able to write themselves into personalities. She has discussed her career and her contemporaries--sometimes inaccurately--in several books: A Girl Like I (The Viking Press, 1966), Kiss Hollywood Good-Bye (The Viking Press, 1974), Cast of Thousands

(Grosset and Dunlap, 1977), and The Talmadge Girls (The Viking Press, 1978). Miss Loos entered films in 1912 by selling a screenplay, The New York Hat, to the American Biograph Company. For Fine Arts, her screenplays include The Wild Girl of the Sierras, The Wharf Rat, The Social Secretary, His Picture in the Papers, The Half-Breed, American Aristocracy, and The Matrimaniac, all released in 1916. Anita Loos "was always hobnobbing with the bigwigs around the studio," remembers Bessie Love. She worked closely with Douglas Fairbanks and John Emerson at Fine Arts, and went with them to Paramount. In 1919, she married John Emerson (q. v.), and in 1921 the couple published a book, Breaking into the Movies.

Anita Loos' other screenplays include A Virtuous Vamp (1919), Polly of the Follies (1922), Gentlemen Prefer Blondes (1928), Red-Headed Woman (1932), San Francisco (1936), The Women (1939), and I Married an Angel (1942).

For more information, see "Written on the Screen: Anita Loos" by Gary Carey in Film Comment (Winter 1970-71), pages 50-55.

BESSIE LOVE

Born, Juanita Horton, Midland, Texas, September 10, 1898. Bessie Love entered films with the Fine Arts Company in June 1915, applying for a summer job while on vacation from school. Her first starring role was in A Sister of Six (1916), but she appeared in many other Fine Arts productions, including The Flying Torpedo, Acquitted, Reggie Mixes In, The Good Bad Man, and Hell-To-Pay Austin, all released in 1916. In its July, 1916, issue, Picture-Play Magazine was asking, "Is she another Pickford?" Bessie Love moved to England in 1935, and has lived there ever since, appearing in several British films and also on the stage.

Among her many, many films are Intolerance (1916), The Aryan (1916), The Sea Lion (1921), Human Wreckage (1923), Those Who Dance (1924), The Lost World (1925), The King on Main Street (1925), Soul Fire (1925), Broadway Melody (1929), Hollywood Revue of 1929 (1929), Good News (1930), The Magic Box (1950), The Story of Esther Costello (1957), Sunday Bloody Sunday (1971), and The Ritz (1976).

(cont'd. on p. 149)

Anita Loos

Bessie Love

In Photoplay (September, 1916), Julian Johnson wrote
of her, "In the bright list of real stars the year has created
I think Bessie Love stands first. Here is a talent more direct, simple and sweetly sincere than any discovered since
Mary Pickford. Mary Pickford and Bessie Love slightly resemble each other, physically; spiritually there is a much
stronger resemblance; mentally--I don't know Bessie Love,
so here I cease. "

For more information, see "Bessie Love" by Harold
Dunham in Films in Review (February 1959), pages 86-99
and From Hollywood with Love by Bessie Love (Elm Tree
Books, 1977).

WILFRED LUCAS

Born, Ontario, Canada, January 30, 1871. Died, Los
Angeles, December 13, 1940. A multi-talented actor and
director in the Teens, Lucas' career petered out in the Twenties. After nine years in grand and light opera and five years
as Rose Stahl's leading man on stage, Wilfred Lucas joined
the American Biograph Company in 1908. His films there
include His Trust (1910), Enoch Arden (1911), The Transfor-
mation of Mike (1911), Man's Genesis (1912), and The Massacre (1912). He directed his first films for American Biograph, and later moved to Universal as both an actor and
director; in 1914, he directed the Universal serial, The Trey
o' Hearts.

He worked with Griffith at Fine Arts from the company's inception. According to Photoplay, "If Griffith wants
a desperado or a saintly priest, a corpulent plutocrat or a
vagabond, a hobo or a Beau Brummel, a seafaring man or a
mountaineer, a David Harum or a Lord Algy, he goes to
Lucas and says, 'Be this character,' and straightway it is in
the way of being accomplished. All that Lucas need do is to
stroll back through the aisles of his well-ordered memory,
take from its niche whichever of the innumerable acquaintances
is desired and fit that person's manner, clothes, expression,
gestures and peculiarities to himself. " On January 8, 1916,
The Moving Picture World announced that Wilfred Lucas had
been promoted to stardom, in recognition of his good work
in The Lily and the Rose, the actor's first Fine Arts film.
Wilfred Lucas' other Fine Arts productions are The Wood
Nymph (1916), Acquitted (1916, and his most important film),
The Wild Girl of the Sierras (1916), Hell-To-Pay Austin

(1916), The Rummy (1916, also screenplay), Jim Bludso (1917, also co-director), A Love Sublime (1917), Hands Up! (1917, also co-director), and Souls Triumphant (1917).

Wilfred Lucas' other films include The Judgment House (1918), The Return of Mary (1918), Soldiers of Fortune (1919), The Beautiful Liar (1921), Trilby (1923), Dorothy Vernon of Haddon Hall (1924), A Broadway Butterfly (1925), Just Imagine (1930), I Cover the Waterfront (1933), Modern Times (1936), Mary of Scotland (1936), and A Chump at Oxford (1940).

For more information, see "How I Became a Photoplayer" by Wilfred Lucas in Motion Picture Magazine (March 1915), page 118, and "Messrs. Wilfred Lucas" by John Aye in Photoplay (June 1916), pages 97-99.

MAE MARSH

Born Mary Warne Marsh, Madrid, New Mexico, November 9, 1895. Died Hermosa Beach, California, February 13, 1968. Mae Marsh entered films in 1912 with D. W. Griffith and the American Biograph Company; her first major screen role was in Man's Genesis, released on July 11, 1912. Her principal films include The Sands of Dee (1912), The Birth of a Nation (1915), Intolerance (1916), The Cinderella Man (1917), The White Rose (1923), The Rat (1925), and Over the Hill (1932).

There have been few performances in silent or sound films to equal those of Mae Marsh as the Little Sister in The Birth of a Nation and the Dear One in Intolerance. She and Robert Harron were paired as a somewhat immature romantic team in Fine Arts productions such as Hoodoo Ann, The Wild Girl of the Sierras and The Wharf Rat, all released in 1916. From the mid-Thirties onwards, Mae Marsh appeared in bit parts in countless films, many directed by John Ford. When Mae Marsh left Fine Arts for Goldwyn, D. W. Griffith cabled her, "I wish you every possible success in your new venture. While I feel that your loss to our company is one that can hardly be replaced I shall be as glad and proud as yourself for all the new successes which I know are sure to come to you."

For more information, see "Mae Marsh" by Harold Dunham in Films in Review (June-July 1958), pages 306-321 and Mae Marsh's delightful volume, Screen Acting, published in 1921 by the Photo-Star Publishing Company of Los Angeles.

TULLY MARSHALL

Born, William Phillips, Nevada City, California, April 13, 1864. Died, Encino, California, March 10, 1943. One of the great character actors of the silent screen. Tully Marshall made his first stage appearance in 1883 at the Winter Garden Theatre, San Francisco, as Fred Carter in Edward Barrett's production of Saratoga. In 1889, he married dramatist Marion Fairfax, who was later to have a considerable screen career as a writer and occasional director. Marshall made his screen debut as Joe Brooks in the 1914 All-Star prodiction of Paid in Full. James L. Hoff in The Moving Picture World (January 24, 1914) wrote, "Mr. Marshall never appeared to better advantage on the stage than he does on the screen."

Tully Marshall

Tully Marshall claimed to have appeared in more than three hundred films, and named his favorite film role as that of Bridger in James Cruze's The Covered Wagon (1923); most film buffs know him for his performance as Baron Sadoja in Erich von Stroheim's The Merry Widow (1925). A-mong Marshall's other films are Intolerance (1916), Oliver Twist (1916), Joan the Woman (1917), M'Liss (1918), Old Wives for New (1918), The Life Line (1919), The Crimson Gardenia (1919), Daughter of Mine (1919), The Slim Princess (1920), What Happened to Rosa? (1921), Hail the Woman (1921), The Hunchback of Notre Dame (1923), He Who Gets Slapped (1924), Smouldering Fires (1925), The Cat and the Canary (1927), Drums of Love (1928), Redskin (1929), The Big Trail (1930), The Man I Killed (1932), A Tale of Two Cities (1935), A Yank at Oxford (1938), and Ball of Fire (1941). He made his last film, Behind Prison Bars, for P.R.C. shortly before his death.

Marshall appeared in the following Fine Arts productions: The Sable Lorcha (1915), Let Katy Do It (1916), Martha's Vindication (1916), A Child of the Paris Streets (1916), and The Devil's Needle (1916).

For more information, see Bert Gray's letter in Films in Review (November 1966), pages 596-597.

BERNARD McCONVILLE

A synopsis of McConville's career appeared in The New York Dramatic Mirror on April 22, 1916, page 30:

> Bernard McConville, the Western reporter and magazine writer, engaged to write scenarios for the D. W. Griffith Fine Arts Films, was associated for years with John S. McGroarty, author of the "California's Mission Play." Was a special writer for the Los Angeles Times and Examiner. Wrote numerous short stories for John McGroarty's West Coast Magazine, among them a detective series, "Tales of a Lapidary Shop," and the Spanish California romances, "En Roscoda," "Wanted a Vaquero," "Marrying Felipe," and other tales of the West. Contributed also to Overland Monthly, Out West, and other magazines.
> Wrote the libretto in English of the three-act Indian grand opera, Atala, composed by Henri

Schoenfeld, the noted composer of the American
prize Symphony, the Lillian Nordica song prize,
and other famous compositions.

As a reporter, Mr. McConville experienced a
broad variety of adventures, which he now finds
readily adaptable to moving picture plays. He believes that melodrama touched with human sentiment is the basis of the photo-dramatic art.

CARMEL MYERS

Born, San Francisco, April 9, 1901. Myers is an
actress with a good head for publicity who has never strayed
far from the public eye. As recently as 1976 she played
cameo roles in Won Ton Ton: The Dog Who Saved Hollywood
and Gus. The daughter of a rabbi, Carmel Myers entered
films after D. W. Griffith had approached her father for ad-
vice concerning the Judaic sequences of Intolerance. Her
mother persuaded Griffith to give her daughter a test, and
the director put her in the Fine Arts stock company at $12.00
a week.

At Fine Arts, Miss Myers appeared in the following
films, all released in 1917: Stage Struck, The Bad Boy, A Love
Sublime, A Daughter of the Poor, and Might and the Man. She is
often credited with an appearance in the Babylonian sequence of
Intolerance, but vehemently denies she was in the film. Motion Picture News (January 6, 1917) reported that Carmel
Myers was "believed by D. W. Griffith to be the most beautiful young woman appearing in pictures. "

Carmel Myers' other films include The Haunted Pajamas
(1917), Sirens of the Sea (1917), A Society Sensation (1918),
My Unmarried Wife (1918), Slave of Desire (1923), Babbitt
(1924), Beau Brummell (1924), Ben-Hur (1926), Tell It to
the Marines (1926), Sorrell and Son (1927), Show of Shows
(1929), Svengali (1931), The Countess of Monte Cristo (1934),
and Lady for a Night (1942). In recent years, she has been
active on television--in the Fifties she had her own New
York-based talk show--and in marketing her own range of
men's cologne, "Carmel. " As early as 1929, she had per-
formed a vaudeville act titled "A Cycle of Songs, " in which
she accompanied herself on the ukulele.

JOHN B. O'BRIEN

Born, Richmond, Virginia, date unknown. Died, Los Angeles, August, 1936. A director who began his screen career as an actor with Essanay. His films include The Angel of Contention (1914), The Foundling (1915), Destiny's Toy (1916), Hulda from Holland (1916), The Big Sister (1916), Maternity (1917), Queen X (1917), A Daughter of Maryland (1917) The Girl and the Judge (1918), The Richest Girl (1918), The Bishop's Emeralds (1919), Impossible Catherine (1919), The Family Closet (1921), Father Tom (1921), Lonely Heart (1921), Those Who Dare (1924), Daring Days (1925), and The Outlaw's Daughter (1925). No credits after 1925.

As Jack O'Brien he co-directed The Flying Torpedo (1916) for Fine Arts, and as John O'Brien he directed Souls Triumphant (1917).

MARY H. (HAMILTON) O'CONNOR

Born, St. Paul, Minnesota, date unknown. Date and place of death unknown. Though a prominent screenwriter with the Fine Arts Company, little is known about Mary H. O'Connor except that she was the sister of character actress Loyola O'Connor (True Heart Susie, etc.) and that her career appears to have ended in 1921. She entered films with Vitagraph in 1913, after an early career as a novelist and a magazine and newspaper writer. Her films include Lure of the Mask (1915), Infatuation (1915), A Man's Prerogative (1915), Up from the Depths (1915), A Yankee from the West (1915), The Mystery Road (1921), and Dangerous Lies (1921).

At Fine Arts, Miss O'Connor scripted the following productions: Jordan Is a Hard Road (1915), The Penitentes (1915), Cross Currents (1916), Daphne and the Pirate (1916), Hell-To-Pay-Austin (1916), A House Built upon Sand (1916), Nina, the Flower Girl (1917), The Girl of the Timber Claims (1917), Cheerful Givers (1917), and Souls Triumphant (1917). From Fine Arts, she joined Famous Players.

SEENA OWEN

Born, Signe Auen, Spokane, Washington, 1894. Died, Hollywood, California, August 15, 1966. Seena Owen began her career with the Alcazar Stock Company in San Francisco, and entered films with the Kalem Company in 1914. Shortly

Seena Owen

thereafter, she joined D. W. Griffith's company, where
George Siegmann nicknamed her "Singy." She eventually
adopted an Americanization of her Danish name, and became
a star thanks to her performance as the Princess Beloved in
Intolerance (1916). She will always be remembered for this
role, but in recent years film buffs have come to know her
as Queen Regina V, whipping Gloria Swanson in Queen Kelly
(1928). Seena Owen's films include The Fox Woman (1915),
A Yankee from the West (1915), Branding Broadway (1918),
A Man and His Money (1919), One of the Finest (1919), Breed
of Men (1919), Victory (1919), Riders of Vengeance (1919),
The Sheriff's Son (1919), The City of Comrades (1919), A
Fugitive from Matrimony (1919), The Life Line (1920), The
Cheater Reformed (1921), Lavender and Old Lace (1921), The

Woman God Changed (1921), At the Crossroads (1922), Back Pay (1922), The Face in the Fog (1922), Sisters (1922), The Go-Getter (1923), The Leavenworth Case (1923), Unseeing Eyes (1923): For Woman's Favor (1924), I Am the Man (1924), Faint Perfume (1925), The Hunted Woman (1925), The Flame of the Yukon (1926), Shipwrecked (1926), The Rush Hour (1927), The Blue Danube (1928), His Last Haul (1928), Man-Made Woman (1928), Sinners in Love (1929), The Marriage Playground (1929), and Officer 13 (1933).

Seena Owen's first Fine Arts appearance after Intolerance was in A Woman's Awakening. "In the role of the girl reared among surroundings reminiscent of a bygone day, who is all too suddenly plunged into a society as shallow as it is advanced," wrote Peter Milne in Motion Picture News (April 7, 1917), "Miss Owen appears to very good advantage. Endowed with an irresistible beauty and an ability that comes naturally to her, she plays the role ... to a degree that warrants no criticism."

For more information, see " 'Owen' or 'Auen' " in Photoplay (March 1916), page 143; "The Camera Is Cruel to Her!" by Delight Evans in Photoplay (May 1920), pages 69-70; "Seena Seen Scenically" by Faith Service in Motion Picture Classic (June 1920), pages 34-35, 69; "Do You Believe in Dimples?" by Adela Rogers St. Johns in Photoplay (June 1921), pages 57, 97-98; and "A Daughter of Denmark" by Truth Astor in Motion Picture Classic (August 1921), pages 66, 83.

EUGENE PALLETTE

Born, Winfield, Kansas, July 8, 1889. Died, Los Angeles, September 3, 1954. A reasonably slim leading man in silent films who developed into one of the plumpest and one of the greatest of character actors with the coming of sound. After a very minor and undistinguished stage career, Pallette entered films circa 1912; he is easily recognizable as a wounded Union Soldier in The Birth of a Nation. He became a leading man at Fine Arts, and played the leading role of Prosper Latour in the French story from Intolerance. In the early Forties, he gained notoriety for the "bombproof retreat" he had built in Oregon, where he intended to hole up should there be a nuclear disaster. The full story is contained in Richard L. Neuberger's article, "Hollywood's No. 1 Hide-Out," in The Saturday Evening Post (December 12, 1942), pages 24-25 and 48-50.

Eugene Pallette's films include The World Apart (1917),
The Marcellini Millions (1917), The Ghost House (1917), A
Man's Man (1918), Tarzan of the Apes (1918), The Amateur
Adventuress (1919), Twin Beds (1920), The Three Musketeers
(1921), North of Hudson Bay (1923), Mantrap (1926), Lights
of New York (1928), The Canary Murder Case (1929), The
Love Parade (1929), Follow Thru (1930), Shanghai Express
(1932), The Kennel Murder Case (1933), The Ghost Goes
West (1936), My Man Godfrey (1936), Topper (1937), The
Adventures of Robin Hood (1938), Mr. Smith Goes to Washington (1939), The Mark of Zorro (1940), The Lady Eve
(1941), and Heaven Can Wait (1943).

While at Fine Arts in February of 1916, Eugene Pallette married his first wife, Ann Slater, who was also with
the company. Robert Harron was the best man, and Lillian
and Dorothy Gish and Mae Marsh were bridesmaids. Eugene
Pallette's Fine Arts films include Sunshine Dad, The Children
in the House, Going Straight, Hell-to-Pay Austin, and Gretchen
the Greenhorn, all released in 1916.

PAUL POWELL

Born, Peoria, Illinois, 1881. Died, Pasadena, California, July 2, 1944. A prolific director at the Fine Arts
Company, Powell was responsible for the following films:
The Lily and the Rose (1915), The Wood Nymph (1916), Acquitted (1916), Little Meena's Romance (1916), Susan Rocks
the Boat (1916), The Marriage of Molly O' (1916), Hell-To-
Pay Austin (1916), The Rummy (1916), The Microscope Mystery (1916), The Matrimaniac (1916), The Girl of the Timber
Claims (1917), Betsy's Burglar (1917), and Cheerful Givers
(1917). Paul Powell was a newspaper reporter with the Chicago Tribune and the Los Angeles Express before entering
films with the Lubin Company in either 1911 or 1912. His
other films include Leap from the Depths (1915), The Wolf
Man (1915), Bred in the Bone (1915), A Society Sensation
(1918), All Night (1918), Who Will Marry Me? (1919), Polly-
anna (1920), The Cradle (1922), The Fog (1923), The Awful
Truth (1925), Jewels of Desire (1927), Death Valley (1927),
and Kit Carson (1928, screenplay only). He directed a series
of talkie shorts for Pathe during 1928 and 1929, and in the
Thirties it appears he worked chiefly as a short film director.
At the time of his death, Powell was managing editor of the
Pasadena Independent.

ALMA RUBENS

Born, Alma Rueben, San Francisco, 1897. Died,
Los Angeles, January 23, 1931. One of the most beautiful
of stars of the Teens, Alma Rubens was said by a 1918 fan
magazine writer to remind him of "red roses in an onyx
vase." She entered films at the suggestion of Rolin Sturgeon
of the Vitagraph Company, and after appearances in some
films with the company, she joined Fine Arts as Douglas
Fairbanks' leading lady in The Half-Breed (1916). She also
appeared in the following Fine Arts productions: The Children
Pay (1916), The Americano (1917), A Woman's Awakening
(1917), and An Old Fashioned Young Man (1917). It appears
that she also was featured in the 1915 production of Peer
Gynt, starring Cyril Maude, but under the name of Mary
Rubens.

Alma Rubens' other films include The Regenerates
(1917), The Crown of Destiny (1917), Under the Red Robe
(1923), Cytherea (1924), East Lynne (1925), and Show Boat
(1929). She died of drug addiction, and the tragedy of her
death, her marriage to actor Ricardo Cortez and her beginnings in films are the subject of an interesting article, "Hollywood's Greatest True Love Story," by James R. Quirk in
Photoplay (April 1930), pages 38-39, 114-115.

ROY SOMERVILLE

A synopsis of Somerville's career appeared in The
New York Dramatic Mirror on April 22, 1916, page 30:

> Formerly newspaperman, editor, actor, and maga-
> zine writer, he joined the Fine Arts' scenario de-
> partment last November. In the fiction world his
> short stories created the lovable character, "Kid
> Ryan," and the whimsical philosopher, "Old Blue-
> nose," while his humorous series of "Devil Chute,"
> put that mining-camp on the literary map.
> Through collaboration with the late John Bunny,
> and with Irvin Cobb in the "Little Mister Fister"
> series, he became interested in motion picture
> work. Since his connection with the Fine Arts,
> his picturization of Acquitted has proven a notable
> success; two original photoplays, The Children in
> the House, and In Search of the Only Girl, will be
> released during the coming month, and several
> others are in the course of production.

PAULINE STARKE

Born, Joplin, Missouri, January 10, 1901. Died, Los Angeles, February 3, 1977. An actress who began her career, while still a teenager, with D. W. Griffith, appearing as an extra in both The Birth of a Nation and Intolerance, and received her first starring roles at Fine Arts. At Fine Arts, she appeared in, among others, The Rummy (1916), The Wharf Rat (1916), The Bad Boy (1917), and Cheerful Givers (1917). Pauline Starke was noted in the Teens for her natural, "country girl" looks, but in the mid-Twenties she became a glamorized M-G-M star, leading Janet French in Photoplay (June 1930) to describe her as "the ugly duckling who became a great beauty." Miss Starke's other films include: Until They Get Me (1917), Eyes of Youth (1919), A Connecticut Yankee in King Arthur's Court (1921), Little Church Around the Corner (1923), and The Viking (1929). She retired, involuntarily, from the screen in 1930, but continued to act on the stage.

For more information, see the column, "Films on 8mm and 16mm" by Anthony Slide in Films in Review (May 1977), pages 305-306 and 310.

MADAME SUL-TE-WAN

Date and place of birth unknown. Died, Woodland Hills, California, February 1, 1959, at the reported age of eighty-five. A Black character actress who worked in The Birth of a Nation and in several Fine Arts productions, including Hoodoo Ann (1916), The Children Pay (1916), and Stage Struck (1917). She was devoted to D. W. Griffith and her collapse at the Hollywood memorial service in honor of the director is often mentioned.

Madame Sul-Te-Wan's real name was Nellie Conley, and she was the grandmother of actress Dorothy Dandridge. Her other films include Manslaughter (1922), The Lightning Raider (1924), The Narrow Street (1924), The Thoroughbred (1930), Mighty Joe Young (1949), Something of Value (1957), Band of Angels (1957), The Buccaneer (1958), and Porgy and Bess (1959).

CONSTANCE TALMADGE

Born, Brooklyn, April 19, 1899. Died, Los Angeles,

November 23, 1973. The youngest of the three Talmadge
Sisters (Natalie, who died in 1969, is perhaps best remembered as one of Buster Keaton's wives), Constance was nicknamed "Dutch," and was, by all accounts, an easy-going,
fun-loving person. She followed her sister Norma to the
Vitagraph Studios, where she made her screen debut in 1911,
and where she first demonstrated a penchant for comedy.
There can be little question that Constance Talmadge never
did anything better than the role of the Mountian Girl in D.
W. Griffith's Intolerance (1916), and none of her later films
appear to show her in a better comedy light. Her major
films, aside from Intolerance, include A Pair of Silk Stock-
ings (1918), A Virtuous Vamp (1919), Polly of the Follies
(1922), East Is West (1922), Dulcy (1923), and Venus (1929,
and her last film appearance). Fine Arts productions featuring Constance Talmadge include The Missing Link (1915),
The Microscope Mystery (1916) and The Matrimaniac (1916).

For more information, see "Constance Talmadge" by
DeWitt Bodeen in Films in Review (December 1967), pages
613-630; The Talmadge Girls by Margaret L. Talmadge (Lippincott, 1924); and Anita Loos' far from reliable book of the
same title, published by The Viking Press in 1978, but which
does include the script by Anita Loos for A Virtuous Vamp.

NORMA TALMADGE

Born, Jersey City, New Jersey, May 26, 1897. Died,
Las Vegas, December 24, 1957. She was a talented dramatic
actress with a hauntingly expressive face; a 1917 fan magazine writer correctly described her as "Our Norma ... of
the serious eyes with unsounded depths." She made her
screen debut with the Vitagraph Company in 1910 and came
to prominence with that company as a result of a tiny role,
that of the girl who rides in the tumbril to the guillotine with
Sydney Carton, in A Tale of Two Cities (1911). On September 22, 1916, Variety carried a photograph of Norma Talmadge on its front cover, and hailed her as "one of theatrical's brightest young women and she is highly regarded in
her chosen profession."

Norma Talmadge's major films include The Battle
Cry of Peace (1915), Panthea (1917), The Forbidden City
(1918), Smilin' Through (1922), The Eternal Flame (1922),
Secrets (1924), Graustark (1925), Kiki (1926), Camille (1927),
The Dove (1928), and The Woman Disputed (1928). Her Fine

Arts productions include Martha's Vindication, The Devil's Needle and The Social Secretary, all released in 1916. She retired from the screen after making two talkies, neither of which was as bad as critics and historians would have one believe, New York Nights (1929) and Du Barry, Woman of Passion (1930).

For more information, see "Norma Talmadge" by Jack Spears in Films in Review (January 1967), pages 16-40; The Talmadge Girls by Margaret L. Talmadge (Lippincott, 1924); and Anita Loos' far from reliable book of the same title, published by the Viking Press in 1978.

FAY TINCHER

Born, Topeka, Kansas, date unknown. Date and place of death unknown. Fay Tincher attended dramatic school in Chicago, and from that progressed to light opera with the Savage Company, also in Chicago. In New York, she appeared with Joe Weber in Dream City, and played the lead in Arthur Hopkins' sketch, "The Dance Dream," on the Keith Circuit. She entered films with D. W. Griffith, being featured as Cleo, the Siren, in The Battle of the Sexes (1914) and as the Worldly Woman in Home, Sweet Home (1914).

She gained fame as a comedienne with her striped parasol and dress in the "Ethel and Bill" series, produced by Komic. Among the films in this series were Ethel Gets the Evidence (1914), Ethel Has a Steady (1914), Bill and Ethel at the Ball (1914), Bill Gives a Smoker (1915), Ethel's New Dress (1915), Ethel Gains Consent (1915), Ethel's Deadly Alarm (1915), Ethel's Doggone Luck (1915), Ethel's Romance (1915), and Ethel's Disguise (1915). In 1925, she appeared as Min, the wife of Andy Gump in the Universal "Gumps" series.

Among Fay Tincher's most important Fine Arts features were Don Quixote and Mr. Goode, the Samaritan, both released in 1916. According to John Lloyd in Photoplay (June 1916), "Out at the Fine Arts studio where Fay Tincher has metamorphosed from a black-and-white cocoon of graphic comedy into a comedienne of finished artistry, whenever light touches are needed for a perplexing part, David Wark Griffith has come to say: 'Let Fay try it.' "

ERICH VON STROHEIM

Born, Erich Oswald Stroheim, Vienna, Austria, September 22, 1885. Died, Maurepas, France, May 12, 1957. One of the greatest and most colorful directors of all time, of whom René Clair commented, "A man whose work is major, and whose life is symbolic." At Fine Arts, von Stroheim worked as an assistant director, advisor and bit player. Erich von Stroheim's films as a director include Blind Husbands (1918, also actor), The Devil's Passkey (1919), Foolish Wives (1921, also actor), Merry-Go-Round (1922), Greed (1924), The Merry Widow (1925), The Wedding March (1928, also actor), and Queen Kelly (1928). As an actor, his films include Hearts of the World (1919), The Heart of Humanity (1919), The Great Gabbo (1929), The Lost Squadron (1932), La Grande Illusion (1937), and Five Graves to Cairo (1943).

For more information, see Hollywood Scapegoat by Peter Noble (Fortune Press, 1951); Stroheim by Joel Finler (Studio Vista, 1967); Von Stroheim by Thomas Quinn Curtis (Farrar, Straus and Giroux, 1971); Stroheim: A Pictorial Record of His Nine Films by Herman G. Weinberg (Dover Publications, 1975); "Erich von Stroheim: 1885-1957" by William K. Everson in Films in Review (August/September 1957), pages 305-314; "Erich von Stroheim: The Legend and the Fact" by Denis Marion in Sight and Sound (Winter 1961/62), pages 22-23 and 51; etc.

CHESTER (CHET) WITHEY

Born, Park City, Utah, 1887. Date and place of death unknown. Withey was a director of apparently considerable talent, but little is known about him. After a career as a stage actor, he worked for the American, Keystone and Reliance-Majestic companies. His films at Fine Arts are Don Quixote (1916, screenplay and actor), Mr. Goode, the Samaritan (1916, screenplay and actor), The Devil's Needle (1916, director and screenplay), The Old Folks at Home (1916, director), The Bad Boy (1917, director and co-screenplay), A Woman's Awakening (1917, director), and Madame Bo-Peep (1917, director). His debut as a director was The Devil's Needle.

His other films include An Alabaster Box (1917), On the Quiet (1918), The Pursuit of Polly (1918), The Hun Within (1918), Maggie Pepper (1919), The Little Comrade (1919),

The Teeth of the Tiger (1919), The New Moon (1919), She
Loves and Lies (1919), Romance (1920, starring Doris Keane
and Withey's most important film), Coincidence (1921), Les-
sons in Love (1921), Wedding Bells (1921), Domestic Rela-
tions (1922), Heroes and Husbands (1922), Outcast (1922),
Richard, the Lion-Hearted (1923), A Cafe in Cairo (1924),
The Pleasure Buyers (1925), Going the Limit (1926), Her
Honor the Governor (1926), The Imposter (1926), The Jade
Cup (1926), Queen o' Diamonds (1926), Secret Orders (1926),
and The Bushranger (1928). Chester Withey's name continued
to appear in Motion Picture Almanac through 1933, but he
does not appear to have directed anything after 1928.

For more information, see "Chet Withey: Builder of
Romance" by Faith Service in Motion Picture Classic (August
1920), pages 84 and 86, and "The Camera Detects Thought"
by Chet Withey in Photoplay (October 1920), pages 29 and
119.

FRANK E. WOODS

Born, Linesville, Pennsylvania, circa 1860. Died,
Los Angeles, May 1, 1939. A close associate and confidant
of Griffith in the Teens. His title with the Fine Arts Company was that of Manager of Production. As Robert C. Duncan described his position in Picture-Play Magazine (September 1916), "He's the head of the scenario department, and,
beside passing judgment on a few million, more or less,
ideas that are submitted to him annually, he keeps a large
force of writers constantly at the task of supplying themes
for the various directors to work out with their companies."
He provided the screenplays for the following Fine Arts productions: The Little School Ma'am (1916, co-screenplay),
The Children Pay (1916), The Bad Boy (1917, co-screenplay),
Betsy's Burglar (1917), A Woman's Awakening (1917), and
An Old Fashioned Young Man (1917). His wife, Ella, is
credited with the screenplay for Martha's Vindication (1916).

Frank Woods was a working newspaperman, who, as
the "Spectator," wrote the first columns of film reviews in
The New York Dramatic Mirror, of which he later became
editor. Leaving the Mirror, he worked as a director with
the Kinemacolor Company and as a scenario editor for American Biograph and Reliance-Majestic. After leaving Fine
Arts, when Griffith deserted the Company, he became Supervising Director at Paramount from 1917 through 1922. Woods

later freelanced, and his films include: Richard, the Lion-
Hearted (1923, co-producer and screenplay), What Shall I
Do? (1924, producer and screenplay), Let Women Alone (1925,
producer and screenplay), and The Awful Truth (1925, pro-
ducer).   He was basically inactive in the industry after 1925.
Frank Woods was one of the founders of the Screen Writers
Guild, the Motion Picture Relief Fund and the Academy of
Motion Picture Arts and Sciences, of which he was the first
secretary from May 1927 through January 1931.

His lecture, "Growth and Development," was published
in Introduction to the Photoplay (first published by the Academy and the University of Southern California in 1929 and
reprinted in 1977).   He was also the author of two 1931 pam-
phlets, Features and Short Subjects, and Improvement of
Screen Entertainment, based on papers he read to the Society
of Motion Picture Engineers.

Appendix B

A COMPLETE LIST OF FINE ARTS PRODUCTIONS DURING THE GRIFFITH REGIME

This list includes all the productions of the Fine Arts Film Company, from its inception in 1915 through its demise in 1917. All films are five reels in length, unless otherwise indicated, and all films were released by the Triangle Film Corporation. Exact release dates for silent films always present something of a problem, since various contemporary sources give varying dates. The dates listed here are from official Triangle publicity material, and do not always coincide with the dates listed in The Moving Picture World and other trade papers.

1915

THE LAMB (November 7)
Director and Screenplay: William Christy Cabanne. Based on a story by Granville Warwick (D. W. Griffith). Photography: William E. Fildew. Music arranged and adapted by Joseph Carl Breil. With Douglas Fairbanks, Seena Owen, Lillian Langdon, Monroe Salisbury, Kate Toncray, Alfred Paget, William E. Lowery, and Eagle Eye. Working Title: THE TEST AND THE MAN.

OLD HEIDELBERG (November 14)
Director and Screenplay: John Emerson. Based on a novel by W. Meyer-Forster and a play by Richard Mansfield. Music arranged and adapted by Joseph Carl Breil. Technical Director on Military Detail: Erich von Stroheim. With Wallace Reid, Dorothy Gish, Karl Fornes Jr., Erich von Stroheim, Raymond Wells, J. W. McDermott, James Gibson, Franklin Arbuckle, Madge Hunt, Erik von Ritzau, Kate Toncray, and Harold Goodwin.

MARTYRS OF THE ALAMO/THE BIRTH OF TEXAS (November 21)
Director: William Christy Cabanne. Screenplay: William
Christy Cabanne and Theodosia Harris. Photography: William E. Fildew. Music arranged and adapted by Joseph Carl
Breil. With Walter Long, Sam De Grasse, Fred Burns,
Alfred Paget, A. D. Sears, Tom Wilson, Juanita Hansen,
Ora Carew, Augustus Carney, John Dillon, Francis Carpenter, and Julia Faye.

THE SABLE LORCHA (November 28)
Director: Lloyd Ingraham. Screenplay: Chester B. Clapp.
Based on the novel by Horace Hazeltine. Photography: Hugh
C. McClung. Music arranged and adapted by Joseph Carl
Breil. With Tully Marshall, Thomas Jefferson, Charles Lee,
Elmer Clifton, Loretta Blake, George Pearce, Hal Wilson,
and Raymond Wells.

DOUBLE TROUBLE (December 5)
Director and Screenplay: William Christy Cabanne. Based
on a novel by Herbert Quick. Photography: William E. Fildew. Music arranged and adapted by Joseph Carl Breil.
With Douglas Fairbanks, Margery Wilson, Tom Kennedy,
Gladys Brockwell, Olga Grey, Kate Toncray, Monroe Salisbury, Richard Cummings, and W. E. Lowery.

THE LILY AND THE ROSE (December 12)
Director: Paul Powell. Based on a story by Granville Warwick (D. W. Griffith). Music arranged and adapted by Joseph
Carl Breil. Miss Dolly's dance by Ruth St. Denis. Miss
Gish's dance by Ted Shawn. Assistant Director: Roy Hiram
Rice. With Lillian Gish, Rozsika Dolly, Loyola O'Connor,
Cora Drew, Wilfred Lucas, Mary Alden, Elmer Clifton, and
William Hinckley.

JORDAN IS A HARD ROAD (December 19)
Director: Allan Dwan. Screenplay: Mary H. O'Connor.
Based on the novel by Gilbert Parker. With Dorothy Gish,
Frank Campeau, Sarah Truax, Owen Moore, Ralph Lewis,
Mabel Wiles, Fred Burns, Lester Perry, Jim Kid, Walter
Long, and Joseph Singleton.

THE PENITENTES (December 26)
Director: Jack Conway. Screenplay: Mary H. O'Connor.
Based on the novel by R. Ellis Wales. With Orrin Johnson,
Seena Owen, Paul Gilmore, Irene Hunt, Josephine Crowell,
F. A. Turner, Charles Clary, A. D. Sears, and Dark Cloud.

1916

CROSS CURRENTS (January 2)
Director: Francis J. Grandon. Screenplay: Mary H. O'Connor. With Helen Ware, Courtenay Foote, Teddy Sampson, Sam De Grasse, and Vera Lewis.

LET KATY DO IT (January 9)
Directors: C. M. and S. A. Franklin. Screenplay: Bernard McConville. Based on a novel by Granville Warwick (D. W. Griffith). Photography: Frank B. Good. Assistant Director: Millard K. Webb. With Jane Grey, Tully Marshall, Charles West, Ralph Lewis, Walter Long, Charles Gorman, George Pearce, Violet Radcliffe, George Stone, Carmen De Rue, Francis Carpenter, Ninon Fovieri, Lloyd Pearl, Beulah Burns, Luray Huntley, and George (André) Beranger. Working Title: MOTHER OF SEVEN.

THE MISSING LINKS (January 16)
Director: Lloyd Ingraham. Screenplay: Marion Clarke. With Thomas Jefferson, Elmer Clifton, Robert Harron, Loyola O'Connor, William Higby, Elinor Stone, Norma Talmadge, Jack Brammall, Hal Wilson, Constance Talmadge, and Robert Lawler.

THE WOOD NYMPH (January 23)
Director: Paul Powell. Screenplay: Granville Warwick (D. W. Griffith). Assistant Director: Roy Hiram Rice. With Marie Doro, Charles West, Wilfred Lucas, Frank Campeau, Cora Drew, Fred Graham, and Pearl Elmore.

THE PRICE OF POWER (January 30)
Director: Jack Conway. Photography: Frank B. Good. With Orrin Johnson, Francis J. McDonald, Marguerite Marsh, Spottiswoode Aitken, Sam De Grasse, Gladys Brockwell, Vera Lewis, Clyde Hopkins, and Daisy Robinson.

ACQUITTED (February 6)
Director: Paul Powell. Screenplay: Roy Somerville. Based on the short story by Mary Rinehart. With Wilfred Lucas, Mary Alden, Bessie Love, Carmen De Rue, Elmer Clifton, Sam De Grasse, W. J. Freemont, Spottiswoode Aitken, James O'Shea, and F. A. Turner.

HIS PICTURE IN THE PAPERS (February 13)
Director: John Emerson. Screenplay: John Emerson and Anita Loos. Photography: George Hill. With Douglas Fair-

banks, Clarence Handyside, Rene Boucicault, Charles Butler, Homer Hunt, and Loretta Blake.

BETTY OF GREYSTONE (February 20)
Director: Allan Dwan. Screenplay: F. M. Pierson. With Dorothy Gish, George Fawcett, Owen Moore, Leonore Harris, Kate Bruce, Grace Rankin, Eugene Ormonde, Macey Harlan, Kid McCoy, and Albert Tavernier.

DON QUIXOTE (February 27)
Director: Edward Dillon. Screenplay: Chester Withey. Based on the novel by Miguel de Cervantes Saavedra. Photography: A. G. Gosden. With DeWolf Hopper, Fay Tincher, Max Davidson, Rhea Mitchell, Chester Withey, Julia Faye, Edward Dillon, Carl Stockdale, William Brown and George Walsh.

DAPHNE AND THE PIRATE (March 5)
Director: William Christy Cabanne. Screenplay: Mary H. O'Connor. Photography: William E. Fildew. 2nd Camera: Karl Brown. With Lillian Gish, Elliott Dexter, Walter Long, Howard Gaye, Lucille Younge, Richard Cummings, and Jack Cosgrave. Working Title: DAPHNE.

THE FLYING TORPEDO (March 12)
Director War Scenes: William Christy Cabanne. Director Other Scenes: Jack O'Brien. Screenplay: Robert M. Baker and John Emerson. Photography: George Hill. With John Emerson, Spottiswoode Aitken, William E. Lawrence, Fred J. Butler, Raymond West, Viola Barry, Bessie Love, Lucille Younge, Ralph Lewis, David Butler and Erich von Stroheim. Working Title: THE SCARLET BAND.

MARTHA'S VINDICATION (March 19)
Directors: C. M. and S. A. Franklin. Screenplay: Ella Woods. Photography: Frank B. Good. Seena Owen's Gowns by Lucille. With Norma Talmadge, Seena Owen, Ralph Lewis, Tully Marshall, Josephine Crowell, Charles West, William Hinckley, Francis Carpenter, George Stone, Alice Knowland, Alberta Lee, Edwin Harley, George Pearce, and Porter Strong.

HOODOO ANN (March 26)
Director: Lloyd Ingraham. Screenplay: Granville Warwick (D. W. Griffith). With Mae Marsh, Robert Harron, William E. Brown, Wilbur Higby, Loyola O'Connor, Mildred Harris, Pearl Elmore, Anna Hernandez, Charles Lee, Elmo Lincoln, Robert Lawler, and Madame Sul-Te-Wan.

THE HABIT OF HAPPINESS (April 2)
Director: Allan Dwan. Screenplay: Allan Dwan and Shannon
Fife. With Douglas Fairbanks, George Backus, Grace Rankin, George Fawcett, Dorothy West, Macey Harlan, and William Jefferson.

LITTLE MEENA'S ROMANCE (April 9)
Director: Paul Powell. Screenplay: F. M. Pierson. With
Dorothy Gish, Owen Moore, Fred J. Butler, Robert Lawler,
Alberta Lee, Mazie Radford, George Pearce, Fred A. Tur-
ner, Kate Toncray, Marguerite Marsh, James O'Shea, and
William H. Brown. Working Title: KATY BAUER.

SOLD FOR MARRIAGE (April 16)
Director: William Christy Cabanne. Screenplay: William
E. Wing. Photography: William E. Fildew and Sam Abel.
With Lillian Gish, Frank Bennett, Walter Long, A. D. Sears,
Pearl Elmore, Tom Wilson, Curt Rehfelt, William Lowery,
Fred Burns, Olga Grey, Monte Blue, and Mike Siebert.
Working Title: MARTA OF THE STEPPE.

SUNSHINE DAD (April 23)
Director: Edward Dillon. Screenplay: Chester Withey and
Tod Browning. Photography: A. G. Gosden. With DeWolf
Hopper, Fay Tincher, Chester Withey, Max Davidson, Eugene
Pallette, Raymond Wells, Jewel Carmen, Howard Gaye, and
DeWolf Hopper, Jr. Working Title: A KNIGHT OF THE
GARTER.

THE CHILDREN IN THE HOUSE (April 30)
Directors: C. M. and S. A. Franklin. Screenplay: Roy
Somerville. Photography: Frank B. Good. Assistant Direc-
tor: Millard K. Webb. With Norma Talmadge, Alice Rae,
Jewel Carmen, William Hinckley, W. E. Lawrence, Eugene
Pallette, Walter Long, George Pearce, Alva D. Blake,
George Stone, Violet Radcliffe, Carmen De Rue, Francis
Carpenter, and Ninon Fovieri.

THE GOOD-BAD MAN (May 7)
Director: Allan Dwan. Based on a story by Douglas Fair-
banks. Photography: Victor Fleming. With Douglas Fair-
banks, Sam De Grasse, Doc Cannon, Joe Singleton, Bessie
Love, Mary Alden, George (André) Beranger, and Fred
Burns.

SUSAN ROCKS THE BOAT (May 14)
Director: Paul Powell. Screenplay: Bernard McConville.

With Dorothy Gish, Owen Moore, Fred J. Butler, Fred A.
Turner, Edwin Harley, Kate Bruce, Clyde E. Hopkins, and
James O'Shea.

A CHILD OF THE PARIS STREETS (May 21)
Director: Lloyd Ingraham. Screenplay: Grant Carpenter.
With Jennie Lee, Carl Stockdale, Tully Marshall, Mae Marsh,
Robert Harron, Loyola O'Connor, and Bert Hadley. Working
Title: THE LITTLE APACHE.

MR. GOODE, THE SAMARITAN (May 28)
Director: Edward Dillon. Screenplay: Chester Withey.
Photography: A. G. Gosden. With DeWolf Hopper, Fay
Tincher, Edward Dillon, Chester Withey, Marguerite Marsh,
Lillian Langdon, and Max Davidson. Working Title: THE
PHILANTHROPIST.

GOING STRAIGHT (June 4)
Directors: C. M. and S. A. Franklin. Screenplay: Ber-
nard McConville. Photography: Frank B. Good. Assistant
Director: Millard K. Webb. With Norma Talmadge, Ralph
Lewis, Ninon Fovieri, Francis Carpenter, Fern Collier,
Ruth Handford, Eugene Pallette, George Stone, Kate Toncray,
Violet Radcliffe, and Carmen De Rue. Working Title:
PLAYMATES.

REGGIE MIXES IN (June 11)
Director: William Christy Cabanne. Screenplay: Roy Somerville. Based on a story by Robert M. Baker. Photography:
William E. Fildew. With Douglas Fairbanks, Joseph Singleton, Bessie Love, W. E. Lowery, Wilbur Higby, Frank Bennett, and A. D. Sears. Working Title: THE BOUNCER.

AN INNOCENT MAGDALENE (June 18)
Director: Allan Dwan. Screenplay: Roy Somerville. Based
on a story by Granville Warwick (D. W. Griffith). With
Lillian Gish, Spottiswoode Aitken, Sam De Grasse, Mary
Alden, Jennie Lee, Seymour Hastings, and William de Vaull.
Working Title: THE SCARLET WOMAN.

THE WILD GIRL OF THE SIERRAS (June 25)
Director: Paul Powell. Screenplay: Anita Loos. With
Mae Marsh, Wilfred Lucas, Maizie Radford, Olga Grey,
Robert Harron, and James O'Shea. Working Title: A CHILD
OF NATURE.

CASEY AT THE BAT (July 2)
Director: Lloyd Ingraham. Screenplay: William E. Wing.

With DeWolf Hopper, Kate Toncray, May Garcia, Carl Stockdale, William H. Brown, Marguerite Marsh, Frank Bennett,
Robert Lawler, Bert Hadley, Hal Wilson, and Frank Hughes.

FLIRTING WITH FATE (July 9)
Director and Screenplay: William Christy Cabanne. Based
on a story by Robert M. Baker. Photography: William E.
Fildew. With Douglas Fairbanks, Howard Gaye, Jewel Car-
men, W. E. Lawrence, George (André) Beranger, Dorothy
Haydel, Lillian Langdon, Wilbur Higby, and J. P. McCarthy.
Working Title: THE ASSASSIN.

THE LITTLE SCHOOL MA'AM (July 16)
Directors: C. M. and S. A. Franklin. Screenplay: Frank
E. Woods and Bernard McConville. Assistant Director: Mil-
lard K. Webb. With Dorothy Gish, Elmer Clifton, George
Pearce, Jack Brammall, Howard Gaye, Josephine Crowell,
Luray Huntley, Millard Webb, Hal Wilson, and George Stone.

STRANDED (July 23)
Director: Lloyd Ingraham. Screenplay: Anita Loos. With
DeWolf Hopper, Carl Stockdale, Frank Bennett, Loyola O'Con-
nor, and Bessie Love. Working Title: THE OLD PLAYER.

THE HALF-BREED (July 30)
Director: Allan Dwan. Screenplay: Anita Loos. Based on
the story, "In the Carquinez Woods," by Bret Harte. With
Douglas Fairbanks, Alma Rubens, Sam De Grasse, Tom Wil-
son, Jack Brownlee, George (André) Beranger, and Jewel
Carmen.

THE MARRIAGE OF MOLLY O' (August 6)
Director: Paul Powell. Screenplay: Granville Warwick
(D. W. Griffith). Photography: John Leezer. With Mae
Marsh, Kate Bruce, Robert Harron, James O'Shea, and
Walter Long.

THE DEVIL'S NEEDLE (August 13)
Director: Chester Withey. Screenplay: Chester Withey
and Roy Somerville. With Norma Talmadge, Tully Marshall,
Marguerite Marsh, F. A. Turner, Howard Gaye, John Bren-
nen, and Paul Le Blanc. Working Titles: THE DOPE FIEND,
DRUGGED HOPES and THE WHITE CURSE.

PUPPETS (August 13)
Director: Tod Browning. With DeWolf Hopper, Jack Bram-
mall, Robert Lawlor, Pauline Starke, Kate Toncray, Edward
Bolles, and Max Davidson. A two-reel short.

HELL-TO-PAY AUSTIN (August 20)
Director: Paul Powell. Screenplay: Mary H. O'Connor. Photography: John W. Leezer. With Wilfred Lucas, Bessie Love, Ralph Lewis, Mary Alden, Eugene Pallette, James O'Shea, Clyde Hopkins, Marie Wilkinson, A. D. Sears, William H. Brown, and Tom Wilson.

PILLARS OF SOCIETY (August 27)
Director: Raoul Walsh. Based on the play by Henrik Ibsen. With Henry B. Walthall, Mary Alden, Juanita Archer, George (André) Beranger, Josephine Crowell, and Olga Grey.

GRETCHEN THE GREENHORN (September 3)
Directors: C. M. and S. A. Franklin. Screenplay: Bernard McConville. With Dorothy Gish, Ralph Lewis, Frank Bennett, Eugene Pallette, Kate Bruce, George Stone, Violet Radcliffe, Carmen De Rue, Beulah Burns, Francis Carpenter, and Tom Spencer. Working Title: GRETCHEN BLUNDERS IN.

THE SOCIAL SECRETARY (September 10)
Director: John Emerson. Screenplay: Anita Loos. Photography: Alfred Huger Moses Jr. Assistant Director: Erich von Stroheim. With Norma Talmadge, Kate Lester, Helen Weir, Gladden James, Herbert French, and Erich von Stroheim.

THE LITTLE LIAR (September 17)
Director: Lloyd Ingraham. Screenplay: Anita Loos. With Mae Marsh, Robert Harron, Olga Grey, Carl Stockdale, Jennie Lee, Ruth Handforth, Tom Wilson, and Loyola O'Connor.

DIANE OF THE FOLLIES (September 24)
Director: William Christy Cabanne. Screenplay: Granville Warwick (D. W. Griffith). With Lillian Gish, Sam De Grasse, Howard Gaye, Lillian Langdon, A. D. Sears, Wilbur Higby, William De Vaull, Wilhelmina Siegmann, Adele Clifton, Clara Morris, Helen Walcott, and Grace Heinz.

MANHATTAN MADNESS (October 1)
Director: Allan Dwan. Screenplay: Charles T. and Frank Dazey. Based on a story by E. V. Durling. With Douglas Fairbanks, Jewel Carmen, George (André) Beranger, Ruth Darling, Eugene Ormonde, Macey Harlan, W. P. Richmond, Norman Kerry, and Adolphe Menjou.

THE RUMMY (October 8)
Director: Paul Powell. Screenplay: Wilfred Lucas. With

Wilfred Lucas, Pauline Starke, William H. Brown, James
O'Shea, Harry Fisher, A. D. Sears, and Clyde Hopkins.

THE OLD FOLKS AT HOME (October 15)
Director: Chester Withey. Based on a short story by Ru-
pert Hughes. With Sir Herbert Beerbohm Tree, Josephine
Crowell, Elmer Clifton, Mildred Harris, Lucille Younge,
W. E. Lawrence, and Spottiswoode Aitken.

FIFTY-FIFTY (October 22)
Director: Allan Dwan. Screenplay: Robert Shirley and Al-
lan Dwan. With Norma Talmadge, J. W. Johnston, Marie
Chambers, Ruth Darling, Harry S. Northrup, Frank Currier,
Dodson Mitchell, and W. P. Richmond.

A SISTER OF SIX (October 29)
Directors: C. M. and S. A. Franklin. Screenplay: Ber-
nard McConville. Photography: David Abel. With Ben
Lewis, Bessie Love, George Stone, Violet Radcliffe, Car-
men De Rue, Francis Carpenter, Beulah Burns, Lloyd Pearl,
Ralph Lewis, Frank Bennett, A. D. Sears, Charles Gorman,
Charles Stephens, and Alberta Lee. Working Title: THE
DEFENDERS.

ATTA BOY'S LAST RACE (November 5)
Director: George Siegmann. Screenplay: Tod Browning.
With Dorothy Gish, Keith Armour, Carl Stockdale, Adele
Clifton, Loyola O'Connor, Fred H. Turner, Tom Wilson,
and Joe Neery. Working Title: THE BEST BET.

AMERICAN ARISTOCRACY (November 12)
Director: Lloyd Ingraham. Screenplay: Anita Loos. With
Douglas Fairbanks, Jewel Carmen, Albert Parker, Charles
De Lima, and Arthur Ortiego.

THE MICROSCOPE MYSTERY (November 19)
Director: Paul Powell. Screenplay: W. E. Wing. With
Constance Talmadge, Wilfred Lucas, F. A. Turner, Winifred
Westover, Pomeroy Cannon, Fred Warren, James O'Shea,
Jack Sealock, Kate Bruce, and Monte Blue. Working Title:
BUGS.

THE CHILDREN PAY (November 26)
Director: Lloyd Ingraham. Screenplay: Frank E. Woods.
With Lillian Gish, Violet Wilkey, Keith Armour, Ralph Lewis,
Alma Rubens, Jennie Lee, Loyola O'Connor, Robert Lokmeyer,
Carl Stockdale, Tom Wilson, and Madame Sul-Te-Wan.

CHILDREN OF THE FEUD (December 2)
Director: Joseph Henabery. Screenplay: Bernard McConville. With Dorothy Gish, A. D. Sears, Sam De Grasse, F. A. Turner, Elmo Lincoln, Alberta Lee, Charles Gorman, Beulah Burns, Violet Radcliffe, George Stone, Tina Rossi, and Thelma Burns. Working Title: THE FEUD BREAKER.

THE WHARF RAT (December 9)
Director: Chester Withey. Photography: A. G. Gosden. Screenplay: Anita Loos. With Mae Marsh, Robert Harron, Spottiswoode Aitken, Pauline Starke, William H. Brown, and Lillian Langdon.

THE MATRIMANIAC (December 16)
Director: Paul Powell. Based on a story by Octavus Roy Cohen and J. V. Giesy. With Douglas Fairbanks, Constance Talmadge, Winifred Westover, Fred Warren, Wilbur Higby, and Clyde Hopkins.

THE HEIRESS AT COFFEE DAN'S (December 23)
Director: Edward Dillon. Screenplay: Bernard McConville. Photography: David Abel. With Bessie Love, Max Davidson, Frank Bennett, Lucille Younge, Alfred Paget, and Alva Blake.

A HOUSE BUILT UPON SAND (December 31)
Director: Edward Morrissey. Screenplay: Mary H. O'Connor. Photography: Philip R. Du Bois. With Lillian Gish, Roy Stuart, W. H. Brown, Bessie Buskirk, Jack Brammall, Kate Bruce, and Josephine Crowell.

> [During the latter part of 1916, a number of two-reel comedy shorts were released by Triangle that appear to have been produced at the Fine Arts studios, with Fine Arts players, but are designated as Keystone productions. One such short is the Douglas Fairbanks vehicle, The Mystery of the Leaping Fish, scripted by D. W. Griffith, and co-starring Bessie Love. Other films include:
>
> EVERYBODY'S DOING IT (Director: Tod Browning. With Howard Gaye, Tully Marshall, Lillian Webster, George Stone, and Violet Radcliffe. Working Title: THE RESCUERS)
>
> MLLE. O'BRIEN (Director: Edward Dillon. With Edward Dillon, Kate Toncray, and Max

Davidson. Working Title: THE PARISIAN MIL-
LINER)

THE DEADLY GLASS OF BEER (Director: Tod
Browning. With Teddy Sampson, Tully Marshall, Jack Brammall, and Elmo Lincoln)

I have been unable to locate accurate release
dates for any of these titles. They do not appear in the regular Triangle release schedule.]

1917

THE LITTLE YANK (January 14)
Director: George Siegmann. Screenplay: Roy Somerville.
With Dorothy Gish, Frank Bennett, Hal Wilson, A. D. Sears,
Robert Burns, Kate Toncray, F. A. Turner, and Alberta Lee.

NINA, THE FLOWER GIRL (January 21)
Director: Lloyd Ingraham. Screenplay: Mary H. O'Connor.
Photography: Frank Urson. With Bessie Love, Elmer Clif-
ton, Alfred Paget, Loyola O'Connor, Jennie Lee, Adele Clif-
ton, Bert Hadley, Fred Warren, Rhea Haines, and Mrs.
Higby.

THE AMERICANO (January 28)
Director: John Emerson. Screenplay: John Emerson and
Anita Loos. Based on the novel Blaze Derringer, by Eugene
P. Lyle Jr. Photography: Victor Fleming. With Douglas
Fairbanks, Alma Rubens, Spottiswoode Aitken, Lillian Lang-
don, Carl Stockdale, Tom Wilson, Tote Du Crow, and Charles
Stevens. Working Title: MR. BREEZE, THE PET OF PAT-
AGONIA.

JIM BLUDSO (February 4)
Directors: Wilfred Lucas and Tod Browning. Based on the
Pike County ballad by John Hay. Photography: A. G. Gos-
den. With Wilfred Lucas, Olga Grey, George Stone, Wini-
fred Westover, Sam De Grasse, James O'Shea, and Monte
Blue.

THE GIRL OF THE TIMBER CLAIMS (February 11)
Director: Paul Powell. Screenplay; Mary H. O'Connor.
Photography: John W. Leezer. With Constance Talmadge,
A. D. Sears, Clyde Hopkins, Beau Byrd, Wilbur Higby, Ben-
nie Schuman, Joseph Singleton, F. A. Turner, Charles Lee,
and Mrs. Talmadge.

THE BAD BOY (February 18)
Director: Chester Withey. Screenplay: Chester Withey and
Frank E. Woods. Photography: David Abel. With Robert
Harron, Pauline Starke, Richard Cummings, Josephine Cro-
well, Carmel Myers, William H. Brown, Harry Fisher,
Mildred Harris, Colleen Moore, Elmo Lincoln, and James
Harrison.

STAGE STRUCK (February 25)
Director: Edward Morrissey. Screenplay: Roy Somerville.
Photography: Karl Brown. With Dorothy Gish, Frank Ben-
nett, Kate Toncray, Spottiswoode Aitken, Jennie Lee, Mazie
Radford, Fred Warren, Josephine Crowell, and Madame Sul-
Te-Wan. Working Title: THE FAILURES.

BETSY'S BURGLAR (March 4)
Director: Paul Powell. Screenplay: Frank E. Woods.
Photography: John W. Leezer. With Constance Talmadge,
Kenneth Harlan, Kate Bruce, Josephine Crowell, Clyde Hop-
kins, Elmo Lincoln, Monte Blue, Kate Toncray, Tom Wilson,
J. Warwick Hall, and Joseph Singleton.

A LOVE SUBLIME (March 11)
Director: Tod Browning. Based on the story, "Orpheus,"
by Samual Hopkins Adams. Photography: A. G. Gosden.
With Wilfred Lucas, Carmel Myers, Fred Turner, Alice
Rae, George (André) Beranger, Jack Brammall, James O'Shea,
Bert Woodruff, Alice Webster, and Alexander McClure.
Working Title: ORPHEUS.

A DAUGHTER OF THE POOR (March 18)
Director: Edward Dillon. Screenplay: Anita Loos. Photo-
graphy: Philip Du Bois. With Bessie Love, Max Davidson,
Carl Stockdale, George (André) Beranger, Carmel Myers,
and Roy Stewart. Working Titles: THE DOLL SHOP and
THE SPITFIRE.

A WOMAN'S AWAKENING (March 25)
Director: Chester Withey. Screenplay: Frank E. Woods.
With Seena Owen, Alma Rubens, A. D. Sears, Charles Ger-
rard, Kate Bruce, Spottiswoode Aitken, Alberta Lee, and
Jennie Lee.

>   [On April 1, Triangle released HER FATHER'S
>   KEEPER, featuring Irene Howley, Frank Cur-
>   rier, Jack Devereux, Jack Raymond, John Hun-
>   neford, and Walter Bussell. It was identified

merely as a Triangle Production, with no indication as to the studio from which it emanated.]

HER OFFICIAL FATHERS (April 8)
Directors: Elmer Clifton and Joseph Henabery. Screenplay:
Roy Somerville. Based on the story, "That Colby Girl," by
Hugh S. Miller. Photography: Karl Brown. With Dorothy
Gish, Frank Bennett, F. A. Turner, Milton Schumann, Sam
De Grasse, Hal Wilson, Jennie Lee, Bessie Buskirk, Richard
Cummings, Fred Warren, and Charles Lee.

AN OLD FASHIONED YOUNG MAN (April 15)
Director: Lloyd Ingraham. Screenplay: Frank E. Woods.
With Robert Harron, Sam De Grasse, Loyola O'Connor, Col-
leen Moore, Alma Rubens, Charles Lee, Wilbur Higby, Bert
Hadley, Tom Wilson, and Adele Clifton. Working Title: A
YOUNG GENTLEMAN OF THE OLD SCHOOL.

CHEERFUL GIVERS (April 22)
Director: Paul Powell. Screenplay: Mary H. O'Connor.
Photography: John W. Leezer. With Bessie Love, Thelma
and Beulah Burns, Tina Rossi, George Stone, Josephine
Crowell, Spottiswoode Aitken, Bessie Buskirk, Pauline Starke,
Winifred Westover, Loyola O'Connor, and William H. Brown.

HANDS UP! (April 29)
Directors: Wilfred Lucas and Tod Browning. With Wilfred
Lucas, Colleen Moore, Monte Blue, Beatrice Van, Rhea
Haines, Bert Woodruff, and Kate Toncray.

MIGHT AND THE MAN (May 6)
Director: Edward Dillon. With Elmo Lincoln, Carmel
Myers, Wilbur Higby, Lillian Langdon, Clyde Hopkins, Carl
Stockdale, Luray Huntley, and Mazie Radford. Working
Title: THE STRONG MAN.

[On May 13, Triangle released THE MAN WHO
MADE GOOD, supervised by Allan Dwan, and
featuring Jack Devereaux, Winifred Allen, Henry
P. Dixon, and Barney Gilmore. It was announced as an East Coast Triangle production,
which should qualify it as a Fine Arts production, but The Moving Picture World (May 12,
1917, page 479) described it as an Ince production.]

SOULS TRIUMPHANT (May 20)
Director: John B. O'Brien. Screenplay: Mary H. O'Connor.

With Lillian Gish, Wilfred Lucas, Spottiswoode Aitken, and
Louise Hamilton.

MADAME BO-PEEP (May 27)
Director: Chester Withey.   Based on a story by O'Henry.
Photography: David Abel.   With Seena Owen, A. D. Sears,
James Harrison, F. A. Turner, Sam De Grasse, Pauline
Starke, Kate Bruce, and Jennie Lee.

Appendix C

MACBETH CREDITS

Director and Screenplay: John Emerson. Based on
the play by William Shakespeare. Photography: George Hill.
New York premiere: Rialto Theatre, June 4, 1916. Los
Angeles premiere: Majestic Theatre, June 6, 1916. Released on a roadshow basis. 8 reels (7,500 ft.)

Sir Herbert Beerbohm Tree	Macbeth
Constance Collier	Lady Macbeth
Spottiswoode Aitken	Duncan
Wilfred Lucas	Macduff
Ralph Lewis	Banquo
L. de Nowskowski	Malcolm
Bessie Buskirk	Donalbain
Jack Conway	Lennox
Seymour Hastings	Ross
Jack Brammall	Seyton
Carl Fornes Jr.	Bishop
Mary Alden	Lady Macduff
L. Tylden	First Witch
Scott McKee	Second Witch
Jack Leonard	Third Witch
Frencis Carpenter ⎫	
Thelma Burns ⎬	Macduff's Children
Madge Dyer ⎭	
Raymond Wells	Thane of Cawdor
George McKenzie	Doctor
Chandler House	Fleance
Olga Grey	Lady

Appendix D

INTOLERANCE: SELECTED COMMENTARY

Because the production of Intolerance is inextricably interwoven with the history of the Fine Arts Company, and because the Griffith masterpiece was shot at the Fine Arts studio, it seems only appropriate to include in this volume materials relating to Intolerance, which received its first performance in California in the form of a preview at the Loring Opera House in Riverside on August 6, 1916, and its New York premiere at the Liberty Theatre on September 5, 1916.

Rather than include still further critical analysis of the film, I have chosen to reprint a selection of contemporaneous reviews, news items, and articles on Intolerance from The Moving Picture World, Motion Picture News, and Photoplay. Additional reprints of contemporary material may be found in George Pratt's Spellbound in Darkness (New York Graphic Society, 1973). Also, full credits, together with a detailed synopsis and critical essay, may be found in The Films of D. W. Griffith by Edward Wagenknecht and Anthony Slide (Crown, 1975).

The following articles are included:

In and Out of West Coast Studios, by Peter J. C. Jensen 181
Griffith Forced to Re-Take Scenes in Mother and Law 182
Intolerance in Review, by Frederick James Smith 183
Intolerance Reaches Apex of Motion Picture Art 189
The Making of a Masterpiece, by Edward Weitzel 193
The Real Story of Intolerance, by Henry Stephen Gordon 197
The Shadow Stage, by Julian Johnson 213
Here's the Chaldean Who Built Babylon 218

IN AND OUT OF WEST COAST STUDIOS*
by Peter J. C. Jessen

<u>Los Angeles, March 18</u>

The greatest scenes yet made for D. W. Griffith's
next subject known under the working title of <u>The Mother</u>
<u>and the Law</u>, were filmed during the past week when on al-
ternate days approximately three thousand extra people were
used.   Director Griffith had as his lieutenants in the making
of these scenes, twenty-eight experienced directors, photo-
players, and nine cameras were in operation practically all
of the time.   The mammoth sets built on the vacant lots opposite the Fine Arts studio were used for these.   The warriors occupied positions at the foot of and on top of the walls,
which stand about ninety feet in height.   During the making
of the battle scenes, several men leaped from the top of the
walls into a fire net below.   Approximately one thousand men
defended the walls of Babylon using instruments of warfare
appropriate to that period.   Below were approximately two
thousand on foot and in chariots that assailed the city with
storms of arrows and papier-mâché boulders.   During one
day the ambulance made more than sixty trips to the company's hospital in charge of Dr. R. K. Hackett, and more
than one hundred people were said to have been injured.   All
were given the first aid.   None of the injuries were of a
serious matter and consisted mostly of scratches and bruises
due to parties being hit with arrows.   On another day about
75 were injured.   One day upwards of fifteen thousand feet
of negative was exposed which ultimately will be trimmed to
a few hundred.   It was declared to be the most successful
day in the history of the studio from the standpoint of securing good results in the making of mob scenes.

*Reprinted from <u>Motion Picture News</u>, Vol. 13, No. 13,
April 1, 1916, page 1892.

GRIFFITH FORCED TO RE-TAKE SCENES IN
MOTHER AND LAW*

Los Angeles, April 5

David W. Griffith has about completed his latest
"masterpiece" entitled The Mother and the Law, dealing with
the life of Christ. For the big crucifixion scene he repaired
to the local Ghetto and hired all the orthodox Hebrews with
long wiskers he could secure.

When the B'nai Brith (the most powerful Hebrew society in the United States) was apprised of it they requested
Griffith to omit that portion of the picture, but he refused.
They then brought pressure to bear upon him through his
associates, but could not move him.

A committee of three members of the society (one
from San Francisco, one from New York and one from Chicago) brought the matter to the attention of Jacob H. Schiff,
Joseph Brandels, Louis Marshall and other prominent Hebrews. Armed with data gathered from colleges, professors
and historians, the committee returned to Los Angeles and
waited upon Griffith with so-called indisputable proofs that
the Jews did not crucify the Saviour, showing that the orthodox method of killings in those days was strangulation and
that the Romans believed in crucifixion. They supplemented
their "proofs" with a 48-hour ultimatum to destroy that portion of the "masterpiece" negative on penalty of a concerted
national campaign of blacklisting and other pressure which
powerful financial and industrial interests might bring to
bear, which included the assertion that censors, governors
of states and even the President would do all in their power
to prevent the showing of the picture with the objectionable
scene.

Confronted with such formidable antagonism Griffith
burned the negative of the scene in the presence of the committee and has retaken it, showing Roman soldiers nailing
Christ to the cross.

---

*Reprinted from Variety, Vol. 42, No. 6, April 7, 1916,
page 3.

INTOLERANCE IN REVIEW*
by Frederick James Smith

It is easy enough, as you catch your breath at the conclusion of Intolerance, to indulge in trite superlatives. Film reviewing has been over superlatived. But this new Griffith spectacle marks a mile-post in the progress of the film. It reveals something of the future of the spectacle, something of its power to create pictures of tremendous and sweeping beauty, drama, and imagination. The future will come when the great writer unites with the great producer.

Intolerance, of course, instantly challenges comparison, by reason of its creator, with The Birth of a Nation. One is the dramatization of a novel, a gripping, even thrilling visualization of a story dealing with a theme of national interest--our own Civil War. On the other hand, Intolerance is the screening of an idea. That alone places it as an advance.

The Screening of an Idea

Mr. Griffith sought a theme which has traced itself through history. He advances the proposition that humanity's lack of tolerance of opinion and speech has brought about the world's woes. Taking four periods of history, he traces the working out of this idea. We have, perhaps, come to assume that our own age is one of singular meddling and busy-bodyism. But Mr. Griffith points out that the thing has been the same through the ages.

Briefly, the periods depicted revolve around the fall of Babylon in 538 B. C. , the coming of the Nazarene and the birth of the Christian era, the massacre of St. Bartholomew's Day in France during the reign of Charles IX, and the present day. Mr. Griffith, of course, handles his four plots at one time. The threads are interwoven. The moments dealing with the life of Christ, it may be noted here, are brief, being in reality rich tableaux of the persecution of the Savior. Griffith has endeavored to humanize Christ.

---

*Reprinted from The New York Dramatic Mirror, Vol. 76, No. 1969, September 16, 1916, page 22.

Alfred Paget as Belshazzar and Seena Owen as The Princess Beloved.

These moments are handled with reverence, dignity, and
beauty of picture.   Indeed, there are moments worthy of
Tissot.   Once, oddly, the director attains a singular effect
of a shadow cross upon the figure of Christ.

The modern theme of Intolerance has a Western town
as its locale.   The owner of a factory reduces wages that
he may make extended--and widely heralded--contributions
to charity.   A strike devastates the town and the workers
are forced to move away.   The boy and the girl of the story,
now married in the city, still remain the playthings of intolerance.   The boy is sent to prison for a crime he never
committed.   In his absence the baby is taken away from the
mother by a charitable society.   The boy, on returning, becomes innocently involved in a murder and through his criminal record, is convicted.   The story finally races to a climax when, as the execution is about to take place, the wife,
aided by a kindly policeman, hurries to the governor with
the confession of the real murderer.   They miss the executive, who has taken a train.   The policeman commandeers
a racing car and they speed after the express.   The execution is stopped just as the death trap is to be sprung.

Spectacle's Appeal Lies in Babylonian Story

The principal appeal of Intolerance, however, lies in
the Babylonian story.   Here we see Belshazzar ruling Babylon with his father, Nabonidus.   He is a kindly, generous
monarch--as kings in those days went--but the high priest
of Bel resents his religious tolerance.   So, when Cyrus,
king of the Medes and Persians, attacks the walled city, the
priest betrays Babylon.   So the city falls, after a mighty
battle such as never before had been conceived in mimicry.

Mr. Griffith has reconstructed the city of Babylon--
according to authentic records and researches, we are told
by the programme and we may well believe.   The city, with
its great walls, three hundred feet high and big enough on
top for two war chariots to pass, its temples, its lofty halls,
its slave marts, and its streets, lives again, seething with
life.   The attack upon Babylon is handled on a tremendous
scale.   We are shown Cyrus's camp in the desert sands.
Then we see his cohorts, his barbarians from distant lands,
his war chariots, his elephants, his great moving towers,
advance upon Babylon.   Great catapults hurl rocks upon the

defenders.   Moulten lead is thrown from the walls.   Showers
of arrows fall.   One great siege tower, black with fighting
men, is toppled over and goes crashing to the ground.   Lad-
ders, manned by warriors, are flung down.   So the battle
goes a day and a night.   Treason finally gives over Babylon,
in the midst of a great bacchanial feast of victory.

This theme is unfolded with Mr. Griffith's fine skill
in handling hundreds and thousands of men.   There is a certain personal note in the spectacle.   Belshazzar, his favorite,
Attarea, the boisterous little mountain girl who loves the
king from afar, and the crafty priest of Bel are finely human-
ized.   The tremendous applause at Intolerance's premiere,
occasioned when Babylon first fought off the invaders, was a
vital compliment to the skill of the producer.   One forgot
that, with the fall of the city, fell the Semitic race, and
that ever afterwards the Aryan people controlled the affairs
of civilization.

Huguenot Theme Least Compelling

The final, and least compelling, theme deals with
Catherine de Medici and her instigation of the massacre of
the Huguenots in Paris in 1572 under the cloak of religion.
The personal side of the story deals with two Huguenot lovers,
victims of the cruel religious persecution.   This theme has
been carefully staged, in the bigness of its court interiors,
the depth of its street scenes, and its handling of the ruth-
less massacre.

The defense of Babylon brings the first half of Intolerance to a big climax, while the last portion is largely
given over to the climax of the modern plot thread.   Finally,
we are shown the idealistic future, with two armies racing
to meet each other, only to throw down their arms and clasp
hands.   This is banal, of course, but Mr. Griffith intends it
to weave the themes together and point to the future, when
tolerance will make war and all evils impossible.

A certain symbolical note is touched by frequent,
half shadowy, glimpses of a woman rocking a cradle.   Mr.
Griffith gives programme explanation of the symbolism:
"Through all these ages Time brings forth the same passions,
the same joys and sorrows, the same hopes and anxieties--
symbolized by the cradle 'endlessly rocking.' "

The Construction of the Four
Plot Threads

Intolerance, let us sum up once more, stands at the outpost of the cinema's advance. It has an idea. It has a purpose. From a structural standpoint, the handling and weaving of the four plots are revolutionary. There is never a moment's lack of clarity. Each story sweeps to its climax. Since the interest is divided, it would be resonable to assume that the dramatic interest might, too, be divided. But the grip of Intolerance, to our way of thinking, surpasses The Birth of a Nation. Power, punch, and real thrills are there--thrills to equal the preceding Griffith spectacle. Its themes are overtopped by spectacular trappings, dwarfing them in a measure. The modern story, in its melodramatic present day-edness, seems a bit below the key of the historical divisions. It is lurid, even conventional, in its final working out. But, in its early moments, it points a caustic finger upon certain phases of modern charity, particularly upon the salaried uplifter. And it is the one vigorous story of the spectacle.

Griffith makes his point in Intolerance. There are obvious moments, moments a bit overdone, lapses to banality, but, on the whole, Intolerance is a mighty thing. Its spectacular appeal is certain.

The musical arrangement of Joseph Carl Breil has impressive moments. There is no strain, however, to equal the barbaric African theme which ran through The Birth of a Nation.

The production has been awaited for new methods of plot handling and production. The mingling of four themes of different periods, told in parallel form, has not been tried before. It was a daring experiment. The method of blending the plots, switching from one to the other, is adroitly done. It will have its effect upon coming productions.

The Production

The spectacle, a number of times reveals close-ups of characters' faces which occupy the whole screen. Sometimes these advance in the camera eye to full screen size. It is an effective way of driving home the dramatic mood of the scene.

We find Griffith making his usual frequent and effective use of detail, as in the flashes of the doves in the shadows of the house as Christ passes, the close-ups of the Hebrews in the Judean streets, the page boy half asleep in French court, and the modern girl tending her pitiful little geranium in her tenement room.

Skillful use is made of camera tricks in handling the seeming hurling of soldiers from the Babylonian walls. We apparently see them strike the ground in front of the camera.

Care has been taken with the sub-titles. The bombastic captions of The Birth of a Nation are absent. Some humor and much historical information are to be found in the sub-captions of Intolerance.

The camera work everywhere is beautifully artistic. We recall, for instance, nothing in screen production more striking than the episode of Christ and the woman taken in adultery.

Cast of "Intolerance" Long and Able

The cast of principals is long and able. Mae Marsh stands pre-eminent for her touching playing of the girl of the modern story. Seena Owen makes a striking and unforgettable figure as Attarea, the favorite of Belshazzar. She lends genuine appeal to the picturesque role. Constance Talmadge gives buoyancy and spirit to the mountain girl. Miriam Cooper sounds a certain poignant note as a modern girl wrecked on the wheel of sordid city life. Margery Wilson has opportunity to reveal little more than prettiness as the Huguenot heroine.

Robert Harron makes the most of his role of the boy of the modern story, almost a victim on the altar of modern intolerance. Alfred Paget's playing of Belshazzar has nobility and humanness. Tully Marshall makes the High Priest of Bel sinister and clean cut.

There are scores of slender roles well done. Prominent among these is the huge faithful warrior of Elmo Lincoln, who dies fighting for his king against hopeless odds. The kindly policeman of the modern story, done by Tom Wilson, stands out. Louis Romaine gives realism to the prison chaplain.

All in all, Intolerance is a stupendous production.   It
has the romance of four civilizations.

INTOLERANCE REACHES APEX OF
MOTION PICTURE ART*

Intolerance, the latest production of D. W. Griffith,
was presented at the Liberty theatre, New York, for the
first time on Tuesday, Sept. 5.   It is without a doubt the
biggest and most startling picture ever offered to the public;
or better still it is the biggest achievement ever presented
in any theatrical line.

Back of the ages of the film business; ages which,
though really only a few short years ago, are considered
too long since for the remembrance of correct dates, David
Wark Griffith produced a two reel subject for Biograph entitled The Reformers.   In this subject the director first
gave evidence of his true feelings toward the intolerance of
social reformers; their dissatisfaction with the progress of
society in broader paths than they themselves were able to
comprehend.   It was a program release and probably not
one in a thousand that know the name of Griffith now, knew
it then.   The germ of The Reformers, nourished and encouraged for approximately five years, now, blossoms forth in
new investments in the shape of Mr. Griffith's gigantic and
stupendous work, Intolerance.

We give this anecdote merely to allow the reader to
grasp the full history of Intolerance.   Mr. Griffith spent
over three years in its production and probably three times
that number in turning over the ideas incorporated in it.
We do not intend to imply that The Reformers and Intolerance are at all alike; they resemble one another only in basic
principles.   The one was the birth of an idea; the other the
idea at full growth--a growth that few ideas attain.

To drive home his belief that Intolerance is the greatest of the world's evils, Mr. Griffith has recourse to the
picturization of four parallel themes, one ancient, one sacred,

*Reprinted from Motion Picture News, Vol. 14, No. 12,
September 23, 1916, pages 1884 and 1887.

one medieval and one modern. These themes have little in
common save for their one underlying idea of the wickedness
of Intolerance. In the ancient theme he depicts the fall of
Babylon, the collapse of one of the greatest civilizations of
the world through Intolerance. In the medieval, the destruction of the kingdom of France at the time of Charles IX is
pictured--again the cause is Intolerance. In the sacred theme
he shows the developments which led to the crucifixion of the
Christ through Intolerance. In the modern, wherein a more
personal story is presented, the intolerance of a band of social uplifters who seek notoriety through misplaced philan-
thropy and who in so doing bring disaster upon a group of
toilers, is portrayed.

Themes Not Developed in Historical Sequence

Instead of relating these four themes in historical
sequence, Mr. Griffith treats first one, then another, then
another, then one and then another; developing each to a certain climax, then switching to the next, developing that to a
point of equal force, then concentrating his attentions on the
next. His ability to concentrate on each theme by turns
enables the audience to follow each trend of action without
confusion. Following this method of procedure he comes to
his closing reels with four climaxes of equal power on his
hands and the intensity of each individual denouement is mul-
tiplied threefold by the intensity of the parallel themes. A
new method of story telling this--another innovation from Mr.
Griffith--one that only he could employ successfully.

Of the individual themes presented, that of the Babylonian period is the most spectacular and thrilling, that of
the birth of Christianity the most impressive, that of the
massacre in France the most tragic and that of the present
time the most humanly interesting. Intolerance truly appeals
to every human emotion--none are neglected.

The siege of Babylon by Cyrus and his hosts with
Belshazzar, the ruler and his followers holding the walls
beggars description. The furious fighting is so realistic that
the onlooker is positively awe-struck. We thought the height
of realism in motion picture warfare had been reached but
Intolerance shatters all previous records. The battling soldiers on the siege towers and the tremendous walls of the
city, the hurling of the firebrands, the pounding of the rams
and the charges of the chariots and the ranks and ranks of

AND THE

D. W. Griffith surveys the <u>Intolerance</u> Babylonian set.

soldiers pouring upon the city--these are shown in flashes of the siege and there is much more besides. Of the settings themselves in these scenes much could be written. The banquet hall which seems to reach a mile in length and the walls, broad enough to accommodate two chariots, are the most expensive. Historical research conducted by Mr. Griffith's under-workers has assured correctness in detail in all these settings. They alone are worth the admission price.

With the massacre of the Huguenots, ordered by Charles IX at the instigation of his mother, Catherine de Medici, there is more of the spectacular and the extreme realistic. The story of the Christ is dwelt on least of all. We see Him at the wedding feast turning water into wine, we see Him with the Magdalene and with the little children. The crucifixion is arranged in double exposure, a method of production that gives the right touch of spiritualism with which such a scene should be endowed.

Sympathetic Touches Skillfully Introduced

But even with such spectacular effects as the fall of Babylon and the medieval massacre, Mr. Griffith has not forgotten his personal touches. He of all others knows the value of introducing an intimate thread amidst the spectacular. He knows that a flash of a baby on the screen will always appeal and he knows what delight an audience gets from the sight of animals. It is his ability to combine the spectacular with the intimate that makes him great--or at least that is part of his greatness.

And so with the Babylonian theme he introduces the story of a mountain girl who worships the sight of Belshazzar. From the time she is introduced ranting in the marriage market until she dies defending her king, she is a constant center of interest. Constance Talmadge in this role creates an exceedingly sprightly and attractive character. The romance of Brown Eyes and her lover so rudely ended by the massacre furnishes the personal interest for the medieval story, while of course the story of the Christ needs nothing personal other than itself.

Modern Story Is Mostly Personal

The modern story is mostly all personal. In it Mr. Griffith takes a hard whack at the mercenary reformists. His plot concerns a young husband and wife who suffer unjustly at their hands, but who come through all right finally after a governor's pardon, thrillingly procured, has arrived just in time to save the husband from the gallows. This part of the picture, too, offers the greatest opportunities for acting, which are most ably taken care of. Mae Marsh as the wife surpassed her wonderful success in The Birth of a Nation and Robert Harron as the husband has seldom appeared to such good advantage.

Other principals who appear in one part of the production or another are Josephine Crowell, Frank Bennett, (excellent as Charles IX), Margey Wilson, Elmer Clifton, Eugene Pallette, Alfred Paget, Seena Owen, Miriam Cooper, Walter Long and Lillian Gish. We find such well known members of the Griffith players as Bessie Love, Howard Gaye, George Walsh, Lloyd Ingraham, Max Davidson, Edward Dillon, George Siegmann and others doing parts that amount to little more than bits.

In a production of such magnitude as Intolerance, the camera work is almost a consideration second to none. It can only be added here that G. W. Bitzer and his staff have done flawless work in every instance. Some of the tints procured on the panoramas are little short of marvellous.

It is natural that many will ask themselves and others whether Intolerance is as good as The Birth of a Nation. From every standpoint it is, certainly. But as for comparisons one might as well attempt to compare the light shed by the moon with that of the sun--the two have an entirely different effect.

THE MAKING OF A MASTERPIECE*
by Edward Weitzel

Sidelights on How D. W. Griffith Conceived and Executed His Great Motion Picture "Intolerance"

After the curtain has descended upon the last scene of D. W. Griffith's colossal spectacle, now being shown at the Liberty theater, New York City, and the mighty palaces of Babylon, the terrible Massacre of St. Bartholomew, the tragedy on Calvary, the impressive story of a modern day, and all the wizardry of a master producer's art is locked up in the small tin boxes that a man may carry away under his arm, the theater on Forty-Second street becomes the scene of long continued and exacting labors. The chief laborer is D. W. Griffith. Since the opening performance of his great picture he has been at the theater from eight in

*Reprinted from The Moving Picture World, Vol. 29, No. 14, September 30, 1916, page 2084.

the morning until two the next morning busily at work. Count-
ing the house attachés, one hundred and thirty'five people are
required to give an exhibition of Intolerance.   When this is
over, the orchestra begins rehearsing new music or the producer and his staff of electricians and photographic experts
try different lighting effects by the use of colored "foots" or
"borders," the rapidly changing scenes on the screen being
lit up with the same care given a performance on the spoken
stage.   Between orders and suggestions to his "crews," after
the matinee one afternoon last week, the tireless but never
ruffled director gave the writer some information as to how
he came to conceive his wonderful photoplay.   The remark,
"You seem to be a very busy man, Mr. Griffith," brought
the smiling reply, "Oh, yes, I'm a day-and-night laborer.
This is the first duty of a director--to be always on the job."

"How did you come to conceive Intolerance?"

"That is a hard question to answer.   It just growed--
like Topsy.   I didn't want to make it, principally on account
of the expense.   It cost four and a half times more than The
Birth of a Nation, and I felt that, after that achievement,
some one else should experiment with such costly productions;
but the subject took possession of me, and I thought it out.
No scenario was ever made for it, you know."

"Do you mean that you carried all the scenes in your
head?"

"Oh, no. I jotted down a general plan and followed
it--at times."

"You are not a believer in the perfect scenario, then?
The working plans, in which every scene, incident and detail of production have been thought out and written down?"

The director's eyes lighted up with an amused smile,
as he shook his head.   "Hardly, the human equation renders
that an impossibility.   It is only when the director gets to
handling his humans, singly or en masse, that he knows
what he wants--or doesn't want.   The unconscious expression
on the face of an actor, a gesture by the leading lady, may
give him a new and greatly improved train of thought."

"How did you dare attempt so revolutionary a scheme
as running four parallel plots in the same picture?"

"Perhaps because it was revolutionary. I felt that
we have not begun to realize the possibilities of the moving
picture art, and such a radical departure from the old rules
promised novel effects, at least. By the way, have you discovered the secret of how we keep from confusing the four
plots in the mind of a spectator? It's by telling such a
short portion of each story at a time and by running them
all at the same tempo. The rate of speed at which the reel
is unwound is a very important factor in showing a picture,
you know. Heywood Broun, in his notice in the Tribune, remarked that the racing chariot of the mountain girl of ancient
Babylon and the rushing train and speeding automobile of today seemed to be very close to each other. The characters
are all on the same errand, and human hearts have been
alike in all ages; only the garments that cover the body dif-
fer. Here again, the same tempo helped to bridge the long
lapse of time. To return to the question of expense. One
of the most costly scenes is the dance of the female slaves
on the steps of the palace in Babylon. We had Ruth St. Denis teaching the movements to the large ballet for days, yet
on the screen the scene lasts only a few seconds. Even a
close-up often requires hours of work, the right expression
being difficult to catch."

"How long were you in getting ready the Babylonian
scenes?"

"We had over three hundred workmen on the job from
July to the following April. The buildings were made of staff,
the same material as that used at the San Francisco exposi-
tion. In preparing the Euphrates, we dammed up a river in
California, and planted reeds and palm trees on its banks.
You would hardly suspect that the scene of the onrush of the
army of Cyrus is not far from Los Angeles. Excuse me
for a moment." Mr. Griffith cast a critical look at the stage.
"Those lights won't do, Bob, they are throwing shadows in
the corners of the scene. Try a different color."

There was no impatience or indication of worry as
the order was given. Mr. Griffith had been at the same work
for days, but his smile was as pleasant and his self-control
as complete as ever. The secret of his success in handling
men and women lies very close to this fact.

"In preparing for Intolerance, Mr. Griffith, did you
follow the method of Sir Henry Irving and call in a number

of famous antiquarians and painters of ancient historical subjects?"

"Not in the flesh. The scenes and incidents are all authentic, but our information was obtained from the writings of the different wise men. The legends of Creation, the Fall and the Deluge are all found in the cuneiform writings of Bal, the High Priest, who betrayed Belshazzar and his city to Cyrus, you are aware, of course?"

"What are you going to produce next, Mr. Griffith? Another supreme effort?"

Again the maker of masterpieces smiled that amused smile of his. "I hope not. I'm willing that some one else should try the experiment. I prefer to make some simple five-reel pictures; they do not tie up large sums of money."

"What about the future of the motion picture?"

"We are only at the beginning of this thing. New and important improvements arc bound to be discovered and the farther we attempt to get away from the art of the spoken stage, the more pronounced will be our advancement. Returning to Intolerance, we are attracting all kinds and conditions of men. The other evening a well known priest of this city came to me, between the acts, and said: 'I must tell you, Mr. Griffith, that I had serious doubts about the propriety of coming here. I was afraid the scenes from the life of the Savior might shock me, but they have been handled with due reverence. As for the rest of the picture, it has made me feel like God, as if I had the power to look down upon all humanity.' At the end of the performance a pugilistic friend of mine stopped me in the lobby to say: 'I'm comin' ag'in tomorrer night, Grif! I don't know much 'bout all yer high brow stuff, but there's something' 'bout th' show that's got me on me ear!'"

It was long after dinner time when the writer bade Mr. Griffith good bye, and the last words which came through the closing door of the theater were: "That is still the wrong shade, Bob; try another color in your border lights." A boundless capacity for work and rubber-tired efficiency are important assets in the makeup of David W. Griffith.

THE REAL STORY OF INTOLERANCE*
by Henry Stephen Gordon

"Often in my atrabiliar moods when I read of pompous
ceremonials," writes Herr Diogenes Teufelsdrockh, ... "and
how the ushers, macers, and pursuivants are all in waiting;
how Duke this is presented by Arch Duke that, and Colonel
A by General B, and innumerable Bishops, Admirals, and
miscellaneous Functionaries are advancing gallantly to the
Anointed Presence; and I strive in my remote privacy to
form a clear picture of that solemnity, --on a sudden as by
some enchanter's wand the, --shall I speak it? the Clothes
fly off the whole dramatic corps; and Dukes, Grandees, Bishops, Generals, Anointed Presence itself, every mother's
son of them, stand straddling there not a shirt on them; and
I know not whether to weep or laugh."

That quality of seeing mankind stripped of its con-
cealments which Herr Teufelsdrockh had in company with
Rabelais, is the fearless theme of D. W. Griffith's latest,
and he says his last, photodrama, --Intolerance.

The Birth of a Nation made him a rich man; money,
gold, at once began to flow toward him, over his shoulders,
--would it submerge him?

Would it drown the poetry which he had coined into
tremendous dividends?

Could he write a second camera epic?

He has.

There is no provision that can determine the event
of an effort which depends on the mood and perception of the
vast many; Intolerance when this is printed will have made
itself, or will have unmade Griffith, judged by the peerless
jury of dollars in the box office.   Judged by the tables of
Verity and of Art, it stands as a terrific arraignment of
fustian humanity, under the indictment brought by implacable
Fact.

*Reprinted from Photoplay, Vol. 10, No. 6, November 1916,
pages 27-40.

Those seventy-five millions of people out of the hundred millions of our population who are writing at scenarios will be interested in knowing where and how this theme was written.

It never was written.

It was created by suffering.

I have told you of Griffith's combat with hypocrisy and imperious traditional Boetianism from the day he stepped forth from the impoverished manse of the Kentucky plantation, to and through his struggle for the survival of The Birth of a Nation; of how in one community the creations of the negro vote, and in others where the negro was not maintained in his odor of martyrdom, the decayed prejudices of the Civil War were venomously injected into the controversy for artistic survival.

"The Truth?   What is Truth?" asked Pontius Pilate.

And all through the centuries since, you and I and the other fellow have been shouting. "Truth is what I believe."

After he had won the scrap and The Birth of a Nation pictured the registering of gold, Griffith determined to do one more photodrama,--and he said then, and says now, only one more,--and in that he would give some manner of response to Mr. Pilate.

He did not look over the card indices of scenarios which Frank Woods had listed, though he did think of the Bible and of the temperamental incident that happened between Cain and Abel because of jealousy and thereby hatred.

But a report of a Federal Industrial Commission fell into his hands and therein he found a large part of his never written scenario.

In that report was a mention of a certain combination of chemical factories,--a business combination under the control of a man who was fervid in charity, acrobatically zealous in ecclesiastical activity.

He did not wear a halo in public, but he was invested with one by all the financial secretaries of Societies for the Propagation of Piety Among the Humble Poor, or for the gratuitous distribution of Tracts to the Hungry.

This official report went on in the coldly mechanical style of an adding machine to tell the profits of this Chemical Trust; the public had previously had described to it how generously the head of the concern used his share for promulgation of Beneficence accompanied by brass tablets bearing the name of the Founder of the particular Beneficence.

With no particular emphasis the report said among other minutiae that the laborers in the plants of the company were paid $1.60 a day; that living conditions had altered may or may not have been indicated, but the workmen wickedly refused to be comforted because their overlord gave hundreds of thousands of the dollars they had aided in the making, to an Evangelical Society for Enlightening Natives of Boroboolaa Gha with Warming Pans.

Those workmen had no objections to the Overlord spending his pocket money for Tracts or Warming Pans or Brass Tablets, but they wanted $2.00 for slowly stifling their souls in the vats of his works.

The Overlord said them nay, and they struck, and the Overlord employed goths and ostrogoths in the guise of deputy sheriffs and constables as is the custom of Overlords since the trade in Hessians and Swiss mercenaries has gone into desuetude; and the wage scale of $1.60 a day was maintained, and the men all came back to work in submission,--all except nineteen.

These nineteen could not testify to their humble change of view because the Overlord's little army of private grenadiers had exercised the military basic principle of Frightfulness; the missing nineteen had had their heads shot off and had thus escaped the righteous punishment of being sent to jail for ingratitude.

On that feeble incident of ignorance of man's kinship, of hatred of gentleness and right, Griffith built the theme of Intolerance; he cast back five thousand years into the supreme civilization of Babylon and there planted one of his incidents; he walked down the aisles of Time to that St. Bartholomew's Day when hatred and fear cut the throat of the best thought and patriotism of France, and there he planted another romantic incident; with the living Christ in Nazareth he finds a living theme; and then to yesterday, or today or tomorrow as you like, he came and rooted there another, making the quadripartite of romance, of truth, and ingenuous fearlessness of the evil that is in all hearts; the substance of his

unanswerable charge is that all the evil, cruelty and wrong
of the world comes from man's implacable belief that what
each man believes to be true, is true, and all else is false,
wicked, and should be destroyed.

In making his first big picture Griffith while using no
scenario, did have the memory of reading the Thomas Dixon
novel to guide his progress, though, as you will remember
the picture is far from following the details of the story.   In
this Intolerance he had little more than his own idea of the
incident in the Industrial Commission's report on the Christian charity of its Overlord, and the intolerable audacity of
those nineteen laborers, who were blinded by their intolerance of believing they were entitled to more of Life than
$1. 60 a day would buy.

At the first "runoff" of this picture in the little pro-
jecting room of his studio, Griffith had as audience one of
the foremost war correspondents of this era,--a man with
not a shred of emotion left to him; a night editor of thirty
years dealing with the dramatic of life, and to whom the
dramatic had become a puerile everyday incident; a city
editor who was on intimate terms with all the grinning skele-
tons of a big city, and a writer of a long life spent in chron-
icling most of the tragedies and comedies of a huge country,
with the machinery of the stage direction of them at his fing-
ers tips.

When the last foot of film had passed these sat silent,
the fibre of their natures torn and ravelled; they could say
nothing; one rose and without phrase grasped Griffith's hand.

Those four world-worn men had been shown not only
the futile hypocrisy of the rest of the world, but their own
as well.

And then from the darkness of the little room came
the sound of the voice of Griffith; possibly he felt from the
silence of his audience that the picture had failed to impress;
possibly he was moved himself; he is as facile in betraying
his emotions as the Sphynx.

He told of his last visit to his Kentucky homestead;
of an admirable, gentle-hearted, Christian-spirited, high-bred
woman of near relationship, of deep orthodox belief; of how
this woman whenever she saw a well-known Christian Scien-
tist of the place approaching, would cross the street; of how

a Catholic priest had installed a chapel of his faith there
and of how all of the other creeds combatted his work.

It was an epitome of the story of Babylon we had just
seen; the glorious city of a glorious civilization where one
of the first and one of the best Bibles had originated,--and
all of it made the victim of hate and jealousy and greed.

Remembering that this later picture attacks with the
precision of mathematics all intolerance, the result of its
effect in the "tryouts" in neighboring places to where it was
produced might give the Devil a richer idea than ever of
the comedy of human seriousness.

So far none of the creeds, theories, or sociological
ideas which the picture eviscerates has had its followers
respond with a single protest; each sees the picture and goes
away thoroughly satisfied that it is not his pet belief which
is assailed, but that of the fellow who believes differently;
Catholic, Jew, Protestant, possible survivors of the Babylonic theogony; prohibitionists, wine-makers, liberals and
conservatists, all have been pleased and flattered by what
they have seen.

What Mr. John D. Rockefeller, the friends of the late
Russell Sage, Mr. Carnegie, and the bounders who have been
founders, will have to say remains locked in the secret now,
of the photoplay's success or failure.

When it is plain as a pike staff that intolerance of
prohibition is a feature of the drama, what are we to think
of prohibition leaders in prohibition Riverside praising the
picture?

When it is equally an assault on money bending thought
and creed to its devices, what deduction follows when a mil-
lionaire who has endowed colleges of sectarian type found
the picture when shown at Pomona altogether admirable?

When in one appalling scene Protestants are shown
savagely slaying Catholics and in another the murders of
St. Bartholomew's Day are depicted in ghastly reality and
Protestants and Catholics both have found the picture to their
taste, what can you think?

Nothing can be thought save that the great drama shown
has undisturbed our universal capacity of seeing only that side
of the shield which reflects ourselves.

"Is this truly to be your last picture?" Griffith was asked.

"It is," he replied; "intolerance that I have met with and fought with in my other picture makes it impossible to ask investment of the tremendous sums of money required for a real feature film with the result dependent on the whim or the lack of brains of a captain of police."

At that "runoff" showing, after the four spectators of fishy capacity for emotion had found their feet again firmly fastened in the clay of the commonplace, one said, "You've made a wonderful picture but you did have to pull the 'old stuff' to send 'em away with a good taste in their mouth.

"You're plucky but you didn't dare finish the picture true to life, and have The Boy executed, as he would have been in real life; Carlyle might well have written your scenario up to that finale; but there you allowed the Despot of the stage to rule and you saved The Boy simply to satisfy the lust for comfort which audiences demand."

"You're one of the fellows who would have stood up and answered Pilate's question, 'What is Truth?' " said Griffith.

"That finale is Truth, and because it is a comfortable truth you thought it false.

"If you had read the newspapers as much as you've written for them, you would know about the Stielow case in New York; Stielow was convicted of a murder and sentenced to die; four times he was prepared for the chair, four times he and his family suffered every agony save the final swish of the current.

"What saved him was exactly what saved 'The Boy' in my picture; the murderer confessed, the final reprieve arrived just as the man was ready to be placed in the chair, his trousers' leg already slit for the electrode."

And picking up the copy of the New York paper containing the account, Griffith read former president Taft's sentence of the criminal law, "The administration of criminal law in this country is a disgrace to civilization."

The man who objected to the conventionally happy

finale did it because he fancied himself just a bit more cultured than most and believed that Art was only true in being disagreeable.

There are no great actors in Intolerance, none whom you will recognize, though Sir Herbert Tree, I am told, in one scene played an extra man's part, just to be in the picture.

DeWolf Hopper for the same purpose in another scene was one of the hundreds in a mob.

Tully Marshall donned the robes of a priest for one brief scene.

But of the players in general, few names will be recognized.

One of them is the woman who rocks the cradle in that mournfully magnificent recurring interlude.

That is Miss Lillian Gish.

Nabonidus the King was done by an extra man.

Out of the sixty-odd thousand people who appear these are probably the ones who will be more or less known to the public.

In the modern story:

> Mae Marsh as The Girl.
> Robert Harron as The Boy.
> Fred Turner as The Father.
> Sam de Grasse as Jenkins, the mill owner.
> Vera Lewis, Jenkins' sister, who creates the "Foundation."
> Walter Long, the Musketeer of the slums.
> Miriam Cooper, The Friendless Woman.
> Tom Wilson, The Kindly Heart.
> Ralph Lewis, The Governor.
> Lloyd Ingraham, The Judge.
> The French period:
> Frank Bennett, as Charles IX.
> Mrs. Crowell as Catherine de Medici.
> Joseph Henabery as Admiral Coligny.
> Margery Wilson as Brown Eyes.

Spottiswoode Aitken as Her Father.
A. D. Sears as The Mercenary.
Eugene Pallette as La Tour.
W. E. Lawrence as Henry of Navarre.
Babylonic period:
Alfred Paget as Belshazzar.
Seena Owen as Princess Atteraia.
George Siegmann (Griffith's chief director) as Cyrus.
Constance Talmadge as The Mountain Girl.
Elmer Clifton as The Rhapsode.
E. Lincoln as The Faithful Guard.
Jewish Period:
Howard Gaye as Christ.
Olga Grey as Mary Magdalene.
Lillian Langdon as Mary.
Bessie Love as The Bride.
George Walsh as The Bridegroom.
William Brown as The Bride's Father.

If you have seen the picture when this appears, or
when you do see it, those are about all the characters you
will recognize as played by known people, if you are the
most erudite "fan."

And you will see thousands on thousands of others,
all apparently expert artists, all trained to the thousandth
fraction of right "registering."

Griffith does not believe that an actor can make a
producer a success, but he has proved that a producer can
make an extra man an actor.

Those fighting scenes of the picture were made by
men trained to the same degree of ferocity that has made
the killers in the Somme region turn the fields of France
into human abattoirs.

During the progress of the making of the picture they
became known as "Griffith's Man-Killers."

The story is told that later Cecil de Mille of Lasky's
wanted some foot soldiers in a fight scene he had to make,
and requisitioned the Man-Killers.

They were to be entrenched, and a column of cavalry
was to sweep down and annihilate them.

They were carefully rehearsed and all went well until the camera was placed and the action began.

Then the cavalry caracoled out and spurred their horses at them.

Some fellow in the trench yelled "Here they come, fellers, now show the dash-blanks what Griffith's Killers can do!"

They did; all the rehearsal directions vanished, they couched their lances and unhorsed every trooper, and then ran them off the field,--and spoiled the scene.

I can well believe the story, for I was a witness of one of the assaults by Cyrus on the walls of Babylon.

The barbarians swept over our spearproof safety coign, and we had to dodge arrows and javelins while scudding for the clear.

George Siegmann, a man as big as two Huns, strove to subdue their onslaught as they were driving the Babylonians too swiftly for the camera, and meanwhile the Babylonians took advantage of the relief expedition by Siegmann and retreated within the city.

Did those barbarians care?

Only so much as to fall on each others neck and crop until there was a riot of directors.

There were only sixty calls for the ambulance that day, but the injuries when examined at the studio hospital did not exceed those pleasing black eyes, bent noses and gallant contusions, which are the croix de guerre of any well-designed scrap.

There was no fatality at all in the taking of the picture, though many times several thousands of warriors had to contend with life-like verity of death.

One man was killed when it was all over.

This by a sardonic freak of Fate was a steeplejack employed because of his surety of foot on heights.

When a small set was being dismantled after the taking of the picture this juggler with altitude was employed as one of the wrecking crew of carpenters.

He was at work on a scaffold eighteen feet from the ground when he made a misstep, fell, and never knew what had happened.

For weeks before he had been stationed on the perilous points hundreds of feet high and had gayly coquetted with death from a station which would make a bluewater sailor dizzy.

I believe that of all the impressiveness of this picture the recurrent scene of Rocking The Cradle will be found most enduring in its elusive poetry of symbolism.

How this came to be created illustrates a Griffith trait.

Years ago when he was in a road company with Wilfred Lucas the two were walking one day when Lucas saw a woman rocking a cradle.

He called the scene to Griffith's attention and quoted the Walt Whitman lines:

> "... endlessly rocks the cradle,
> "Uniter of Here and Hereafter."

"Who wrote that?" asked Griffith.

"That's from Walt Whitman," said Lucas, "you'll find it somewhere in his 'Leaves of Grass.'"

Griffith said nothing but darted away and found a book store, bought a copy of Whitman, and it happened as he opened the book the leaves parted at the very passage.

That was twelve or fifteen years ago.

But when the idea of Intolerance came to his mind Griffith recalled those lines, imagined the picture of the eternal cradle, and there you have Walt Whitman's thought photographed.

This chronicler is far from being a hero worshiper; I

The cover of the original souvenir program for <u>Intolerance</u>.

have been on much too intimate terms with far too many
heroes to fondle any illusions about them; they often wear
patent leather shoes with spats, and sometimes they bandoline
their hair, and often they are careless about marriage vows
and going to church, and paying debts, and occasionally I've
met the best of them who can adroitly eat peas with his knife,
and a lot of them wear wrist watches, and some use perfum-
ery, but when a man can make a camera fasten to a negative
film Walt Whitman's intellect he is none of these types but
a man hero, and I kow-tow to him as being no less a poet
than Whitman himself.

Beyond argument the measure of achievement today
is that of money.

How much did it cost?   will be the prime question
about this work of beauty.

I know exactly and I will tell you exactly.

This picture of Intolerance cost five times as much
as The Birth of a Nation.

But what the latter cost no one but those who paid
the cost know.

The press agents concerned, claimed all manner of
figures from $250,000 up to half a million.

An estimate from a number of those expert in judging, places the expenditure for The Birth of a Nation close
to $100,000, some going as high as $200,000, none going
much below the first figure.

This last picture has been two years in the actual
making, and work on the preparatory stages was begun over
three years ago; considerably more than sixty thousand people
were engaged at one time and another in the acting, and more
in the various forms of effort outside of the acting.

I do happen to know authoritatively that much over
300,000 feet of film was used in the making and that this
was cut in the "assembling" to the present limit of the picture of between 12,000 and 13,000 feet.

As for carefulness, it is a fact that the captions have
been set and changed close to two thousand times.

As for Griffith himself, he has put his heart's substance into the labor.

I saw him the day before he left for New York; he was brave, even gay mentally, jesting and debonair; but he was gaunt and excited though in thorough self command.

I asked him, "Now that your work is over what is your idea of your future?   What is your next ambition?"

He looked frankly at me and said unsmilingly.   "My idea of life now is a tremendously large bed, in some place where no telephone, no messenger boy, no newspaper, no telegram, no voice, can reach me, and to sleep for a solid week, only waking very occasionally long enough to eat a good dinner, and then roll over and again sleep. "

"What will you do if <u>Intolerance</u> fails?"   I asked.

Blandly smiling, he said, "I'll seek the Jersey coast and try to find one of those man-eating sharks. "

"And what if it wins?"

"I have told you before that this will be my last picture.

"That is as true as anything can be which the future holds. "

"The speaking stage, producing drama?"

"I have told you before that such was my desire; if the picture succeeds it will not, it cannot, make the money that in fabulous fashion pictures are credited with making; theatres cannot hold as much money as some newspapers say some pictures make.

"The matter of the money to be made is very like the fellow blowing the bassoon in the orchestra who was told to blow louder; 'That's all very well,' he replied, 'but where is the wind to come from?' "

He says he intends to take up the stage next as a means of finding expression unhampered, but when asked what he would do, and how, he side-stepped.

"There will never be any combination of the speaking
and the photo drama," he added with a tang at satire, "not
if audiences can help it.

"The stage is perfect now, to my mind, because it
enables us to make moving pictures so much easier than it
might.

"I'm sorry that Mansfield, that Daly, that Irving, are
dead, but as a moving picture man I am glad, for the movies'
sake, that they are gone. If those men were now alive, we
of the movies would have to work harder than we do, and
I don't know how that could be done, for I figure that now
we work fourteen and fifteen hours a day, but if the stage
were different we would have to work thirty-six hours in the
twenty-four; so we are glad that competition with the stage
is not fiercer than it is."

"Don't you regard the modern part of your picture
as an attack on the courts, on judges?"

"I certainly do not, because it is not.

"That Stielow case in New York is exactly like the
murder case in the story; only reality goes the picture three
better in the way of reprieves. Stielow and his family faced
death-suffering four times, and three times the reprieve came
at the very last minute.

"If I had shown scenes like that on the screen it
would have made the public laugh as impossible, but the
people should not laugh at the courts; judges do not make
the laws, you, I, everyone, are responsible for the laws.

"I have met several judges and have always found
them very nice and often very wonderful men. Real gentlemen, in fact.

"What has seemed peculiar to me about the law is
that after so prolonged an experiment with the principles of
Christianity we still find as was found through all the ages
that justice demands if a man kills another he in turn should
be murdered.

"No, I am far from attacking the courts or judges,
for the only thing that has stood between the pictures and

the censors and thereby prevented the pictures from utter extinction, has been the courts. "

Here are his reasons as dictated by himself, for making no more feature pictures.

"It appears that henceforth there will be no middle ground in the pictures; there will be the ten, twenty and thirty cent pictures, and the big two dollar ones.

"The first classification does not attract me, and the second offers too many stupid, cruel, costly and apparently ineradicable offensives.

"Of necessity the stage must tell the truth more freely than any other method of expression. It is the only means existing today of even attempting to portray the truth.

"I do not mean the drama as it is known to Broadway, but the drama as it is known to dramatists.

"I have tried to tell the truth in my new picture.

"But I find that what we call the Movies are less free now than ever, and are more and more dependent on the censor, and on that account I feel inclined to stop.

"There are but a few means of conveying what we believe to be truth; the college is seriously handicapped, as too many of the universities are endowed by a few rich men whose brain power has been used only to acquire wealth; these have little or no knowledge beyond their immediate needs; they have never taken the time to gain knowledge of human nature in the little nor in the mass; they have their own ideas of life and deride everything foreign to their own little circles; they know little of the present and less of the past.

"There is very little doubt that most college professors' opinions on morals, politics, and even on history, are very different in their private and their public capacities.

"Who can believe that a man dependent on a university will have an opinion for the public which is not more or less sicklied with the pale cast of thought about the men who put up the money for the institution?

"The world can hope for no boldness of verity from the colleges.

"The preacher of today is as always, swayed to some extent by the majority of the sect to which he belongs; he can seldom speak as an individual, and of necessity he cannot launch what may seem a new truth that infringes on what was an old truth, and remain in his denomination.

"I wondered recently at the daring of a certain professor of Assyriology who said in a little-read magazine that the average normal being of today would find himself with more decent associates and in happier surroundings in Babylon, or ancient Egypt, than in any intervening period of the world's history, up to the Eighteenth Century.

"The newspaper and magazine appeal to a certain clientele which they must please, and are forced to listen as a rule to the hydra-headed monster called Public Clamor, more than to her gentler sister, Public Opinion.

"But the producer of a feature picture depends on a much larger audience than any of these means; he does not have to defer to what Mrs. Smith thinks, or what Mr. Jones believes, for he has a million Mrs. Smiths and a million of Mr. Jones, and he is far more certain to get a fair hearing, or he would be if it were not for the censor.

"Isn't the folly of it all palpable?   Because a new idea is expressed people are not forced to accept it.   But certainly in this country there should be no objection to the discussion of all subjects.

"What kind of people, what sort of race, can continue to exist that is afraid of discussion?

"The politics of the world is founded on so much hypocrisy that everything is done, not for what is right, nor even against what is wrong, but for the effect on a majority of the people.

"That is why all Europe is slaughtering.

"That is why 'Christian' nations will murder Turks and crucify pagans and slay with zest 'foreigners.'

"A 'foreigner' is always a man with a head so dense that he will not think as we think.

"The story for Truth as we see it has become barred from the pictures, so that anyone who has a real idea to express should not look to the moving picture as a means, but if he has enough money, to the stage.

"We of the moving picture craft admit our defeat; it is impossible for us to take any big subject of interest without the fear of the autocrats above us taking away our property.

"I now contemplate turning to the stage in making an attempt to find freedon of expression."

This ends what I have to tell about David W. Griffith.

THE SHADOW STAGE*
by Julian Johnson

The metropolitan critics who preceded me in learned discourse upon Mr. Griffith's sun-play, Intolerance, shot away all the superlatives which were our common property. Thus deprived of the communal ammunition I must lay about me with a week-day set of words and present facts garnished neither with rhapsody nor raillery.

Intolerance is a collective story of the penalties paid through the centuries to those "who do not believe as we believe." It occupied its maker's entire attention for at least a year and a half. Both the notion and the generalship are his. Intolerance is more than the world's biggest photoplay. In size and scope it is the biggest art-work of any description in a decade.

Here is a joy-ride through history; a Cook's tour of the ages; a college education crammed into a night. It is the most incredible experiment in story-telling that has ever been tried. Its uniqueness lies not in a single yarn, but in the way its whole skein of yarns is plaited.

Its distinct periods are four: Babylon, at the end of the regency of Prince Belshazzar; Judea, in the time of Christ;

---

*Reprinted from Photoplay, Vol. 11, No. 1, December 1916, pages 77-81.

France under the inquisitorial high tide of St. Bartholomew's;
and the American Now, with the intolerances of capital, labor,
and the courts.   None of these tales runs straightaway.   You
stand in medieval France and slip on the banana-peel of ret-
rogression to Chaldea.   You are sure America has you--a
wind has aviated you back to Palestine.   It is much like lis-
tening to a quartette of excellent elocutionists simultaneously
reading novels by Arnold Bennett, Victor Hugo, Nathaniel
Hawthorne and Elinor Glyn.

Any of these carnivorous legends would fang you emo-
tionally if you were left long enough in its cage.   But just
as it is about to bite, out you come, slam goes the door,
and you are thrust among the raveners of another century.

There has never been such scenery, anywhere, as
the edifices reared for the Babylonian episode.

Pictorially, the greatest filmings are the Judean scenes,
perfect in composition, ideal in lighting, every one in effect
a Tissot painting of the time of Christ.

The Chaldean visions will teach history to college professors.

Altogether, the accuracy and authority of Intolerance's
historic information is stupendous.

The finest individual acting accomplishments are Mae
Marsh's.   The unique figure is Constance Talmadge, as The
Mountain Girl; the most poignantly beautiful, Seena Owen, as
Attarea, favorite of Belshazzar.   But there are no male as-
sumptions even approaching the chief portrayals in The Birth
of a Nation.

Mr. Bitzer's photography, devoid of anything sensa-
tional, flows like the transparent, limpid style of a finished
writer.   It is without tricks, and without imperfections.

An attempt to assimilate the mountainous lore of this
sun-play at a sitting results in positive mental exhaustion.
The universally-heard comment from the highbrow or no-
brow who has tried to get it all in an evening: "I am so
tired!"

Profoundest of symbols is the Rocking Cradle--"uniter
of here and hereafter"-- which joins the episodes.   This

mysterious ark of life, the stuff of a dream in the dimness
of its great shadowed room, almost belongs to infinity.   Lillian Gish is the brooding mother.

The music is sadly inefficient--the most inefficient
music a big picture ever had.

Thousands upon thousands of feet of this photoplay
never will be seen by the public.   In the taking, this story
rambled in every direction, and D. W. G. relentlessly and
recklessly pursued each ramble to its end.   At least half a
dozen complete minor stories were cut off before the picture
was shown at all.

In all probability, Intolerance will never attain the
popularity of The Birth of a Nation.   It has not that drama's
single, sweeping story.   It appeals more to the head, less
to the heart.

Babylon is the foundation-stone, and seems to have
been the original inspiration, of this visual Babel.   Its mighty
walls, its crowds, its army, have won many long-drawn
"Ahs!" of sky-rocket admiration.   But these were not es-
sentially Griffith--anyone with money can pile up mobs and
scenery.   Mr. Griffith's original talent appears in recreating
the passions, the ambitions, the veritable daily life of a
great people so remote that their every monument is dust,
their every artwork lost, their very language forgotten.   This
is more than talent; it is genius.

You were taught that the Jewish Jehovah traced destruction's warning in letters of fire on the wall of Belshazzar's palace; and that Cyrus, to get in, drained the Euphrates
river and walked on its bed under Babylon's gates.   See this
picture and get the facts.   Babylon was peacefully betrayed
by the priests of Marduk long after it had successfully with-
stood as frenzied a siege as the Persian conqueror could
bring.

Not content with rearing the vast barriers and marvellous gates you have seen illustratively reproduced in these
pages, the California necromancer showed life as it ran its
slender course among the poor more than twenty-five centuries ago.   Always of this undercurrent is The Mountain
Girl, a wild, wonderful little creature, to be followed from
semi-slavery through the civic courts to the marriage market,
where she is released by an impress from the roll-seal Bel-

shazzar has strapped upon his wrist.   Thereafter she is, to
the death, a sweet Amazon in the service of her great Sar.
The camp of Cyrus, with the "Institution" of the Medes and
Persians, is as instructive as a West-Asiatic history.   The
attack upon Babylon, with its terrible towers, its demoniac
"tank" of Greek fire--flaming prophecy of the Somme jug-
gernauts!--its ferocious personal encounters, is unparalleled
in battle spectacles.   Behold the vivid though perhaps dubious
realism of gushy closeups on sword-thrusts.   Heads literally
fly off above shearing swords, hot lead sears, rocks crush,
arrows pierce horridly--and withal there is the unconquerable
animation and fury of ultimate conflict.

        Otherwheres, the sensuous glory of the Chaldean
court.   No brush-master has painted more Oriental splendors
than those boasted by the golden bungalow of Nabonidus, quaint
father of the virile voluptuary, Belshazzar.   Beauty blooms
in wildest luxuriance in this New York of the Euphrates.
The dances of Tammuz, god of springtime, flash forth in
breath-taking nudity and rhythm as frank as meaningful.   They
are flashes, only; that is why they remain in the picture.
One cannot imagine a more beautiful thing than Seena Owen
as Attarea--veritable star of the East.   The tiny battle-chariot
with its cargo of a great white rose, drawn down the table
to Attarea's Belshazzar by two white doves, chances to remain the only untouched thing in the palace of death which
Cyrus enters.   There is pathos!   Tully Marshall as the High
Priest of Bel, Elmer Clifton as the Rhapsode, George Siegmann as Cyrus--three players who are especially redoubtable.

        The magical David pounds his points home by contrast.
From the solemn grandeur of Ishtar's high altar, with its
costly burnt offering of propitiation, he flashes to an aged
widow offering her all to the same deity--three turnips and
a carrot, covered with a little oil.

        The France which our filmetcher rears for the mas-
sacre of St. Bartholomew is as fine a France as Stanley
Weyman pictured in words.   Griffith spares neither exactness
nor feeling.   With delicate touches he builds up keen interest
in the home of Brown Eyes--then slaughters the whole family.
Wonderful characters here are Josephine Crowell's Catherine
de Medici; and Charles IX, as played by Frank Bennett.

        Much has been taken from the Judean scenes, but so
much remains to hail as optic poetry that the loss is negli-
gible.   I can think of nothing finer in the handling of light,

nor in the massing and moving of figures, than the "marriage in Cana." More education! The complete wedding rite, with its odd observances according to Hebrew tradition, is a transcription from Minor Asia such as one cannot find outside the pages of Josephus. Stirringly dramatic, yet faithful to the letter of the gospels, is the scene in which Jesus faces those who would stone the woman taken in adultery. There is a scene of The Christ laughing, conversing, supping, interchanging views--a man among men. And there is the <u>Via Dolorosa.</u>

The modern story is, among other things and preachments, as attack upon the arrogance of "Foundations," and that tyranny of some organized charities which makes their favored more victims than beneficiaries. In its essence, the modern tale seems to me a dull, commonplace movie melodrama. In it Mr. Griffith seems to lose his perspective of character. He makes commonplace types and personifications, not his usual creatures: thinking, feeling men and women.

Mae Marsh and Robert Harron Portray victims of poverty, lack of education and evil surrounding. Both are driven from the home town by strike participation. The boy turns cadet--eventually reforms to marry Mae. His underworld master, "The Musketeer of the Slums," frames him criminally for this desertion, and, in the language of the caption, he is "intolerated away for awhile." In the interim, the Musketeer endeavors to "make" the boy's wife, who has lost her baby to intolerant uplifters. In the grand encounter of Musketeer, Musketeer's girl, boy and wife, the monster is shot, the boy is blamed though the mistress did it, and the capital sentence is carried out--nearly, but not quite-- in the perfect gallows-technique of San Quentin penitentiary.

Best in the modern spectacle are not the dull details of things that happen, but the lifelike performances of those to whom they happen. Mae Marsh's flirtation in court with her husband as the jury deliberates his life away--she a scared, drab little figure of piteous noncomprehension--here is a twittering smile more tragic than the orotund despairs of Bernhardt. Miriam Cooper, as the Musketeer's mistress, gives an overwhelming pastel of jealousy and remorse. All actresses who honestly provide for home and baby by the business of vamping and gunning, would do well to observe Miss Cooper's expressions and gestures. Miss Cooper is police dock--she is blotter transcript. Her face is what you

really see some nights under the green lamps. Harron is
ideal as the boy, and Walter Long, as the Musketeer, approaches but does not equal his performance of Gus, in The
Birth of a Nation.

        Spades are not once termed garden implements in this
sector, nor are the kisses paternal or platonic.

        In this stupendous chaos of history and romance the
lack of a virile musical score is the chief tragedy. Proper
melody would have bound the far provinces of this loose em-
pire of mighty imagination into a strong, central kingdom.

        I wish Mr. Griffith had worked out a whole evening
of this great Babylonian story. Sticking to this alone, he
would have added an art-product to literature as enduring as
Flaubert's Salammbo.

        If I may predict: he will never again tell a story in
this manner. Nor will anyone else. The blue sea is pretty
much where it was when the sails of the Argonauts bellied
tight in the winds of a morning world, and so are the people
who live in the world. Still we wish to follow, undisturbed,
the adventures of a single set of characters, or to thrill
with a single pair of lovers. Verily, when the game is hearts
two's company, and the lovers of four ages an awful crowd.

HERE'S THE CHALDEAN WHO BUILT BABYLON*

        If you wish to know who built Babylon--said to have
been quite a lovely Manhattan when Mare Island was a colt--
you can buy a big black book for fifteen or twenty dollars
which will tell you that nobody knows just who built it. When
interviewed, the Assyrian nobleman depicted below upon the
throne of a chef of the period called this just darned ignorant
hedging. He knows who built Babylon. He built it himself.

        Translated from its nebuchadnezzarish syllables into
our tongue his name is really very simple: "Huck" Wortman.
Yet the ancients have been called such a difficult people to understand!

_____

*Reprinted from Photoplay, Vol. 11, No. 3, February 1917,
page 83.

The present location of Babylon is the Fine Arts back lot, near Hollywood. Huck's oriental metropolis was erected just for shooting, and now all Hollywood is sore because he won't tear it down. If you are in the vicinity of <u>Intolerance</u> any evening you can behold his right nifty little town in all its pristine glory.

Sar Wortman has many interesting reminiscences of his old pal Belshazzar, and all of them fellows. "One day me and Bel," says he--but that's another story.

D. W. Griffith, said to have been the Babylonian prime minister before the days of Lloyd George, one day discovered that his Grand Edificer has been working on the great construction for nearly three months without so much as a Sunday at home.

"Get out of here!" he exclaimed. "I'll bet you'll hardly know your wife and children."

So Huck went home. Three hours of miserable, pacing restlessness followed. Suddenly Mrs. Huck seized the broom.

"Oh, go back to the job if you can't get your mind off it!" she admonished. "You were never made for the idle life."

Perfectly happy, Huck trotted back to the lot. He has indulged in no more dangerous ventures.

BIBLIOGRAPHY

1. "Aitken Returns to New York from West Coast," Motion Picture News, Vol. 13, No. 13 (April 1, 1916), page 1876.

2. "Allan Dwan Now at Work in East," The Moving Picture World, Vol. 32, No. 3 (April 21, 1917), page 409.

3. "Anita Loos Writes the Titles," The Moving Picture World, Vol. 30, No. 9 (December 2, 1916), page 1337.

4. "As Triangle Plan Matures 25 Houses Sign for Service," Variety, Vol. 40, No. 1 (September 3, 1915), page 17.

5. Ball, Robert Hamilton. Shakespeare on Silent Film. New York: Theatre Arts, 1968.

6. Barry, Iris and Eileen Bowser. D. W. Griffith: American Film Master. New York: Museum of Modern Art and Doubleday, 1965.

7. Blaisdell, George. "Douglas Fairbanks in New York," The Moving Picture World, Vol. 28, No. 13 (June 24, 1916), page 2213.

8. Bogdanovich, Peter. Allan Dwan: The Last Pioneer. New York: Praeger, 1971.

9. Brown, Karl. Adventures with D. W. Griffith. New York: Farrar, Straus and Giroux, 1973.

10. Cohn, Alfred A. "What They Really Get--Now," Photoplay, Vol. 9, No. 4 (March, 1916), pages 27-30.

11. "Coming Triangle Attractions," The Moving Picture

World, Vol. 26, No. 11 (December 4, 1915), page
1803.

12.   "Douglas Fairbanks in Fine Arts Pictures," The Moving
      Picture World, Vol. 26, No. 1 (October 2, 1915),
      page 86.

13.   Duncan, Robert C.   "The Fine Arts Studio," Picture-
      Play Magazine, Vol. 5, No. 1 (September, 1916),
      pages 88-94.

14.   "Effective and Novel Presentation Ideas Introduced at
      Model Theatre by Rothapfel," The Triangle, Vol. 1,
      No. 14 (January 22, 1916), pages 1 and 7.

15.   "Fairbanks at $15,000 Weekly Tops All Picture Salar-
      ies," Variety, Vol. 45, No. 7 (January 12, 1917),
      page 3.

16.   "Fairbanks Endeavors to Break Contract with Triangle,"
      Motion Picture News, Vol. 15, No. 4 (January 27,
      1917), page 546.

17.   "Fairbanks Faces Suit for Breaking Contract," Motion
      Picture News, Vol. 15, No. 9 (March 3, 1917),
      page 1368.

18.   "Fairbanks Retires from Triangle," The Moving Picture
      World, Vol. 31, No. 4 (January 27, 1917), page
      537.

19.   "Fairbanks Wants to Make a Few Pictures in South
      America," Motion Picture News, Vol. 13, No. 25
      (June 24, 1916), page 3884.

20.   "Fine Arts Plant and Studios Spreading Very Rapidly,"
      The Triangle, Vol. 2, No. 5 (May 20, 1916), page
      3.

21.   "Fine Arts Plays with Popular Stars," The Triangle,
      Vol. 1, No. 7 (December 4, 1915), page 3.

22.   Gish, Lillian (with Ann Pinchot).   Lillian Gish: The
      Movies, Mr. Griffith and Me.   Englewood Cliffs,
      N. J. : Prentice-Hall, 1969.

23.   _____ (with James Frasher).   Dorothy and Lillian
      Gish. New York: Charles Scribner's Sons, 1973.

24. Griffith, D. W. "Fine Arts Making Film Test 'Twixt Star and Legit," Variety, Vol. 40, No. 4 (September 24, 1915), page 17.

25. "Griffith Bids Mae Marsh Godspeed," The Moving Picture World, Vol. 30, No. 12 (December 23, 1916), Page 1787.

26. "Griffith Leaves Triangle and Signs with Artcraft," Motion Picture News, Vol. 15, No. 13 (March 31, 1917), page 1987.

27. "Griffith Out of Triangle," Variety, Vol. 46, No. 3 (March 16, 1917), page 27.

28. "Griffith to Contribute to Artcraft," The Moving Picture World, Vol. 31, No. 13 (March 31, 1917), page 2074.

29. "H. E. Aitken Announces Triangle Merger," Motion Picture News, Vol. 13, No. 12 (March 25, 1916), page 1767.

30. Hampton, Benjamin B. History of the American Film Industry. New York: Covici Friede, 1931 (reprinted in 1970 by Dover Publications).

31. Herndon, Booton. Mary Pickford and Douglas Fairbanks. New York: W. W. Norton and Company, 1977.

32. "Historical Accuracy Is Aim for Macbeth," Motion Picture News, Vol. 13, No. 11 (March 18, 1916), page 1606.

33. Hopper, DeWolf (in collaboration with Wesley Winans Stout). Once a Clown, Always a Clown. Boston: Little, Brown, and Company, 1927.

34. "How Flying Torpedo Was Supervised," The Triangle, Vol. 1, No. 20 (March 4, 1916), page 6.

35. "Ince Definitely Out of Triangle," The Moving Picture World, Vol. 32, No. 13 (June 30, 1917), page 2071.

36. "The Ince-Triangle Deal," The Moving Picture World, Vol. 32, No. 12 (June 23, 1917), page 1941.

37. "Is She Another Pickford?" Picture-Play Magazine,
     Vol. 4, No. 5 (July, 1916), page 228.

38. "Kessel-Bauman-Aitken," The Moving Picture World,
     Vol 25, No. 1 (July 3, 1915) , page 824.

39. Lahue, Kalton C. Dreams for Sale. South Brunswick
     and New York: A. S. Barnes, 1971.

40. Lindsay, Vachel. The Art of the Moving Picture. New
     York: Macmillan, 1915.

41. Loos, Anita. The Talmadge Girls. New York: The
     Viking Press, 1978.

42. Love, Bessie. From Hollywood with Love. London:
     Elm Tree Books, 1977.

43. Macgowan, Kenneth. Behind the Screen. New York:
     Delacorte, 1965.

44. "Mae Marsh at Work," The Moving Picture World, Vol.
     26, No. 12 (December 11, 1915), page 1985.

45. Milne, Peter. "The First Knickerbocker Triangle Pro-
     gram," Motion Picture News, Vol. 12, No. 14 (Oc-
     tober 9, 1915), pages 84-85.

46. "New Triangle Exchange Proposition," The Moving Pic-
     ture World, Vol. 30, No. 2 (October 14, 1916),
     page 214.

47. "Norma Talmadge, Selznick Star," The Moving Picture
     World, Vol. 30, No. 3 (October 21, 1916), page 410.

48. "One Hundred Thousand Dollar Mob Scene," The Tri-
     angle, Vol. 1, No. 7 (December 4, 1915), page 6.

49. Owen, K. "Their Lieutenants," Photoplay, Vol. 9,
     No. 4 (March, 1916) , pages 42-48.

50. Ramsaye, Terry. A Million and One Nights. New
     York: Simon and Schuster, 1926.

51. "Reopening Triangle-Fine Arts Studio," The Moving Pic-
     ture World, Vol. 32, No. 10 (June 9, 1917), page 1619.

52. "Roy Stuart," The Moving Picture World, Vol. 30, No.
     12 (December 23, 1916), page 1791.

53. "Sennett Probably Out of Triangle: Radical Future
     Plans," Motion Picture News, Vol. 15, No. 26
     (June 30, 1917), page 4057.

54. "Shakespeare Wrote Screen Plays?" The Moving Pic-
     ture World, Vol. 27, No. 7 (February 19, 1916),
     page 1137.

55. " 'Sig,' $4,000,000 Producing Company, Is Launched,"
     Motion Picture News, Vol. 12, No. 2 (July 17, 1915),
     page 87.

56. "Sir Herbert Tree Arrives in Los Angeles," The Tri-
     angle, Vol. 1, No. 12 (January 8, 1916), page 2.

57. "Sir Herbert Tree Leaves Los Angeles," The Moving
     Picture World, Vol. 27, No. 12 (March 25, 1916),
     page 1988.

58. "Stage Stars Are on Wane for Picture Productions,"
     Variety, Vol. 41, No. 2 (December 10, 1915), page
     3.

59. "Studio Improvements for Tom Ince," The Moving Pic-
     ture World, Vol. 32, No. 1 (April 7, 1917), page
     102.

60. "They're Just Shooting Douglas Fairbanks," Photoplay,
     Vol. 11, No. 4 (March, 1917), page 109.

61. The Triangle, Vol. 1, No. 1 (October 23, 1915) - Vol.
     1, No. 26 (April 15, 1916).

62. _____, Vol. 2, No. 1 (April 22, 1916) - Vol. 2,
     No. 26 (October 14, 1916).

63. "Triangle Blazes Way for Regular $2 Seats," Motion
     Picture News, Vol. 12, No. 14 (October 9, 1915),
     page 41.

64. "Triangle Completes First Releasing Plan," Motion
     Picture News, Vol. 12, No. 9 (September 4, 1915),
     pages 41-42.

65. "Triangle Film Incorporated," The Moving Picture
     World, Vol. 25, No. 5 (July 31, 1915), page 824.

66. "Triangle Opening Announced," The Moving Picture
     World, Vol. 25, No. 10 (September 4, 1915), pages
     1622-1623.

67. "Triangle Opening at Colonial," The Moving Picture
     World, Vol. 27, No. 11 (March 18, 1916), page
     1804.

68. "Triangle Plans to Change Its Distributing Scheme,"
     Motion Picture News, Vol. 14, No. 15 (October 14,
     1916), pages 2347-2348.

69. "Triangle Reorganizes; Ince Out--Sennett May Withdraw,"
     Motion Picture News, Vol. 15, No. 25 (June 23,
     1917), page 3893.

70. "Triangle Rumors Set at Rest by Griffith, Ince and
     Sennett," Motion Picture News, Vol. 14, No. 7
     (October 28, 1916), page 2654.

71. "Triangle to Produce Specials Once a Month," Motion
     Picture News, Vol. 15, No. 16 (April 21, 1917),
     page 2478.

72. "Triangle Turns the First Birthday Mark," Motion Pic-
     ture News, Vol. 14, No. 20 (November 18, 1916),
     page 3128.

73. "Triangle Will Produce Two Reel Subjects," Motion Pic-
     ture News, Vol. 13, No. 20 (May 20, 1916), page
     3041.

74. "Triangle's Auspicious Opening," The Moving Picture
     World, Vol. 26, No. 2 (October 9, 1915), pages
     233-234.

75. Von Harleman, G. P. "Bessie Love One Year in Pic-
     tures," The Moving Picture World, Vol. 30, No. 13
     (December 30, 1916), page 1948.

76. _____. "Douglas Fairbanks Bids Goodbye to Califor-
     nia," The Moving Picture World, Vol. 31, No. 1
     (January 6, 1917), page 85.

77. _____. "Griffith Leaves Fine Arts," The Moving
     Picture World, Vol. 31, No. 13 (March 31, 1917),
     page 2087.

78. _____. "Griffith Regime Passes at Fine Arts," The
     Moving Picture World, Vol. 32, No. 1 (April 7,
     1917), page 79.

79. _____ and Clarke Irvine. "Beerbohm Tree Reaches
     Coast," The Moving Picture World, Vol. 27, No. 2
     (January 8, 1916), pages 228-229.

80. _____. "Julius Caesar Production," The Moving
     Picture World, Vol. 28, No. 11 (June 10, 1916),
     page 2213.

81. _____. "Sir Herbert Tree Returns to Los Angeles,"
     The Moving Picture World, Vol. 29, No. 4 (July 22,
     1916), page 620.

82. _____. "Triangle Producers Return to the Coast,"
     The Moving Picture World, Vol. 30, No. 4 (October
     28, 1916), page 557.

INDEX

Abel, David 127, 173, 174,
176, 178
Abel, Sam 169
Acquitted 78-82, 146, 149,
157, 167
Ade, George 49
Aitken, Harry E. 1, 2, 4, 5,
7, 12, 17, 46, 47, 63, 93,
95, 100, 101, 105, 110,
123
Aitken, Spottiswoode 64, 100,
116, 167, 168, 170, 173,
174, 175, 176, 177, 178,
179, 203
Aladdin and His Wonderful
Lamp 76
Alden, Mary 4, 21, 79, 166,
167, 169, 170, 172, 179
Ali Baba and the Forty Thieves
76
Allen, Winifred 177
American Aristocracy 54, 61,
132, 144, 146, 173
American Biograph Company
1, 79, 88, 130, 138, 140,
141, 146, 149, 150, 163
American--That's All 121
Americano, The 54, 63-65,
135, 158, 175
Anna Lucasta 123
Arbuckle, Franklin 165
Arbuckle, Roscoe "Fatty" 29,
93
Archer, Juanita 172
Armour, Keith 173
Artcraft 68, 118, 119
Aryan, The 84
Atta Boy's Last Race 92, 173
Autumn Leaves 123
Avenging Conscience, The 2

Babes in the Wood 76

Backus, George 169
Bad Boy, The 116, 127, 142,
153, 159, 162, 163, 176
Baker, Robert M. 168, 170,
171
Barry, Viola 12, 168
Barrymore, John 54
Barrymore, Lionel 28
Battle Cry of Peace, The 83
Battle of the Sexes, The 2,
161
Baumann, Charles O. 2, 3, 5
Beach, Rex 54
Beban, George 5, 51
Belasco, David 93
Bennett, Frank 88, 113-114,
116, 197, 170, 171, 172,
173, 174, 175, 176, 177,
193, 203, 216
Beranger, George (André) 59,
128, 167, 171, 172, 176
Berlin, Irving 54
Betsy's Burglar 115, 129, 157,
163, 176
Betty of Greystone 91, 168
Big A Film Company 109
Biography Company see Ameri-
can Biograph Company
Birth of a Nation, The 1, 2,
7, 14, 16, 18, 19, 20, 27,
47, 48, 49, 67, 71, 78, 88,
113, 118, 119, 138, 141, 142,
144, 150, 156, 159, 183, 187,
192, 193, 194, 197, 198, 208,
215
Bitzer, Billy 21, 129, 193, 214
Blackton, J. Stuart 83, 93
Blake, Alva D. 169, 174
Blake, Loretta 52, 166, 168
Blue, Monte 128-129, 169,
173, 175, 176, 177
Boland, Mary 5
Bolles, Edward 171

Bouchier, Arthur   109
Boucicault, Rene   168
Bound in Morocco   56
Brammall, Jack   167, 171, 174,
    175, 176, 179
Brandels, Joseph   182
Breil, Joseph Carl   21, 165,
    166, 187
Brennen, John   171
Brockwell, Gladys   166, 167
Brown, Karl   21, 129-130,
    168, 176, 177
Brown, Lucille   21, 129
Brown, William   168, 169,
    171, 172, 173, 174, 176,
    177, 203
Browning, Tod   37, 42, 117,
    130, 169, 171, 173, 174,
    175, 176, 177
Bruce, Kate   168, 170, 172,
    173, 176, 178
Burke, Billie   54, 76, 84, 93
Burns, Beulah   73, 167, 172,
    173, 174, 177
Burns, Fred   166, 169, 170
Burns, Robert   113, 175
Burns, Thelma   174, 177, 179
Buskirk, Bessie   174, 177, 179
Bussell, Walter   176
Butler, Charles   168
Butler, David   168
Butler, Fred J.   168, 169
Byrd, Beau   175

Cabanne, William Christy   6,
    14, 21, 23, 27, 46, 48, 49,
    58, 59, 83, 92-93, 130-132,
    165, 166, 168, 169, 170,
    171, 172
Campeau, Frank   4, 28, 166,
    167
Cannon, Doc   169
Cannon, Pomeroy   173
Carew, Ora   23, 166
Carmen, Jewel   38, 59, 60,
    132-133, 169, 171, 172, 173
Carney, Augustus   25, 166
Carpenter, Francis   73, 76, 98,
    166, 167, 168, 169, 170, 172,
    173, 179
Carpenter, Grant   170
Casey at the Bat   39-42, 144,

170
Cassidy   121
Chambers, Marie   173
Cheerful Givers   154, 157, 159,
    177
Child of the Paris Streets, A
    86, 87, 144, 152, 170
Children in the House, The
    74, 136, 140, 145, 158, 169
Children of the Feud   174
Children Pay, The   19, 88-89,
    144, 145, 157, 158, 159,
    163, 173
Christy, Howard Chandler   5
Civilization   110
Claire, Madame   92
Clapp, Chester B.   166
Clark, Marguerite   18
Clarke, Marion   167
Clary, Charles   166
Clifton, Adele   172, 173, 175,
    177
Clifton, Elmer   21, 110, 115,
    166, 167, 171, 173, 175,
    177, 193, 203, 216
Clune's Auditorium   7
Cobb, Irvin S.   6, 54, 62, 93
Cohan, George M.   54
Collier, Constance   100, 102,
    105, 106, 109, 179
Collier, Fern   170
Columbia   123
Conspiracy   83
Conway, Jack   21, 29, 122, 167,
    179
Cooper, Miriam   60, 188, 193,
    203, 217-218
Corbin, Virginia Lee   76
Cosgrave, Jack   168
Coward, The   5, 6, 7
Cross Currents   91, 140, 154,
    167
Crowell, Josephine   21, 29,
    110, 166, 168, 171, 172,
    173, 174, 176, 177, 193,
    203, 216
Cummings, Richard   166, 168,
    176, 177
Currier, Frank   121, 173, 176

Dalton, Dorothy   65
Daphne and the Pirate   78, 87,

93, 130, 142, 145, 154, 168
Dark Cloud 166
Darling, Ruth 172, 173
Daughter of the Poor, A 128,
    133, 153, 176
Davidson, Max 21, 38, 39, 168,
    169, 170, 171, 174, 175,
    176, 193
Davis, H. O. 121
Dazey, Charles T. and Frank
    172
Deadly Glass of Beer, The 175
Dean, Julia 5
De Grasse, Sam 25, 166, 167,
    169, 170, 171, 172, 174,
    175, 177, 178, 203
De Lima, Charles 173
DeMille, Cecil B. 112, 204
de Navaro, Mary Anderson 98
de Nowskowski, L. 179
De Rue, Carmen 73, 79, 167,
    169, 170, 172, 173
Desmond, William 65
Despoilers, The 35
de Vaull, William 170, 175
Devereux, Jack 121, 176, 177
Devil's Needle, The 89, 152,
    161, 162, 171
Dexter, Elliott 4, 78, 168
Diane of the Follies 87, 132,
    142, 172
Dillon, Edward 14, 21, 34, 119,
    133-134, 168, 169, 170, 174,
    176, 177, 193
Dillon, John 166
Dingman, H. 69
Diplomacy 78
Dixon, Henry P. 177
Dixon, Thomas 200
Dolly, Rozsika 29, 166
Don Q, Son of Zorro 44
Don Quixote 10, 34-36, 133,
    161, 162, 168
Doro, Marie 4, 76-78, 167
Double Trouble 130, 141, 166
Down to Earth 54
Dresser, Louise 5
Drew, Cora 166, 167
Drew, Sidney 37
Du Crowe, Tote 175
Dwan, Allan 9, 14, 21, 28, 54,
    55, 57, 91, 120, 121, 134,
    166, 168, 169, 170, 171, 172,

173, 177
Dyer, Madge 179

E and R Jungle Film Company
    38
Eagle Eye 165
Edwards, Walter 65
Elmore, Pearl 167, 168, 169
Emerson, John 4, 12, 13, 14,
    21, 51, 52, 54, 61, 63, 68,
    82, 83, 92, 100, 105, 106,
    107, 108, 109, 134-135, 146,
    165, 167, 168, 172, 175, 179
Epoch Producing Company 2
Erlanger, A. L. 93
Escape, The 2, 20
Everybody's Doing It 174

Fairbanks, Douglas 4, 5, 6,
    44-68, 84, 86, 92, 93, 105,
    132, 134, 135, 158, 165, 166,
    167, 169, 170, 171, 172,
    173, 174, 175
Fall of Babylon, The 127
Famous Players-Lasky 78, 94
Farnum, Dustin 5, 6, 105
Farnum, William 195
Fawcett, George 168, 169
Faye, Julia 25, 166, 168
Fife, Shannon 169
Fifty-Fifty 173
Fighting Blood 71
Fildew, William 93, 165, 166,
    168, 169, 171
Fisher, Harry 173, 176
Flagg, James Montgomery 6
Fleming, Victor 169, 175
Flirting with Fate 56, 59-61,
    128, 132, 170
Flying Torpedo, The 12-14,
    16, 82-83, 130, 146, 154,
    168
Foot, Courtenay 167
Foot, Edward 21
Fornes, Karl, Jr. 165, 179
Fovieri, Ninon 73, 167, 169,
    170
Fox, William 75, 93
Fox Film Company 5, 6, 119
Foy, Eddie 5
France, R. W. 118

Franklin, C. M. (Chester)
    14, 21, 70-76, 135-136,
    167, 168, 169, 170, 171,
    172, 173
Franklin, S. A. (Sidney) 14,
    21, 70-76, 136, 167, 168,
    169, 170, 171, 172, 173
Freemont, W. J. 167
French, Herbert 172
Frohman, David 93
Furst, William 5

Garcia, May 171
Garden of Allah, The 98
Gaye, Howard 21, 23, 59,
    98, 168, 169, 171, 172,
    174, 193, 203
General Film Company 5
Gerard, Charles 176
Gest, Morris 93
Ghosts 92
Gibson, James 165
Giesy, J. V. 174
Gillette, William 96
Gilmore, Barney 177
Gilmore, Paul 166
Gish, Dorothy 4, 21, 26, 28,
    74, 113, 114, 116, 117,
    130, 136-138, 165, 166, 168,
    169, 170, 171, 172, 173,
    174, 175, 176, 177
Gish, Lillian 4, 9, 10, 21,
    29, 78, 84, 87-89, 98,
    119, 130, 138, 157, 166,
    168, 169, 170, 172, 173,
    174, 178, 193, 203, 215
Going Straight 74, 136, 140,
    145, 170
Good, Frank B. (Butcher)
    138-140, 167, 168, 169,
    170
Good Bad Man, The 56, 58,
    93, 128, 134, 146, 169
Goodwin, Harold 165
Goodwin, Nat 51
Gorman, Charles 167, 173,
    174
Gosden, A. G. 168, 169,
    170, 174, 175, 176
Gottschalk, Louis 21
Grab Bag Bride, A 116
Grafters 121

Graham, Fred 167
Grandon, Francis J. 140, 167
Gretchen the Greenhorn 74,
    136, 157, 172
Grey, Jane 4, 71, 72, 140-
    141, 167
Grey, Olga 21, 117, 141, 166,
    169, 170, 172, 175, 179, 203
Griffith, D. W. 1, 2, 3, 4, 6,
    7, 8-19, 20, 21, 23, 32, 46,
    54, 56, 65, 66, 67, 69, 70,
    71, 75, 76, 77, 78, 79, 93,
    94, 96, 98, 100, 105, 110,
    112, 118, 119, 120, 123,
    128, 129, 130, 134, 136, 138,
    141-142, 145, 149, 150, 153,
    155, 159, 160, 161, 163, 165,
    166, 167, 168, 170, 172, 180,
    181, 182, 183, 185, 186, 187,
    188, 189, 190, 191, 192, 193,
    194, 195, 196, 197, 198, 199,
    200, 202, 204, 205, 206, 209,
    215, 216, 218, 219

Habit of Happiness, The 54,
    56, 57, 134, 169
Hackett, Dr. R. K. 180
Hadley, Bert 144, 170, 171,
    175, 177
Haines, Rhea 175, 177
Half-Breed, The 54, 55, 56-
    57, 128, 132, 134, 146,
    158, 171
Hall, J. Warwick 176
Hamburger, Mose 90
Hamilton, Louise 178
Handforth, Ruth 170, 172
Hands Up! 150, 177
Handyside, Clarence 168
Hansen, Juanita 23, 25, 166
Harlan, Kenneth 115, 176
Harlan, Macey 168, 169, 172
Harley, Edward 168, 170
Harris, Leonore 168
Harris, Mildred 84, 116, 168,
    173, 176
Harris, Theodosia 166
Harrison, James 176, 178
Harron, Charles 142
Harron, Robert 4, 9, 10, 21,
    69, 85, 87, 113, 116, 119,
    142, 150, 157, 167, 168,

170, 171, 172, 174, 176,
177, 188, 192, 203, 217,
218
Hart, William S. 4, 5, 49, 65,
84, 122
Hastings, Seymour 170, 179
Haunted House, The 121
Haydel, Dorothy 60, 171
He Comes Up Smiling 56
Hearst, William Randolph 5
Heart Strategy 116
Hearts of the World 118, 136
Heinz, Grace 172
Heiress at Coffee Dan's, The
127, 133, 174
Hell-To-Pay Austin 146, 149,
154, 157, 172
Henabery, Joseph 115, 174,
177, 203
Her Father's Keeper 120-121,
176
Her Official Father 115, 177
Hernandez, Anna 168
Hichens, Robert 98
Higby, Mrs. 175
Higby, Wilbur 167, 168, 170,
171, 172, 174, 175, 177
Hill, George 167, 168, 179
Hinckley, William 166, 168,
169
His Deadly Undertaking 116
His Picture in the Papers
28, 51-54, 135, 146, 167
Hitchcock, Raymond 5, 6, 29
Hite, C. J. 2
Hodkinson, W. O. 121
Home, Sweet Home 2, 161
Hoodoo Ann 16, 84-86, 142,
144, 150, 159, 168
Hopkins, Clyde 167, 170,
172, 173, 174, 175, 176,
177
Hopper, DeWolf 4, 10, 32-43,
46, 84, 98, 101, 105,
168, 169, 170, 171, 203
Hopper, DeWolf, Jr. 32, 169
Hopper, Hedda 32, 120
Hopper, William see Hopper,
DeWolf, Jr.
House, Chandler 179
House Built upon Sand, A 9,
89, 154, 174
Howey, Walter 10

Howley, Irene 121, 176
Hughes, Frank 171
Hughes, Rupert 6, 110, 173
Hunneford, John 176
Hunt, Homer 168
Hunt, Irene 166
Hunt, Madge 165
Huntley, Luray 167, 171, 177

IMP Company 1
In Again, Out Again 54
Ince, Thomas H. 2, 3,
4, 5, 6, 8, 17, 65, 67, 92,
93, 94, 112, 119, 120, 121,
122
Ingraham, Lloyd 14, 28, 61,
88, 116, 119, 143-144, 166,
167, 186, 170, 171, 172, 173,
175, 177, 193, 203
Innocent Magdalene, An 87, 170
Intolerance 8, 10, 11, 14, 16,
20, 42, 49, 54, 69, 73, 74,
84, 112, 114, 116, 118, 119,
123, 127, 130, 132, 141, 142,
146, 150, 153, 155, 156
Iron Mask, The 56
Iron Strain, The 6
Irving, Sir Henry 101

Jack and the Beanstalk 76
James, Gladden 172
Janis, Elsie 54
Janitor's Wife's Temptation, A
29
Jefferson, Thomas 4, 166, 167
Jefferson, William 169
Jim Bludso 117-118, 129, 130,
150, 175
Joan the Woman 112
Johnson, Orrin 5, 29, 166,
167
Johnston, J. W. 173
Jordan Is a Hard Road 28,
145, 154, 166

Kahn, Otto 5
Keenan, Frank 35
Kennedy, Tom 166
Kerry, Norman 172
Kessel, Adam J. 2, 3, 5

Kessel, Charles 2
Keystone Company 4, 5
Kid, Jim 166
Kilgore, Joseph 120
Klaw, Marc 93
Knickerbocker Theatre 4, 6,
    93
Knowland, Alice 168

Laemmle, Carl 1, 2
Lamb, The 6, 21, 46-49, 57,
    130, 142, 165
Langdon, Lillian 1, 65, 170,
    171, 172, 174, 175, 177,
    203
Lawler, Robert 167, 168, 169,
    171
Lawrence, W. E. 12, 168,
    171, 173
Le Blanc, Paul 171
Lee, Alberta 21, 168, 169,
    173, 174, 175, 176
Lee, Charles 166, 168, 175,
    177
Lee, Jennie 21, 86, 88, 116,
    117, 170, 172, 173, 175,
    176, 177, 178
Lee, Raymond 76
Leezer, John 171, 172, 175,
    176, 177
Leonard, Jack 179
Lester, Kate 172
Let Katy Do It 16, 19, 70-71,
    74, 128, 136, 140, 142,
    145, 152, 167
Lewis, Ben 173
Lewis, Ralph 21, 88, 100,
    144-145, 166, 167, 168,
    170, 172, 173, 179, 203
Lewis, Vera 144, 167, 203
Lily and the Rose, The 4,
    21, 29, 78, 142, 149, 157,
    166
Lincoln, Elmo 168, 174, 175,
    176, 177, 188, 203
Lindsay, Vachel 86
Little Liar, The 141, 144,
    172
Little Meena's Romance 157,
    169
Little School Ma'am, The 74,
    136, 163, 170

Little Yank, The 19, 113-115,
    175
Lokmeyer, Robert 173
Long, Walter 23, 25, 70, 78,
    145, 166, 167, 169, 171,
    193, 203, 218
Loos, Anita 47, 51, 52, 54,
    57, 62, 63, 68, 86, 135,
    145-146, 147, 167, 168, 170,
    171, 172, 173, 174, 175, 176
Love, Bessie 8, 9, 12, 13,
    21, 42, 56, 61, 73, 78, 79,
    83, 84, 115, 144, 146-149,
    167, 168, 169, 170, 171,
    172, 173, 174, 175, 176,
    177, 193, 203
Love Sublime, A 128, 150,
    176
Love under Cover 116
Lowery, William 165, 166,
    169, 170
Lubin, Sigmund 93
Lucas, Wilfred 21, 78-82,
    100, 117, 120, 149-150,
    166, 167, 170, 172, 173,
    175, 177, 178, 179, 206
Lucille 168
Lynch, S. A. 121

Macbeth 15, 96-110, 135, 179
McCarthy, J. P. 171
McCarthy Brothers 83
McClung, Hugh 166
McClure, Alexander 176
McConville, Bernard 119, 152-
    153, 167, 169, 170, 171, 172,
    173, 174
MacCormack, Florence 5
McCoy, Kid 168
McDermott, J. W. 165
McDonald, Francis J. 167
Mace, Fred 5, 6, 29
Mack, Willard 29
McKee, Scott 179
McKenzie, George 179
MacMahon, Henry 5
Madame Bo-Peep 122-123,
    162, 178
Mlle. O'Brien 174
Majestic Company 1, 2, 68
Majestic Theatre 90, 179
Male Governess, The 116

Man Hater, The 121
Man Who Made Good, The 121,
    177
Manhattan Madness 54, 56,
    57-58, 128, 132, 134, 172
Mark of Zorro, The 44
Markey, Enid 6, 29, 35
Marriage of Molly O', The 86,
    145, 171
Marsh, Mae 5, 9, 16, 17, 78,
    84-87, 93, 98, 116, 150-151,
    157, 168, 170, 171, 172, 174,
    188, 192, 203, 214, 217
Marsh, Marguerite 21, 89, 167,
    169, 170, 171
Marshall, Louis 182
Marshall, Tully 5, 29, 71, 72,
    89-90, 151-152, 166, 167,
    168, 170, 171, 174, 175, 188,
    203, 216
Martha's Vindication 74, 136,
    140, 145, 152, 161, 163,
    168
Martyrs of the Alamo 4, 21,
    23-28, 47, 73, 129, 130,
    166
Matrimaniac, The 63, 146,
    157, 160, 174
Menjou, Adolphe 172
Messinger, Buddy and Gertrude
    76
Metro 92, 114, 132
Mickey 7
Microscope Mystery, The 90-
    91, 157, 160, 173
Might and the Man 153, 177
Missing Links, The 16, 69,
    89, 142, 144, 160, 167
Mr. Fix-It 56
Mr. Goode, the Samaritan 16,
    39, 133, 161, 162, 170
Mitchell, Dodson 173
Mitchell, Rhea 168
Modern Musketeer, A 56
Moore, Colleen 10, 116, 176,
    177
Moore, Owen 1, 21, 28, 166,
    168, 169, 170
Morosco-Pallas 100
Morris, Clara 172
Morrissey, Edward 116, 174,
    176
Moses, Hugo, Jr. 172

Mother and the Law, The see
    Intolerance
Mutual Film Corporation 1, 2,
    3
My Valet 6
Myers, Carmel 9, 153, 176,
    177
Mystery of the Leaping Fish,
    The 46, 61, 92, 174

Naulty, J. N. 5
Neery, Joe 173
New York Motion Picture Com-
    pany 2, 3, 122
Nina, the Flower Girl 114,
    144, 154, 175
Noble Fraud, A 116
Normand, Mabel 5, 6, 7
Northrup, Harry S. 173
Nurnberger, Joseph E. 21

O'Brien, Jack/John 12, 13,
    83, 154, 168, 177
O'Connor, Loyola 88, 154, 166,
    167, 168, 170, 171, 172, 173,
    175, 177
O'Connor, Mary H. 119, 154,
    166, 167, 168, 172, 174,
    175, 177
Old Fashioned Young Man, An
    10, 116, 142, 144, 158, 163,
    177
Old Folks at Home, The 110,
    172
Old Heidelberg 4, 7, 21-23,
    26, 47, 134, 138, 165
Ormonde, Eugene 168, 172
Ortiego, Arthur 173
O'Shea, James 167, 169, 170,
    171, 172, 173, 175, 176
Other Man, The 93
Owen, Seena 6, 29, 90, 122,
    154-155, 165, 166, 168, 176,
    178, 184, 188, 193, 203, 214,
    216

Paderewski, Ignace 5
Paget, Alfred 21, 23, 47, 165,
    166, 174, 175, 184, 188,
    193, 203

Pallette, Eugene   38, 74, 156-
    157, 169, 170, 172, 193
Panthea   91
Paramount Pictures   5, 114
Parker, Albert   121, 173
Pathe, Charles   93
Pearce, George   166, 167,
    168, 169, 171
Pearl, Lloyd   73, 167, 173
Peggy   76, 93
Penitentes, The   21, 29-31,
    154, 166
Perry, Fred   166
Pickford, Mary   1, 18, 84,
    94, 135, 149
Pierson, F. M.   92, 168, 169
Pillars of Society   92, 128,
    172
Pipe of Discontent, The   116
Porter, Edwin S.   93
Powell, Paul   14, 21, 29, 76,
    78, 90, 157, 166, 167, 169,
    170, 171, 172, 173, 174,
    175, 176, 177
Powers, W. M.   5
Price of Power, The   29, 91,
    140, 167
Private Life of Don Juan, The
    44
Puppets   42-43, 171

Radcliffe, Violet   73, 167,
    169, 170, 172, 173, 174
Radford, Mazie   169, 170,
    176, 177
Rae, Alice   169, 176
Rankin, Grace   168, 169
Ray, Charles   5, 49
Raymond, Jack   176
Raynes, J. A.   21
Reaching for the Moon   54
Reformers, The   189
Reggie Mixes In   58, 132, 146,
    170
Rehfelt, Curt   169
Reid, Wallace   21, 26, 165
Reliance Company   1, 2, 14,
    15, 113, 144, 162, 163
Reliance Studios   28
Rialto Theatre   93, 106, 179
Rice, Roy Hiram   166, 167
Richmond, W. P.   172, 173

Richter, Millie   93
Rise and Fall of Free Speech
    in America, The   18-19
Road Agent, The   116
Robin Hood   56
Robinson, Daisy   167
Romaine, Louis   188
Romance of Happy Valley, A
    19, 88
Rork, Sam   90
Ross, E.   69
Rossi, Tina   174, 177
Rosson, Arthur   120, 121
Rothapfel, S. L.   93
Roxy   see Rothapfel, S. L.
Rubens, Alma   64, 119, 158,
    171, 173, 175, 176, 177
Rummy, The   150, 157, 159,
    172

Sable Lorcha, The   2, 28, 144,
    152, 166
St. Denis, Ruth   29, 166
Salisbury, Monroe   165, 166
Sammis, George W.   5
Sampson, Teddy   167, 175
Saunders, P. W.   69
Schenck, Joseph   91
Schertzinger, Victor   21
Schiff, Jacob H.   181
Schulberg, B. P.   93
Schuman, Bennie   175
Schumann, Milton   177
Sealock, Jack   173
Sears, A. D.   23, 113, 166,
    169, 170, 172, 173, 174,
    175, 176, 178, 203
Selznick Company   91
Sennett, Mack   2, 3, 4, 5, 6,
    8, 17, 67, 92, 93, 94, 116,
    120
Shawn, Ted   29, 166
Sheehan, Winfield   75
Sheriff, The   70
Sherry, J. Barney   4
Shirley, Robert   173
Shubert, J.   93
Schubert, Lee   93
Siebert, Mike   169
Siegmann, George   19, 113, 173,
    175, 193, 203, 216
Siegmann, Wilhelmina   172

Sig Motion Picture Company
  3, 4
Singleton, Joseph 166, 169,
  170, 175, 176
Skinner, Otis 96
Slater, Ann 157
Social Secretary, The 90, 135,
  146, 161, 172
Sold for Marriage 87-88, 129,
  130, 141, 145, 169
Somerville, Roy 90, 113, 117,
  119, 158, 167, 169, 170,
  171, 175, 176, 177
Sothern, Edward H. 96, 109
Souls Triumphant 150, 154,
  177
Spencer, Tom 172
Stage Struck 116-117, 153,
  159, 176
Starke, Pauline 159, 171, 173,
  174, 176, 177, 178
Stephens, Charles 173, 175
Stewart, Roy 176
Stielow Case 202, 210
Stockdale, Carl 37, 64, 85,
  88, 168, 170, 171, 172, 173,
  175, 176, 177
Stolen Magic 7
Stone, Elinor 167
Stone, George 73, 98, 117,
  167, 168, 169, 170, 171,
  172, 173, 174, 175, 177
Stranded 42, 144, 171
Strong, Porter 168
Stuart, Roy 89, 174
Successful Failure, A 121
Sullivan, C. Gardner 122
Sully, Beth 56
Sul-Te-Wan, Madame 84, 159,
  168, 173, 176
Sunshine Dad 36-39, 133, 157,
  169
Susan Rocks the Boat 16, 157,
  169
Sweet, Blanche 2

Talmadge, Constance 69, 90-
  91, 115, 127, 159-160, 167,
  173, 174, 175, 176, 188,
  192, 203, 214
Talmadge, Mrs. 175
Talmadge, Natalie 160

Talmadge, Norma 5, 69, 74,
  89-91, 160-161, 167, 168,
  169, 170, 171, 172, 173
Tavernier, Albert 168
Telephone Bell, The 116
Tempest, The 98
Terry, Ellen 96
Thief of Bagdad, The 44
Three Musketeers, The 44
Thurston, Eugene 93
Tincher, Fay 21, 36, 38, 92,
  133, 161, 168, 169, 170
Tolhurst, Louis H. 91
Toncray, Kate 21, 165, 166,
  169, 170, 171, 174, 175,
  176, 177
Townsend, J. 69
Treasure Island 76
Tree, Sir Herbert Beerbohm
  5, 15, 34, 95-111, 173, 179,
  203
Tree, Iris 98
Triangle Film Corporation 1,
  4, 5, 18, 20, 28, 32, 66, 68
Triangle Kiddies, The 73-76
Truax, Sarah 5, 166
True Heart Susie 19, 88, 154
Turner, F. A. (Fred) 166,
  167, 169, 171, 173, 174,
  175, 176, 177, 178, 203
Tylden, L. 179

Universal 2, 5, 6, 92, 149
Urson, Frank 175

Van, Beatrice 177
Village Scandal, The 29
Vitagraph Company 5, 89, 113,
  158, 160
von Ritzau, Erik 165
von Stroheim, Erich 21, 23,
  90, 105, 162, 165, 168, 172

Walcott, Helen 172
Wales, R. Ellis 21, 101
Walsh, George 34, 84, 168,
  193, 203
Walsh, Raoul 172
Walthall, Henry B. 92, 172
Ware, Helen 5, 98, 167

Warner, Henry B.   5
Warren, Fred   173, 174, 175,
   176, 177
Warrington, C. S.   69
Warwick, Granville   <u>see</u>   Grif-
   fith, D. W.
Webb, Millard K.   167, 169,
   170, 171
Weber, Lois   89
Weber and Fields   5
Webster, Alice   176
Webster, Lillian   174
Weir, Helen   172
Wells, Raymond   38, 165, 166,
   169, 179
West, Charles   167, 168
West, Raymond   168
Westover, Winifred   9, 173,
   174, 175, 177
Wharf Rat, The   86, 112, 142,
   146, 150, 159, 174
When Hearts Collide   116
Whitman, Walt   206
Whitman Bennett Studios   28
Wild and Woolly   54
Wild Girl of the Sierras, The
   86, 141, 146, 149, 150, 170
Wiles, Mabel   166
Wilkey, Violet   88, 173
Wilkinson, Marie   172
Willat Studios   28
Williams, Kathlyn   105
Wilson, Hal   113, 166, 167,

171, 175, 177
Wilson, Margery   21, 49-50,
   166, 188, 193, 203
Wilson, Tom   21, 23, 166, 169,
   171, 172, 173, 175, 176, 177,
   188, 203
Wing, William E.   39, 91, 169,
   170, 173
Withey, Chester   89, 90, 109,
   110, 122, 162-163, 168, 169,
   170, 171, 173, 174, 176
Woman's Awakening, A   156,
   158, 162, 163, 176
Won by a Foot   116
Wood Nymph, The   16, 76-78,
   142, 149, 167
Woodbury, J. E.   69
Woodruff, Bert   176, 177
Woods, Ella   74, 163, 168
Woods, Frank   10, 14, 17, 20,
   21, 74, 88, 119, 163-164,
   171, 173, 176, 177
Wortman, "Huck"   218-219
Wright, W. S.   69

Younge, Lucille   168, 173, 174

Zeidman, Bennie   92
Ziegfeld, Florenz   93
Zukor, Adolph   5, 68, 93, 119